Implementing

ISO 9001 : 2000

Implementing

ISO 9001 : 2000

Pradeep Kumar Mathur
Technical Director &
Management Representative
Verny Group of Companies
Hyderabad

VIKAS® PUBLISHING HOUSE PVT LTD

VIKAS® PUBLISHING HOUSE PVT LTD
E-28, Sector-8, **Noida**-201301 (UP) India
Phone: +91-120-4078900 • Fax: +91-120-4078999
Registered Office: 576, Masjid Road, Jangpura, **New Delhi**-110014. India
E-mail: ***helpline@vikaspublishing.com*** • Website: ***www.vikaspublishing.com***

- **Ahmedabad** : 305, Grand Monarch, 100 ft Shyamal Road, Near Seema Hall, Ahmedabad-380051 • Ph. +91-79-65254204, +91-9898294208
- **Bengaluru** : First Floor, N S Bhawan, 4th Cross, 4th Main, Gandhi Nagar, Bengaluru-560009 • Ph. +91-80-22281254, 22204639
- **Chennai** : E-12, Nelson Chambers, 115, Nelson Manickam Road, Aminjikarai, Chennai-600029 • Ph. +91-44-23744547, 23746090
- **Hyderabad** : Aashray Mansion, Flat-G (G.F.), 3-6-361/8, Street No. 20, Himayath Nagar, Hyderabad-500029 • Ph. +91-40-23269992 • Fax. +91-40-23269993
- **Kolkata** : 82, Park Street, Kolkata-700017 • Ph. +91-33-22837880
- **Mumbai** : 67/68, 3rd Floor, Aditya Industrial Estate, Chincholi Bunder, Behind Balaji International School & Evershine Mall, Malad (West), Mumbai-400064 • Ph. +91-22-28772545, 28768301
- **Patna** : Flat No. 101, Sri Ram Tower, Beside Chiraiyatand Over Bridge, Kankarbagh Main Rd., Kankarbagh, Patna-800020 • Ph. +91-612-2351147

Implementing ISO 9001 : 2000
ISBN: 978-81259-1377-1

First Published 2003
Reprinted several times
First Reprint 2014

Printed in India.

To

My Mother Shanti Mathur
and
Late R. V. Rangayyamma

Foreword

The opening of the world economy has thrown up immense challenges to us. The biggest challenge is to survive and stay competitive. In the wake of this challenge, the focus on quality has assumed greater importance as this provides the leading edge to the industry. Quality, therefore, is no more the sole responsibility of quality assurance department; it is everyone's business in the organisation. In fact in world-class companies, it is an ingrained culture.

ISO 9000 series provides a building block to establish and maintain a culture of quality in any organisation and lends a robust framework for managing quality. These standards were released in 1987 and have undergone two revisions in line with the changing requirements. The latest version, ISO 9001:2000, is built around eight 'quality management principles' which brings it very close to business excellence models adopted by world-class companies. With changing business environment, it maintains the focus on 'doing things right' as in the earlier versions. Great emphasis is given to 'doing the right thing', with stress on systematic analysis of data and continual improvement. The process approach provides a strong foundation for quality management in any organisation.

I congratulate P.K. Mathur for bringing out the book on *Implementing ISO 9001:2000* which details all requirements of the latest standard in a comprehensive and lucid manner. Being a practitioner, P.K. Mathur has injected his practical insights on developing the quality management system in line with the latest version, which I am sure will be of immense help to the readers. Those in the process of implementing the quality management systems or upgrading their existing systems will find the procedures and the sample manual given in the book extremely useful for their own documentation.

I am sure the book will find a wide readership. I wish the book all success.

Dr. T. Mukherjee

Deputy Managing Director (Steel),
Tata Iron and Steel Company Limited,
Jamshedpur, India.

Preface

In any field of activity, the power to survive, sustain, grow and progress comes primarily from the quality of one's output. Therefore, systematic management of the processes generating these outputs is the most effective means of surpassing competition. Be it a battle between foes or a game between competitors, the quality of a systematically managed and executed maneuver, even of one's opponent, cannot be, but admired. This leads us to the conclusion that 'Quality Outputs' are the result of systematic management of processes. Managing organizations systematically requires establishing, maintaining and constantly improving processes and systems. This capability is easily acquired through understanding, application and utilization of ISO 9000 standards.

Having started my career with the Bureau of Indian Standards (BIS), an organization dedicated to promoting quality at the national level, the culture of this organization got rubbed into my system during the formative years. After resigning from the BIS, I have been working for the last 10 years for Verny Containers Ltd., an organization reputed for its absolute commitment to quality. It is here I gained indepth knowledge. The motto of Verny is "Strive for the best in your product even if it is not required or expected by the customer." In other words, do not strive for mere compliance by doing what the customer asks for but give him much more. Interestingly, this leads to customer delight.

ISO 9001:2000 when used in 'word and spirit' is the best tool for establishing and operating a Quality Management System for bringing about improvements by 'Exceeding Customer Expectations'. I therefore did a lot of reading and analysis to understand this standard.

With the insight I gained while preparing my organization towards certification, I realized that there were many aspects that required clear understanding. The learning experience was extremely satisfying. It therefore seemed right that I pen down whatever I have learnt to assist other aspiring organizations. These lessons have been learnt from so man people over the last so many years. Hence there is a urge to share my thoughts and views with others. After all, I too have learnt from others.

I tried to make every chapter comprehensive. Certain points may therefore appear to have been repeated, but it is intentional for the sake of continuity of information in a particular chapter. I hope this will help readers understand the subject and reduce further reference.

I do not claim to be an expert on the ISO 9000 standards, rather a user of the standard. Whatever I presented here is basically an organized presentation of the copious notes I have taken over time and the discussions I had with my colleagues, friends and many quality experts.

Pradeep Kumar Mathur

Acknowledgements

It is indeed very difficult to express my gratitude to all those who directly or indirectly inspired, encouraged and supported me during the writing of this book. I'm deeply indebted to them for all their help.

This book however could not have seen the light of day without the direct involvement, encouragement and help of the following, whom I wish to specially thank:

Dr. T. Mukherjee A technical stalwart of the steel industry yet so humble, who so gladly consented to write the Foreword for this book. I'm indeed greatly indebted to him for his kindness and the wonderful Foreword for my first effort. Despite his busy schedule, he took the pains to go through this entire book.

Dr. Shravan Kumar My trainer during the Initial Lead Assessor training and also Transition Auditor training of M/s Nigel Bauer & Associates, UK, who set my thoughts in the right direction and put my concepts in the correct perspective.

Mr. R.V.K. Ranga Rao His belief in my capabilities has helped me reach where I am today. He taught me by absolute belief in the power of quality. His favorite statement, "Have a Lakshman Rekha (Line of Self Control), never to be stepped across," is expected to be the future of ISO 9001 too.

Mr. Dayal Prasad Mathur My father and best critic, for so painstakingly and tirelessly editing my numerous drafts and weeding out all those tiny slips I made.

Mr. R.V.S.M. Chinna Rao My counterpart in Verny who was kind enough to take on a part during my writing days.

Vasanta Mathur My wife, without whose encouragement and support I could not have undertaken or finished writing this book.

Rijuta and Harshini My daughters whose rightful time I spared for this book, yet in their innocence are quite amused, in fact even a little proud of the fact that their daddy could have finished this book earlier but for their interruptions and questions.

Engineering Staff College of India, Hyderabad and M/s Nigel Bauer & Associates, United Kingdom The training organizations for their detailed and informative Lead Assessor training and Transition Auditor training that set me on the right course.

Mr. S. Ravishankar of BIS Whose orientation programs on the 2000 version of ISO 9001 I had attended.

Mr. H.L. Upendar of BIS Whose brain I've never hesitated to pick being my friend as always.

Mr. Raj Kapoor of M/s Suprint Ad Media, Hyderabad His artistic and imaginative skill converted my concept into an appealing cover design.

Mr. Venkatesh of M/s Suprint Ad Media, Hyderabad His efforts in drawing the illustrations so well.

The British Library, Hyderabad The ever available treasure house of knowledge and information.

Staff of the British Library, Hyderabad A team of extremely polite and courteous people who are ever helpful.

Vikas Publishing House Pvt Ltd All the members for their help and support in bringing out this book.

Last but not least, my former and present colleagues, who have primarily been responsible for shaping my thoughts, through their association. In addition to the above my sincere thanks to C. Ram Prasad, K. Rajendra Prasad and S.S.V. Subba Rao of Verny for helping me with word processing.

Above all I would like to thank those countless teachers, writers and experts whose names unfortunately I do not remember, but who have molded my thoughts and taught me whatever I have endeavored to present.

Pradeep Kumar Mathur

Contents

LIST OF FIGURES

LIST OF TABLES

Section

I

Fundamentals

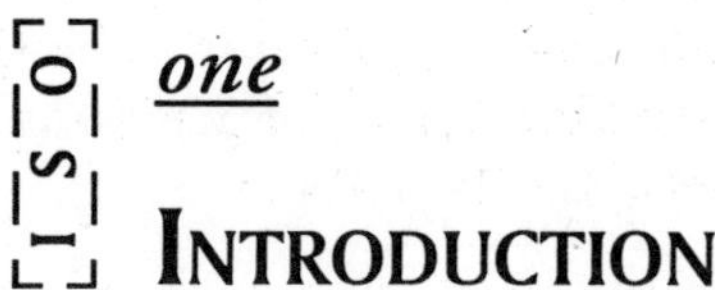

one

INTRODUCTION

1. WHAT IS ISO

ISO in short stands for the 'International Organization for Standardization' functioning from Geneva in Switzerland as a worldwide federation of national standards organizations. It is made up of representatives from more than 107 countries who represent their National Standardization Bodies. The Indian representative in ISO is the Bureau of Indian Standards (BIS).

Founded in 1946 to develop industrial standards to facilitate international trade, the ISO does the work of preparing these international standards through its technical committees numbering over 130.

Interestingly, the Greek word "isos" means equal and from this has been derived the English prefix "iso" meaning equal or identical as in isotherm (equal temperature), isobars (equal pressure), isohytes (equal rainfall), isometric (equal dimension), isosceles triangle (with two equal sides), etc. It is for this reason the word ISO was adopted as the acronym to represent the organization, which is extremely apt, since the very purpose of this organization is to standardize, i.e. equalize.

2. WHAT IS ISO 9000 FAMILY

ISO 9000 family refers to the group of international standards of ISO brought out for the management of Quality Systems in organizations. Members of TC 176, the Technical Committee for the Quality System related standards at ISO, while numbering these standards, felt that it would be better to number all these related standards in a consecutively numbered series for convenience. Normally standards are numbered as they are made and the numbers allotted are sequential, with the next higher available number being given to any newly prepared standard ready for allotment of a number. By the time these Quality System related standards were ready, ISO had already made more than 8000 standards. Although reserving of a block of numbers was a deviation from practice, it was still done, in the interest of user convenience. Thus, having decided to number these standards in a series, by even keeping numbers of this series free for future use, the next higher available series of numbers being 9000, it was blocked for quality system related standards. These standards were thus called the, "ISO 9000 Series of Standards". This series of standards has now been renamed the "ISO 9000 Family of Standards". They consist of ISO 9000, ISO 9001, ISO 9004 and ISO 19011.

ISO 9000 family of standards, are related to the Quality Management System and not to the products. They aim at controlling and improving processes that help produce products rather than controlling the products themselves. They can be applied to any organization, producing any product or service, and are truly generic in nature.

3. WHAT IS ISO 9001

ISO 9001 is the international standard, which lays down the requirements for a Quality Management System (QMS). This QMS in the simplest of terms is defined as,

The process of Management of the Systems of an organization, with regard to its Quality related activities, for 'meeting and enhancing customer satisfaction' and also taking care of all other interested parties such as legislative and regulatory bodies, shareholders, suppliers, employees, etc.

This International Standard is based on:

1) The "8" Quality Management Principles
   a) Customer Focus,
   b) Leadership,
   c) Involvement of People,
   d) Process Approach,
   e) System Approach to Management,
   f) Continual Improvement,
   g) Factual Approach To Decision Making, and
   h) Mutually Beneficial Supplier Relationships
2) The "Plan-Do-Check-Act Improvement Cycle"

The QMS Principles are such that they are applicable and common to every type of organization, be it in the manufacturing or service sector. Therefore, although the standard remains the same, each organization interprets the standard in its own way and then implements it to suit its requirements. This means that the standard being generic, there are a variety of ways the same standard can be applied, specific to each organization.

The "Plan-Do-Check-Act Improvement Cycle" is the most fundamental and basic method of viewing any activity where the motive is, 'to do the job well and improve it continually'. This cycle can be used to breakdown, analyze, understand and then improve even the most complex of activities. This cycle is known as the Deming PDCA Circle, named after its originator W. Edward Deming.

At the basic level, this cycle can be described as under:

- Decide what you want to do.
- Do it.
- Verify, whether whatever you have done is in line with what you had decided to do.
- Review your earlier decision and correct wherever needed.
- Look for possibilities to improve whatever you are doing.

In conclusion, the QMS is a dynamic system, based on good business management practices for producing and supplying good quality products through continual improvement for achieving and enhancing, satisfaction and perceptions of the customer together with the interest of all interested parties.

Thus a system exclusively designed and tailored as per the policies of an organization provides its people with an environment suitable for their needs. This harmony of the system and its people is essential.

We ought to remember that, requirements always depend upon needs. For instance,

- If a person needs to skate, his requirement is ICE
- If he needs to snow-ski, his requirement is SNOW
- If he needs to water-ski, his requirement is WATER
- If he needs to swim, his requirement is WATER
- If he needs to have a sauna, his requirement is STEAM and COLD WATER
- If he needs to have a steam bath, his requirement is STEAM.

We observe it is the same water, which is required in a different form each time based on a different need. Similarly ISO 9001:2000 too being generic, is as fluid and flexible as water and molds itself to different organizational requirements as per their needs.

4. WHY ISO 9001

The common reasons why organizations take up ISO 9001 are as follows:

- Fulfil customer requirements
- Keep-up with competition
- Gain a market advantage
- Provide a better framework for development and growth
- Improve the image
- Gain publicity
- Comply with export market requirement
- Create a system for identifying and defining requirements, and
- Build public confidence

Whatever be the initial reasons, it is essential that once this project of establishing, implementing, maintaining and improving a system as per ISO 9001 is taken-up, it should be whole-hearted. If attempted reluctantly, it will do more harm than good and will become a long, difficult and unrewarding experience leading to frustration within the organization.

The greatest advantage of this standard is, that it helps organizations to,

- discipline their systems
- ensure controls
- manage their growth and
- continually improve themselves.

5. DEVELOPMENT OF ISO 9001

The origin of ISO 9001 can be traced back to the combined influence of the United States Military Standard - MIL-Q-9058A, the North Atlantic Treaty Organization (NATO) quality standard - AQAP1 and the British Standards Institute (BSI) Quality Management standard BS 5750. The International Organization for Standardization, through its technical committee TC 176, has now brought out the 'Third edition dated 2000-12-15' of this Quality Management System standard, as its latest revision.

In the ISO 9000 family of standards, it is ISO 9001 which lays down the requirements for the quality system. Over the years, through its three revisions, the standard has also undergone change and developed into a powerful document. Adopting this standard would now help organizations establish, implement and improve their own Quality Management System.

TABLE 1

ISO 9001 System Requirements and Purpose

Standard	System Requirements	Purpose
ISO 9001:1988	Quality System	Quality Assurance
ISO 9001:1994	Quality System	Quality Assurance
ISO 9001:2000	Quality Management System	Quality Assurance & Customer Satisfaction

Thus ISO 9001:2000 scores in a major way over its previous versions because it aims at both Quality Assurance and Customer Satisfaction.

6. QUALITY SYSTEM AND QUALITY MANAGEMENT SYSTEM

The quality system of an organization basically consists of its structure, procedures, processes and resources required for adequate and effective management of all its quality related activities. This quality system is created by the organization primarily, to satisfy its own internal requirements, for determining and implementing its quality policy, and fulfilling its objectives for survival and growth. The quality system functions through the well-defined structure of responsibility, authority and relationships for implementing and practising quality planning, quality control, quality assurance and quality improvement.

Every organization has a system of management, which basically consists of, 'a set of interrelated or interacting elements that help it in establishing its policy and objectives and achieving these objectives'. This management system is made up of many smaller systems such as the financial management, the environmental management system, the quality management system, etc.

The Quality Management System (QMS) is that part of the organization's management system, which focuses on the achievement of results, in relation to the quality objectives, to satisfy the needs, expectations and requirements of all interested parties. The QMS thus directs and controls all quality related activities of the organization.

The quality objectives that the QMS aims to achieve, compliment other objectives of the organization such as those related to growth, funds, profitability, the environment, occupational health and safety, etc.

7. 'QUALITY ASSURANCE' AND 'QUALITY ASSURANCE & CUSTOMER SATISFACTION'

Quality Assurance is that part of Quality Management, which focuses on providing confidence on behalf of the organization, to all interested parties, that all specified quality requirements shall be met.

Quality Assurance coupled with Customer Satisfaction, however, is that part of Quality Management which focuses not only on providing Quality Assurance on behalf of the organization, but also on achieving and enhancing customer satisfaction and perception regarding the degree of success in meeting and exceeding customer requirements.

8. MISCONCEPTIONS REGARDING ISO 9001

(i) Being a self-declaration standard, one can literally declare poor quality and get away by having an ISO 9001 certification.

This is in fact, possible. An organization can declare lower standards, comply with it, and obtain certification. However, in practice it would be unlikely, since the planning, effort put in, production, testing done, checks exercised, etc. are all the same irrespective of whether the organization declares a lower or higher standard. After all this effort no organization gains anything by declaring a poor standard. Of course it is possible that what appears a low standard could be the organization's best effort to comply with the requirement of "Fitness for use".

This fitness for use is like, " One man's food is another man's poison".

Consider the case of an organization making 'low cost toys of plastic or even clay' for selling in village fairs. The quality of these toys may appear poor, but what the organization is selling, has to fit the pocket of the buyer and yet give joy to the child. The organization succeeds in both. Thus, apparently what appears to be an organization making poor quality toys is in fact an organization meeting its customer requirements.

(ii) An organization already recognized to be consistently producing good quality products does not need to prove it.

An organization does not necessarily have to prove its capability to existing loyal customers in relation to existing competition, but it definitely needs to fight new competition. This is where the certification helps. Also, for getting new customers, the certification helps. Moreover, in the absence of the certificate, competition is able to sway and snatch away customers by telling them that, the organization has not taken the certification because it could not comply with the ISO requirements. The customers may not fully believe this, but a doubt is definitely created in their minds.

(iii) An organization with a good QMS in existence does not need a certificate.

The value of an independent unbiased assessment need not be emphasized or elaborated. The certificate, if not anything else, at least helps give evidence of capability.

(iv) Certification is expensive for small organizations.

Bureau of Indian Standards always gives the small scale industries a discounted fee structure to encourage them to take up certification. Similarly, most of the other certifying bodies too, help the small companies, in this regard.

The Govt. of India also gives a subsidy to the tune of Rs. 75,000/- to small scale industries.

(v) Our customers want poor quality, which depends on their paying power.

Poor quality is different from fitness for use. The customer may want cheaper product but it is for the organization to give him the best possible, and work towards quality improvement without increasing price.

Going back to the example given in 'Misconception No. 1', the customer no doubt wants a cheap plastic or clay toy for the child. However, if the organization were to use toxic paints for decorating the toy, just because these paints are cheap, then this would be an incorrect interpretation of customer requirements.

(vi) It results in lot of unnecessary paperwork.

Though most organizations already have a lot of paperwork such as purchase orders, billing, material receipt records, sales records, pay roll, etc. lack of other useful records fail to provide readily, the vital information needed when its holder is not available. Thus documentation helps make the jobs, independent of individuals. Obviously, efficiency improves. In order to convey the spirit behind the standard this version has also reduced the mandatory procedures to 6 (Table 12, Sl. No. 15). This does not in anyway mean that, even those procedures that are needed by the organization can also be done away with just because they are not mandatory.

(vii) The standard expects you to document what you practise and practise what you document.

This is not true. The sequence of steps in fulfilling what the standard expects you to do is as follows:

- Document what you do.
- Compare the practice against the requirements of the standard.
- Determine the shortcomings of the practice in vogue.

- Align practice to requirements of the standard by overcoming the deficiencies.
- Document this new upgraded practice.
- Establish this as THE PRACTICE.

Therefore, 'what you do' corresponds to THE PRACTICE, which is the "aligned correct practices" and not the "earlier existing practice". Of course, if the existing practice has elements that are superior to the requirements of the standard, then they need not be downgraded to align them to the standard.

(viii) Having a Quality Control Manager is mandatory.

This is not correct since the need is for 'control of quality' and not the availability of this manager. Actually the best method of controlling quality is for the process owners themselves to do it. The creation of this post of a Quality Control Manager is with the intention of taking advantage of his knowledge, experience and capability. Also having him helps centralize this technical knowledge, expertise and control.

(ix) All job descriptions must be documented and people's competence must be evaluated for them.

Only "key or critical" job descriptions need to be documented—not all jobs. In every organization, people's competence is in any case evaluated while allotting jobs. The only possibility is that, this evaluation may not be formal. What needs to be done is to ensure that, formal competence evaluation is definitely done for the 'key or critical jobs' of the organization.

(x) Everyone in the organization must be able to repeat the quality policy verbatim.

This is not essential. The Quality Policy is the top management's statement affirming its own policy commitment given to the people of the organization. It gives a direction to them, and what is required is, that people should know, understand and be able to explain this direction in relation to their function. Many a time, it is not possible for uneducated workers to explain the policy to demonstrate compliance to this requirement. The verbatim repetition is basically a method of circumventing this deficiency by ensuring they are at least able to repeat it.

Think back to the time, when we as children were required to repeat the prayer or the pledge in school. The purpose of being able to repeat then, was to ensure that when required to explain, we were able to explain it, using memory.

(xi) All outdated documents must be removed from the place of use.

It is not the availability of these obsolete documents that is prohibited but their use even by mistake, that has to be prevented. Actually the best method of controlling this unintended use is to remove the obsolete documents from the place of use. However, if the organization has a system by which their use can be controlled by some other means, even while the obsolete documents are at the place of use, it would be acceptable.

In certain cases, it is possible that an obsolete document may be required to be used, even at a later date and so would be available at the place of use. In such a case, as long as this is a conscious decision, its use is acceptable. Take the case of a product model that gets replaced with many newer ones over a period of time. Now, if the organization receives a request for a replacement component for the earlier obsolete model, obviously they will have to use its obsolete drawing. This is a conscious and intended use, and the availability of the obsolete drawing at the place of use, as such, would be acceptable.

(xii) All Purchase orders have to be signed.

Here again, the requirement is for the purchase orders to be controlled by proper procedure for authorization, preparation, verification, approval and issue. The signatures are for the purpose of ensuring these. No doubt, even when an individual signs he can do so without reading the document but it is presumed that if he has signed he has read it. Actually if an organization can demonstrate that their computer—generated purchase orders have proper checks and controls through passwords, it would be acceptable even if the purchase order is not signed.

Also, from the suppliers' angle, the question as to how they would know whether a purchase order is genuine or not may arise, and hence the insistence on signature.

(xiii) Documents have to carry an approval signature.

Here again the logic mentioned in point (xii) above applies.

(xiv) All measurements have to be made with calibrated instruments.

The emphasis is on the measurement being reliable and hence made with reliable instruments, and not on calibrated instruments. Calibration is merely the means of ensuring reliability, accuracy and correctness. If an organization can show that they have a methodology to ensure accuracy and correctness even without calibration for a specific application, it would be acceptable. This reliability of measurement is ensured through insistence on 'National or International traceability' for the calibration done.

Moreover, where measurements are for indication purpose only, the instrument used need not be calibrated.

(xv) All auditors have to undergo a formal training.

The formal training is the means of ensuring knowledge of the standard and methods to be adopted for carrying out the audits. The requirement is for the auditors to be knowledgeable.

9. MAKING ISO 9001 WORK FOR YOU

If you really want the standard to work for you, stop viewing it as a set of rules to be followed to solve all your problems. Just treat and view it as a tool, which if used in the right manner, will give better results. Develop a framework for operating, analysing and improving your own organization as the primary motive. Also, do the following:

- Do things in a systematic and organized manner
- Document things to get out of the trap of dependence on only specific individuals
- Control key documents
- Maintain genuine records
- Check regularly for errors and scope for improvement
- Act to correct and prevent and
- Continually strive for improvements.

10. CERTIFICATION

Even after establishing, implementing and successfully maintaining the QMS as per ISO 9001, it is still essential for the organization to be able to demonstrate and prove this periodically. The organizations can achieve this through 'Third Party QMS Certification', whereby their QMS gets assessed and certified by an authorized independent body, which would issue a certificate indicating the scope and validity of certification. Moreover, during the period of the certificate's validity, it is obligatory for the certifying body to assess the organization periodically. Therefore this certificate, issued by the certifying body indicating the scope and validity of the certification, would give the organization the necessary evidence that can be furnished for proving successful implementation and maintenance of the QMS.

There are a number of certifying bodies, which undertake this certification such as BIS (Bureau of Indian Standards), BVQI (Bureau Veritas Quality International), LRIS (Lloyd's Register Industrial Services), etc.

Bear in mind, "Getting certified is easy but continuing to remain certified is not so easy".

Section

II

"Eight" Quality Management Principles

two

CUSTOMER FOCUS

1. THE POWER OF FOCUS

Have you ever seen a child use a magnifying glass to burn paper, out under the Sun?

Yes, most of you have. In fact, you yourselves may have had paper burnt this way, as a child.

What is it that happens out there? What is it that causes the paper to burn under the magnifying glass?

Actually, the heat energy of the Sun, which feels terrible but bearable even on a very hot day and positively welcome on a cold day, is not as weak as it appears. It is merely un-focused. Once focused using a converging lens, the rays get concentrated at the focal point and become powerful enough to burn the paper.

This power does not come from the lens but from, 'the concentration of energy'. Focus of the energy therefore is the 'Power Giver' to the child.

In one word, the answer to the above questions is FOCUS.

For organizations too, focus provides the capability to bring together their divergent energies by concentrating them towards the single-minded achievement of desired goals.

"Focus" gives organizations the power to not only perform well but also to excel.

2. 'CUSTOMER FOCUS' ORIENTATION

A customer is the most important visitor on our premises.
He is not dependent on us. We are dependent on him.
He is not an interruption on our work. He is the purpose of it.
He is not an outsider on our business. He is a part of it.
We are not doing him a favour by serving him.
He is doing us a favour by giving us an opportunity to do so.

— Mahatma Gandhi

It is indeed extremely significant that, like a true visionary, more than half a century ago, Mahatma Gandhi put forth this philosophy of 'customer satisfaction'. I first saw this quote in a bank, about 25 years ago. It literally read like the bank's oath to me then. Mahatma Gandhi's statement, even when it was made, was not a new discovery but an acknowledged fact. Right down the ages, perceptive people have known and practised this principle of customer orientation. However, what makes this statement by Mahatma Gandhi significant is that, he who preached for the acquiring of handloom weaving skills by the masses, also acknowledged and propagated 'Customer Focus' as a need, even for the cottage industries he championed.

Thus, the shift towards 'Customer Focus', which has been emphasized in the 2000 version of this international standard, only means that the 'ISO quality movement' is moving in the right direction. The earlier 1994 version required the organization to have a 'Quality Assurance oriented Quality System' to demonstrate 'Conformance to Specified Requirements'. The present standard however targets development of a 'Quality Management System' to demonstrate 'Conformance to Customer and Regulatory Requirements as also enhancement of Customer Satisfaction through Continual Improvement'.

In order to better understand this change in focus, it is essential to understand the importance of customer satisfaction which arises only by ensuring the following:

(i) Meeting customer's and regulatory requirement,

(ii) Assuring conformance of product quality consistently, and

(iii) Exceeding customer expectations by constantly enhancing quality levels.

ISO 9000:2000 emphasizes that organizations depend on their customers and therefore should understand their current and future needs, should meet customer requirements and should strive to exceed customer expectations.

The focus of the standard being on the customer, it is essential for the organization,

(i) To identify and understand the customers,

(ii) To determine their requirements and expectations, and

(iii) To establish the means of meeting and exceeding these requirements and expectations.

For any organization in today's competitive environment, developing true Customer Focus is not an option but a necessity for survival. No organization can afford to forget that customers always have the choice to source their requirements elsewhere. The alternative therefore for the organization is between satisfying customers or facing decline and possible extinction.

Although the days of selling or marketing are not over yet, the thrust presently is on Customer Focus that literally means the organization should form a kind of partnership with the customers by providing solutions to their needs, expectations and desires.

The traditional *Paanwala* (Beetle leaf seller) of any town has a very large number of habitual consumers of Paan (Beetle leaf) as his daily customers, yet he recognizes every one of them individually. On any day, when a Mr. Mishra walks up to him and tells him, " My usual" the Paanwala only just glances up and then prepares the *Paan* exactly the way this Mishraji likes it. If it is a Mr. Pandey who has come, he gets his *Paan* to his liking. Mind you, there are more than 50 different permutations and combinations, and the *Paanwala* remembers what Mishraji or Pandeyji likes. In fact I have seen instances when a gentleman seated in a bus halted at a bus-stop, has shouted for his *Paan* from the window of the bus, and the *Paanwala* has, by merely resorting to voice recognition, prepared the required Paan and sent it to the customer, all in a matter of less than a minute. Hats off to this unique individual for, *"he truly knows his customers, their needs and expectation."*

Similarly, on a much larger scale, most hotels maintain a 'Customer Profile' database, consisting of details of each individual's requirements, preferences, tastes, likes and dislikes, etc. This database helps the management and staff, display customer recognition. This recognition in turn is aimed at exhibiting to the customers, that the hotel considers them special enough to be remembered and that their patronage is valued. All this effort eventually aims at seeking continued patronage by the customers. Based on these examples we can formulate a rule for any organization which would read,

Little things that make you know customers better
are significant, not trivial,
So attention to these make all the difference

Customers today are enlightened, discerning and perceptive with quite high expectations and cannot be taken for granted. True customer focus also requires the organization to communicate to its people the actual feedback received, from the customers, be it good or bad. This alone can help the people of the organization, to act upon the feedback as a basis for further improvement.

The key to building customer focus is the ability to anticipate the needs of:

- Existing loyal customers
- Potential customers
- Dissatisfied customers and
- Competitor loyal customers.

3. OUR CUSTOMER

Traditionally the word 'customer' has been used to define those people, external to the organization who purchase the organization's product. Today however the word customer is used more broadly and includes even the people working within the organization.

Our customer is any individual or group of individuals, who receive our product either directly or through a series of intermediaries. The receiver of our product therefore need not only be the user. He could be the consumer (person who uses our product), client (who uses our service), end-user (who ultimately uses our product), retailer (who uses our product by buying and then selling it again), beneficiary (who benefits from the uses of our product) and purchaser (who purchases our product and not necessarily uses it). In fact the definition has been further widened to cover everyone on whom, directly or indirectly our product has an effect.

Thus, the customer is anyone on whom our product has an effect.

For instance, for a 'Pharmaceuticals Company' its customer is not merely the patient who takes the medicine. The customer list ought to contain everyone on whom 'the value addition of the product' has an influence and so includes all those listed below:

- The patient who takes the medicine
- The doctor who prescribes it
- The hospital that buys it
- The nurse who administers it
- The retail pharmacy that sells it
- The wholesaler who bulk-stocks it
- The patient's relative who pays for it directly
- The patient's organization, which pays for it indirectly
- The insurance company, which covers the patient's health insurance and
- The drug controller who approves it.

Or for a 'Biscuit manufacturing Company' the customer list would probably run as follows:

- The child who eats the biscuits
- The grandmother who feeds the child
- The mother who buys them
- The father who pays for them

- The retailer who sells them
- The wholesaler who bulk-stocks them
- The health inspector who certifies the company and
- The third party Certifying Agency which certifies them.

3.1 Our External Customer

The external customers are not part of our organization, but on whom, the purchase of our product has an effect. They can be the buyer, users, ultimate users, government agencies, the public at large, etc. All of them get influenced directly or indirectly by the purchase of the product and so are to be treated as customers.

3.2 Our Internal Customer

The internal customers are part of our organization, and are in fact users of 'Our In-process Outputs', which are our process intermediates. Thus each stage of activity within our organization, adds value to the inputs received and, after value addition, passes it on to the next stages, which become their internal customers.

4. UNDERSTANDING THE CUSTOMER

Although 'understanding the customer' as a concept sounds difficult, it is an extremely simple requirement to practise to perfection. Remember, customers are people just like us and they are human. Most of them are just ordinary people. They want quality, appreciate courtesy, feel nice when people are good or kind to them, dislike dishonesty, and would love to be recognized and pampered. No doubt customers as individuals are different, but then, they come from different backgrounds with different experiences, moods and prejudices based on which they view their needs and expectations. If they sometimes appear unpredictable, irrational, illogical and emotional, so what? So are we. We all are Human, with human failings. They therefore as customers are entitled to their failings and expectations.

Never get disturbed by the apparent lack of logic, rationale or predictability of a customer. The absolute truth is that,

Our customer is the reason for the existence of our Organization

Learn to 'Think like a customer' and question yourself on what you would have liked, if roles were reversed. Know them, cherish them and be fair to them. It is for us, as the supplier, to understand them, for which we must seek answers to the following:

(i) Who are our customers?

(ii) What are their needs and expectations / aspirations?

(iii) How do we meet these needs and expectations / aspirations? and

(iv) How do we exceed these needs and expectations / aspirations?

Answers to these questions are to be essentially determined on a continuous basis to keep ahead of competition. However in addition to determining the above, and trying to meet the requirements, we must also ensure that,

(i) We never break our promises

(ii) We never promise more than what we can do

(iii) We give them a little more than they require or expect and

(iv) We never underestimate competition.

A customer has certain rights which every organization must essentially accept and honour. These rights are as follows:

(i) Right to proper and adequate education

(ii) Right to complete, correct and honest information

(iii) Right to health and safety

(iv) Right to decide and select products as per choice

(v) Right to be heard

(vi) Right to enjoy the products purchased

(vii) Right to re-dressal in case of dissatisfaction.

4.1 Customer Requirements (Needs and Expectations)

Determination of these attributes is extremely important, as they are the goals that the organization has to meet and exceed. It is meeting and exceeding these attributes that leads the organization to ensuring and enhancing customer satisfaction and delight. These can be classified as follows:

TABLE 2

Customer Satisfaction and Delight Related Attributes

S.No.	Attribute	Nature of Attribute	Purpose
1.	Stated needs	These correspond to the determined, specified, communicated and stated needs of the customer that are **vital** in nature and have to be met by the product	They are necessary for the design and development, production, delivery and assessment of the product for its **basic functioning**
2.	Implied needs	These correspond to the known and required needs of the product, are **essential** and also have to be necessarily met	They are also necessary but for the **safe & satisfactory performance** of the product
3.	Expectations	These correspond to those additional attributes wished to be built into or accompanying the product which are **desired** yet never stated or implied	They are add-ons to the product to hold onto existing and pulling in newer customers by **pleasing** them
4.	Delight	These correspond to those absolutely **unexpected** but pleasing tangible or intangible attributes that are given away as free accompaniments	They are surprises for **delighting** customers to hold onto the existing and pull in newer customers

4.2 Determining the Needs

With regard to the requirements it should be ensured that:

(i) They give complete and detailed information,

(ii) They are adequate for the purpose,

(iii) They are clear and unambiguous,

(iv) They are measurable with known accuracy and precision,

(v) They give tolerances of acceptable and achievable levels,

(vi) They specify methods of measurement and test, which can be undertaken,

(vii) They provide acceptance and rejection criteria, and

(viii) They provide future requirement details, to enable forward planning.

4.3 Determining the Expectations

The point to be remembered in determining customer expectations is, to make sure they are understood from the 'CUSTOMER'S VIEWPOINT'. The customers can themselves inform us of their views on the relative importance of each of the following attributes normally used to determine expectations:

- Performance
- Features
- Conformance
- Reliability
- Durability
- Serviceability
- Aesthetics
- Perception

4.4 Meeting Customer Needs and Expectations

The entire purpose of emphasizing and focusing on the customer is to ensure that all our activities function with the objective to 'meet and exceed customer needs and expectations'. If customers are kept dissatisfied, no organization could prosper let alone maintain itself, and may even cease to exist.

Keep your customers coming back, not your products

In areas of the organization where there is no customer contact and they are mere faceless-entities, the need is to create a situation that brings about people involvement internally with 'a customer and goals' approach. To overcome this situation the internal customer approach has been adopted, whereby everyone is linked to each other and has a physical customer available, who can be satisfied. This approach is extremely easy to understand, because only if each stage supplies a correctly completed, satisfactory product to the next stage, the finished product, can lead to customer satisfaction. This 'Internal Customer Approach' leads to a 'Customer Driven' organization that ensures every stage treats the next stage or person, as its internal customer and itself as the customer of the previous stage.

TABLE 3

Normal Customer Expectations from Products (Goods and Service)

From Goods	From Service
Better Performance Better Features Better Reliability Better Conformance Better Durability Better Serviceability Better Aesthetics Better Perceived Quality Better Assurance Better Availability	Better Timeliness Better Reliability Better Competence Better Communication Better Credibility Better Security Better Understanding Better Courtesy Better Cooperation Better Assurance Better Availability Better Conformance Better Effectiveness & Efficiency
Lower Price	Lower Price
	Faster Accessibility Faster Responsiveness Faster Delivery

5. MEETING REGULATORY REQUIREMENTS

Regulatory requirements basically have a protective role. Exploitation of workers was one of the first to cause a hue and cry, while of late the environment has taken its place. What is expected of any law-abiding organization is, that it should determine, follow, monitor and endeavor to improve upon all regulatory requirements not only in letter but also in spirit.

An organization that does not follow regulatory requirements cannot be expected to follow voluntary requirements in the true spirit

6. MEETING SOCIETY REQUIREMENTS

Every organization must no doubt be customer-oriented, but service to the customer is incomplete without an orientation of service to society and this must also be essentially fulfilled. This basically means the organization while taking care of the needs of the customer must be concerned about the needs of the society as well, and should not work against them in any way. The general areas of concern for any society are as follows:

- Protecting the environment,
- Conserving the resources, and
- Avoiding wasteage in any form.

Thus a good organizational system not only ensures a satisfied customer but also exercises internal controls for achieving and meeting society requirements.

No Organization can claim to have a Quality Culture
If it lacks honest concern, supported by sincere actions,
towards its responsibility to society

7. EXCEEDING CUSTOMER REQUIREMENTS DELIGHT

The entire purpose of meeting customer needs and expectations is 'to retain the existing and attract new customers'. But what does an organization do when its competitors also begin to meet customer needs and expectations? In such a business environment, the competitive edge developed by the organization gets lost. In such a situation, there is the possibility of, competitors luring away customers by offering marginally better benefits. The businesses then would begin to operate merely based on small incentives given to customers.

This is the time to, exceed customer's expectations and achieve what is called 'Customer Delight'. The advantage is, delighted customers are now not sure of what will be given next but are sure it will be more than what they expect. This is the region of imagination and leads to fulfilment of dreams. One should not forget that what delights them today would become an expectation tomorrow and then one has to look for a new delight parameter. Thus constant innovation to stay ahead of customer expectation is required. All delight parameters necessarily do not cost extra, but even if they do, they are necessary for the organization to stay on top and are the factors that propel an organization towards continual improvement.

Here, I am reminded of an incidence that occurred to me, while writing this book, which appropriately explains the difference between a customer's stated needs, implied needs, expectations and delight.

My darling daughters, Rijuta Mathur who is 14 years old and Harshini Mathur who is 11 years old learned from my wife that their names would figure in the acknowledgements of this book. They rushed to me and chanted in unison, "Daddy, is it a fact that our names will come in the book?"

When I said, "Of-course. Your names will definitely be in the Acknowledgements of my book" they were absolutely thrilled.

Then came the tricky question from Harshini, "Daddy, will all the readers of the book really read my name and will I become famous?"

To this Body-line bowling, I had to honestly reply with, "No darling, most people do not read the acknowledgements of a book".

She was disappointed, but gamely went-on, " Doesn't matter. We ourselves shall show it to our friends".

This conversation set me thinking the whole evening. After considerable analysis I realized there was a valuable lesson to be learnt from this simple conversation with my daughters.

My children were my customers in this instance. It was for me as the processor to understand their innocent expressions, where they had actually expressed the following:

(i) A stated need that their names should figure in this book.

(ii) An implied need that readers read their names.

(iii) An expectation that they become famous.

(iv) An unexpected hope that their fame would spread whereby even a few of their friends might get to know of it.

Thus by merely putting in their names in the acknowledgement I would have never achieved the objective of satisfying, let alone delighting them. Thus by bringing their names here into the text of the book, which readers are bound to read I have satisfied and delighted them by fulfilling their dream.

Such may be the means required to be adopted by organizations to delight customers, and when done, will definitely lead them to success.

In simple words, if the customer gets just a wee bit more, than he expects and is promised, he would be surprised by what he gets hence delighted. Delight is sometimes called the 'WOW factor as, whenever one is delighted, he reacts with, " WOW, this is a wonderful surprise!" or " WOW, that was a great service!"

There is another Wow episode that occurred one busy day when, I drove my car into a petrol filling station to fill-in petrol. The attendant there not only filled-in petrol for me, but also cleaned the wind shield of the car and checked the wheel pressure, as a complimentary service. I was pleasantly surprised and said to myself, "Wow, this is indeed very nice, I should patronize this filling station, in future too". This continued for a couple of months and then the service was discontinued one day. I was disappointed, but the attendant was highly apologetic while informing me of the discontinuing of service and so possibly covered-up for my disappointment. Moreover by then, I was habituated to filling-up there and so have continued to do so.

The exact opposite of WOW is the 'OUCH factor'. This results from an undesirable occurrence or episode, which is remembered even long after it has occurred, merely for its negative impact.

Imagine you are on a vacation with your family. You walk into a hotel, where you have a confirmed booking for a room with a sea-view. However, when you enter your room you find it does not face the sea, rather it gives you a view of the town, how would you feel? You would definitely be upset. Moreover, if in this situation, the hotel staffs attitude is also casual and unconcerned about the foul-up, you would obviously be more than upset. You would be hurt and would think, "Ouch, this is bad service and worse handling of the situation. I would rather stay elsewhere in future". You may even walk-off in a huff and move to another hotel, just because they couldn't give you a room of your choice. This is an 'Ouch situation' you would remember all your life for it's negative attributes.

If however after this foul-up the staff approach is highly apologetic with a promise to change your room to a sea-view the very next day and they make your first day's room stay complimentary, how would you feel? The hurt, although still there, would have been made less painful and bearable.

If further they also make your entire first day's other expenditures in the hotel also complimentary, you would certainly feel satisfied and would happily stay-on.

This is known as 'Recovery of an Ouch situation'.

Ouch situations although undesirable are unavoidable and recovery being the only solution, it has to be essentially adopted. This recovery saves the good reputation of the organization from being tarnished, which would lead to bad publicity. It also strengthens customer's belief in an organization's commitment to customer satisfaction and delight.

This type of Recovery of ouch situation helps retain old customers and gain new customers.

TABLE 4

Comparison of Stated Needs, Implied Needs, Expectations and Delight

No.	Stated / Real Needs	Implied / Perceived Needs	Expectations	Delight
1.	These aspects of the product are requirements that have been stated clearly, defined and are measurable and needed by the customer.	These aspects of the product are requirements that although not stated, still the customer needs them to be fulfilled.	These aspects of the product are neither stated nor implied, yet expected by the customer.	These aspects of the product are neither required nor expected by the customer and their presence pleasantly surprises and delights the customer.
2.	Specification, use, purpose, application, performance, etc.	Safety, life, perception, installation, delivery, warranty, service, security, etc.	Satisfaction, response, follow-up, competence, courtesy, etc.	Any unexpected pleasant thing associated with the product.

8. CUSTOMER PERCEPTION OF QUALITY

Perception of Quality from the customer's point of view is defined as, "what they feel about the quality". Understanding this feeling requires aligning our understanding with their perception. Ultimately the customer's perception whether 'acceptable or unacceptable', 'right or wrong', 'reasonable or unreasonable', 'just or unjust', 'logical or illogical', 'real or imaginary', still determines the perceived quality of our product. There is no scope to disagree with this perception. It is their opinion and their perception and so it is final.

There are however a few rules given below that would help an organization maintain and improve customer perceptions:

(i) Deliver whatever you promise and do not promise more than you can deliver.

(ii) Provide help, support and care for the customers.

(iii) Accept faults and endeavour to avoid repeating them.

(iv) Display knowledge of your field with humility.

Remember, 'Quality is what the customer says it is, not what the organization writes down as the specifications or procedures'. Product quality after-all is totally 'Customer Perception' related.

9. CUSTOMER COMPLAINTS

Customer complaints are opportunities to convert dissatisfied customers into satisfied and even delighted customers. This conversion is possible only if the complaint is attended to at the highest priority and with full sincerity. Further, the process of resolving and handling the complaint at all levels should be done in a trained and professional manner.

Often it may not be possible for the individual who receives a complaint to redress the complaint on his own, as its decision may be beyond his authority level. In such a case he may seek help from a higher level but this does not mean that he can get away by using this as an excuse. He should respond quickly, agree with the complainant, exhibit and demonstrate genuine regret (as perceived by the complainant) for the occurrence and actively continue to make all efforts to find a solution coupled with, positive concern and efforts, to set things right. In resolving the complaint it must be ensured that the customer ultimately gets what was originally promised. This however will not result in customer recovery.

Recovery does not mean merely giving the complaining customer, just what he had the right to get in the first instance. Recovery requires making the customer feel that the episode was a genuine error and the organization regrets it and would make all efforts to prevent recurrence. It also requires the organization to give the custormer something more, not merely to compensate for the inconvenience but to exhibit the genuineness of the regret. This type of recovery in-fact not only brings back the lost customer but also results in a free advertisement for the organization.

Failure to fulfil customer NEEDS results in a DEFINITE complaint and
Failure to meet customer EXPECTATIONS leads to a PROBABLE complaint
However, both result in loss of face

In the past, there was an unwritten rule that, 'one dissatisfied customer will definitely narrate his experience to at-least five of his acquaintances leading to tarnishing of an organization's reputation. In todays electronic era, the rule has changed and 'the dissatisfied customer on account of the ease of communication, will now narrate his experience to 500 or even 5000 friends'. Thus customer dissatisfaction is not to be allowed at all. In-fact, the opportunity is to be used to make the customer more loyal than before, by doing much more than he expects. Remember, successful handling of complaints, to the complete satisfaction of customers, leads to long-term customer relationships.

10. CUSTOMER SATISFACTION

Customers are not necessarily regular BECAUSE they are satisfied,
Customers are definitely regular IF they are satisfied

Satisfaction requires evaluation of emotion. It results from the fulfillment of requirements and expectations of the customer. Thus, like most subjective things, customer satisfaction also has different meanings for different people. Yet here is its most appropriate definition:

'Customer satisfaction is a combination of quality of performance of 'the product and associated service'.

Ensuring and enhancing customer satisfaction is the purpose of any organization for retaining existing customers and endeavouring to get new customers. The organization's success in achieving this customer satisfaction leads to excellence in performance. The emphasis should be on enhancing and not merely ensuring customer satisfaction. After all, customers could be satisfied and still do not return for a repeat purchase, because the competition could be offering a still better product and service. Thus despite 100% of the organization's customers being satisfied it could still be losing customers. It is only the process of continually enhancing the level of satisfaction and keeping ahead of competition that ensures customer retention.

Pursue Profits and success will evade you,
Pursue Customer Satisfaction and success will seek you.

Monitoring and measuring this customer satisfaction is no doubt important but it is basically an activity of postmortem. After all this measurement is done after the activity has taken place or a product has been delivered and put to use. Therefore although measuring and monitoring this is necessary, it is not the most important activity for ensuring customer satisfaction.

Customer retention and expansion comes not from reactive and reflex handling but from proactive and reflective handling of their problems.

Many Quality experts also lose sight of this fact and lay undue stress on the monitoring and measurement of customer satisfaction. Do not stray from the goal. Our interest ought to be in the present and future, rather than the past.

Thus the rule is,

Concentrate on Customer Care and Support
Not merely on Monitoring and Measuring Customer Satisfaction

11. NATIONAL CUSTOMER SATISFACTION INDEX

Many individual organizations monitor customer satisfaction on a regular basis, but not many of us know that in 1989 Sweden was the first country to monitor this on a National Level. The Customer Satisfaction Barometer (CSB) as a national index was set-up to measure customer satisfaction based on an annual survey of more than 100 leading corporations of the country, covering around 30 industry sectors. The introduction of this new index, CSB was intended to be complimentary to the other indices in existence, especially the productivity index. Thus, whereas earlier only the quantitative aspect was being measured, this inclusion brought-in measurement of the qualitative aspect of industry. CSB could therefore be used to provide information about industry trends with regard to the quality related progress and growth of Swedish industry. Moreover, this CSB, which is still used is itself kept dynamic. Following Sweden's example many countries continue to adopt CSB to monitor customer satisfaction at their national levels.

This demonstrates that monitoring customer satisfaction even at the national level has been recognized as an important requirement by many countries. Therefore at the organizational level it is not merely important but imperative to monitor customer satisfaction.

12. CUSTOMER CARE AND SUPPORT

Customer care requires instilling a feeling of confidence in customers that the organization really likes and values them. This feeling can only result if the organization through their thoughts, words and actions displays a genuine concern and responsibility towards the interests of their customers. It also requires the organization to exhibit protectiveness towards the customer's interests and a willingness to even go out of the way to satisfy and delight them.

Customer Support requires subordinating the organization's interests to those of the customers, again through thought moke both though, word plural, word and actions. This subordination can result only if, the organization is prepared to do every thing within their power, to fulfill and provide for their requirements and expectations. It expects the organization to be truly in their favor - mentally, physically and emotionally.

12.1 Reasons for Providing Customer Care and Support

Any customer when he buys, 'buys a product'. The quality of the product must therefore be such that, it is capable of standing on its own, for satisfying the customer.

An ideal situation for any organization would be when its customers, being happy with the quality of its products (goods and services), buy more and more of the products but have nothing to complain about at all. In practice however, the actual facts are that customer satisfaction is not always achieved. This is because, product quality does not remain the same throughout and is quite often found to be lacking in some aspects, leading to an expression of dissatisfaction by the customer. Any organization can have confidence in their product quality, only if they produce, 'Right first time, every time'. This however is the ideal situation mentioned above while in real life situations product quality is, 'Not right every time in the first attempt' and many a time it is, 'Not right at all'.

To eliminate customer dissatisfaction the organization needs to set, 'those things right that have gone wrong'. The organization therefore has to determine the reason for the dissatisfaction and rectify it, on the basis of feedback from all possible sources.

However often the dissatisfaction of the customer is not with the product supplied, but involves other extraneous factors such as:

(i) An unavoidable situation beyond the control of an organization occurs and they let their customer down. Consequently the customer, on account of their dependence on the organization which has failed them, themselves get forced into a chain reaction failure, towards their own onward commitments, to their customers.

(ii) Although the organization's product quality is as promised, the competitors have raised their level of product quality, thereby lowering the organization's quality level relatively.

(iii) The competitors raise their level of 'Customer Care and Support'.

(iv) The competitors play foul to take away the organization's regular customers.

Hence the organization even with excellent product quality finds itself losing customers. This is where 'Customer Care and Support' helps an organization. The product on the merits of its own quality along with customer care & support are jointly necessary. Thus we can safely conclude that a customer who buys the organization's products does so for the following reasons:

(i) The Quality of the Product,

(ii) The 'Care and Support' given to him by the organization.

It is quite apparent that 'Customer Care & Support' although an add-on benefit extended to retain customers and to bring them back for repeat orders, plays a crucial role not withstanding quality advantages. Despite its importance, mere 'Customer Care and Support' alone is not enough to hold customers. Outstanding 'Product Quality' coupled with equally good 'Customer care and support' are necessary to remain competitive.

Thus every organization accepts the process of 'Customer Care & Support' as its Key Macro Process to achieve its twin fundamental objectives i.e.

(i) Customers buy more and more, and

(ii) Customers don't complain.

12.2 Rules for Customer Care and Support

A few helpful rules that would assist organizations gain customer confidence & ensure top class 'Customer Care & Support' are listed below:

- Determine customers' requirements and always give them what they want.
- Design and implement systems that ensure jobs are done right first time every time.
- Commit less and give more.
- Don't contradict customers rather endeavor to understand them and educate them.
- Give customer complaints the highest priority and take remedial actions with sincerity.
- Become extra cautious when complaints stop coming as this could mean cover-ups.
- Imitate positively oriented best practices without any shame.
- Value and respect people of the organization and those not connected directly too.
- Continually improve products, processes and system based on feedback from all sources.

[I S O] *three*

LEADERSHIP

1. LEADERSHIP

A leader has confidence in his own abilities and he trusts his people's capabilities

In any war, a true leader can turn the tables, even with a weaker army under his command, through strategic understanding of his people and exploiting their actual potentials and capabilities to the fullest. This is true for an success of the organization. In fact, leadership determines and controls an performance of the organization . After all, if the person at the top does not lead the organization in the right way, success eludes. It is for this reason that ISO 9001:2000 has shifted its focus towards the top management and imposed innumerable responsibilities on them.

The role of the top management has now become the hub around which the organization is expected to revolve. The top management is expected to hold together, the rim of the rotating organizational wheel, despite the forces pulling them away under the dynamics of motion. Just as the hub maintains all parts of the rim balanced, equally so also the top management is expected to treat all parts of the organization as equal, without playing favourites. After all, every part of the organization exists on account of its need to the organization and all of them are equally important, none more, none less.

Leadership is a personal quality and cannot be delegated. It is essential that the top management for this reason should be personally involved and be "seen and heard to be involved" by the people of the organization. This means the top management should get actively involved with details, right at the operational levels and not merely sit in their ivory towers. Leadership is not authority, but the ability to roll up the sleeves and get the hands dirty, in order to accomplish what the leader has set out to do by example, so that people 'by their own free will, want to follow the leader'.

An organization therefore, would be a reflection of the attributes of the top management (with personal involvement of the Chief Executive).

2. A TRUE LEADER

A true leader is an individual who has the following qualities:

- Vision
- Culture and Values
- Commitment
- Planning
- Appreciation
- Leadership in Community

2.1 Vision

Dr. S. Radhakrishnan, the second President of India, who was a noted philosopher also, while writing his interpretation of Mahatma Gandhi's message to mankind, stated:

Civilization is based on a dream. Its codes and conventions, its way of life and habits of mind are poised on a dream. When the dream prevails, civilization advances; when the dream fails, civilization goes down.

What is true of any 'civilization' is also true of an 'organization'. If in this statement of Dr. S. Radhakrishnan's we substitute all 'civilization' related words with corresponding 'organization' related equivalents, we have the following statement emerging out:

An organization is based on a vision. Its policies and procedures, its system of operation and practices are supported in balance by the vision. When the vision is successfully achieved, the organization advances; when the vision fails, the organization goes down"

This statement therefore shows that an organization depends on the vision of its leader.

Vision is a short and crisp statement, which contains the following:

"What we will look like in the future" or "What we want to become."

Vision therefore, is what makes an organization. Only if there is a vision actions would be taken to achieve it. Without a vision an organization may survive, but it would be mere survival and nothing more. Progress comes only from aiming high and striving for it.

We in India, who believe in reincarnation and plan our karmas, from one birth to the next and the next, should be able to adapt to this philosophy of long-term vision with ease.

An organization's vision should inspire its people to strive and rise above their normal levels of performance. This can happen only if people learn to enjoy their work and know what they are trying to achieve.

The doorman of an organization should feel he is, 'A one man reception committee' and not 'Someone who just opens and shuts the door'. He will then enjoy his work and take pride in it.

There is this tale of a King, who while riding through a quarry in his kingdom, saw a family of workers consisting of a grandfather, a father and a son working there chiseling stones. He stopped to talk with them, to enquire about their welfare.

When the King individually asked each of them, "Who are you and what are you doing?" their replies were as follows:

The son retorted, "Are you blind? Can't you see I'm a stone chipper breaking stones to earn a living?"

The father replied, " Sir, I'm a stone carver and shaping stones to construct a building."

The grandfather smiled and spoke," O' Lord, I'm a sculptor and giving life to a temple."

The grandfather here is a visionary who will excel at his work, because he has a dream, which he enjoys bringing to life, with his work.

No leader can succeed unless he has a vision and he plans ahead. To build a strong, dynamic and progressive organization their must be a vision. It is this vision, which gives direction to the organization for achieving the primary goals of the organization. These primary goals cover all areas of the business, of which quality is one part. Hence, the quality policy is developed to express the primary quality goals of the organization based on the vision statement.

To sum up the sequence in the successful operation of any organization starts with a Vision, which leads to the Primary Goals of the organization. These in turn lead to the Quality Policy, which then give rise to the Quality Objectives to be achieved by the people within the organization. The Quality Plans provide the means of achieving these quality Objectives.

2.1.1 Primary Goals These are the fundamental goals that any organization wishes to achieve irrespective of the nature of its activity. Basically the primary goals can be thought of as generic objectives. They therefore are the reasons for the setting of organization specific objectives and are as follows:

- Ensure customer satisfaction and strive for delight
- Improve effectiveness and efficiency in every activity
- Ensure that with passage of time the level of performance does not fall but is maintained equal to or better than competitors' level
- Continually improve performance with time
- Have a means of measuring and comparing own performance
- Provide a framework for formulation of strategies and policies
- Have a basis for acquiring, allocating and utilizing resources and
- Provide clarity in the direction the organization should take.

2.1.2 Policy Policy is actually the starting point for planning of any system and so is accorded the highest place within the system. This policy is developed to express the primary goals of an organization.

The Quality Policy of an organization has an essentially significant role to play within its QMS. However since this QMS is a part of the whole Business Management System of an organization, and Quality is an important and essential tool for organizational success, Quality Policy is placed at the core of the Overall Business Policy of the organization.

2.1.3 Objectives

The Objectives of any organization are
those time-bound measurable quality targets
towards the achievement of which
the entire resources and processes are utilized

While the Quality Policy is a general statement, Quality Objectives give the specific details of practical actions for focus. These objectives are the first step in the planning, since only after knowing the objectives the means of achieving them could be decided. Fixation of measurable objectives and in-fact, their very existence, has a significant impact on performance improvement, both at the organization level as well as the lower levels within the organization. These objectives, act as the organization's own reference standard against which, they can measure and assess their own performance. Further the objectives should be attainable and not be fixed beyond reach. They should not be at a very low level either. The rule is to keep them just out of reach and at a respectable level. Most importantly the objectives are to be set in measurable terms.

2.2 Culture and Values

'Organizational Culture' is a complex combination of interrelated beliefs regarding the way the organization should function and 'Organizational Values' are those moral principles to which the organization attaches importance and considers worthy for establishing its own codes of conduct. Although it appears to vary amongst organizations, 'Culture itself actually depends upon Values'. Thus, values exhibited and propagated by the top management mold the culture of the organization and influence the behavior of its people. For instance, the habit of following rules, putting quality before profits, being customer oriented, working right first time every time, fulfilling social objectives, etc. are all part of the culture of an organization depicting the organizations values.

Profits ought to be the need, not the purpose and
amongst a culture and profits clash, culture should prevail
while between a value and culture clash, value should prevail

When elders teach children, they are bringing about a cultural change in the children. Similarly if the organization takes it upon itself to teach and propagate these values, the people themselves could bring about a cultural change in the organization's operations.

Performance improvement through cultural change requires the following from any leader:

- A creative discontent with the existing system
- A desire to improve continually
- A spirit of learning
- A habit of asking questions
- A willingness to seek answers
- A practice of teaching people
- A readiness to provide opportunities for gaining new knowledge and skills
- A total lack of shame, in learning from subordinates or competitors
- A willingness to work as a team for the common good and
- A practice of acting on facts rather on hearsay.

2.3 Commitment

An organization depends on its people, for resolving its difficulties and only their commitment can achieve this. A leader who himself cannot show this quality, can never expect to make demands on his people.

The quality objectives and the quality policy are the top management's demonstrations of commitment. If the people in the organization see that the actions taken by the management are contradictory to the policy and the objectives, doubts regarding their commitment would arise. Like a good teacher in the school, the top management becomes a role model for its people. When the people see the top management turn a blind eye to deficiencies, the entire quality movement of the organization becomes a hoax. Difficult decisions they may be, but the ability to stay firm in the interest of the quality movement needs commitment. Thus, actions rather than mere lip service are required. Also the leader's commitment to the cause should be, not only made known to all levels, but also visible through actions. Suppose necessary resources are not available and there is no logical justification for this deficiency, obviously people's confidence in the management's commitment would receive a severe blow. People are not fools and are extremely perceptive. They are capable of making their own judgment, based on observations.

2.4 Planning

This is one of the most important parts of any successful endeavor. In fact a properly planned activity flows along smoothly not because it does not have problems, but usually because solutions to the anticipated problems have already been thought-out, planned for and could be implemented within no time when a problem crops up. Planning basically requires answering the following questions:

1) Where do we want to go?

2) Where are we now?

3) How do we reach there or at-least reduce the gap?

In order to decide on its Objectives the organization should list out its Primary Goals. Having identified the Primary Goals the next step is to determine the Present Status. This present status can be determined by self-assessment. Finally, the means of achieving the Primary Goals or at-least reducing the gap between goals and status is done by practising continual improvement.

Most of us have either read or heard of the book "Alice in Wonderland" by Lewis Carroll. It is indeed quite an interesting book from which even Senior Managers can learn numerous philosophical lessons of management. The need for advance planning for successful decision-making is demonstrated by the following extremely logical narration in the book.

Alice is at a cross road and wonders which way to go. She sees the Cheshire Cat sitting on a nearby tree.

"Which way do I go?" Alice asks her

"Where do you want to go?" the cat counter questions her.

"I don't know" Alice replies back.

"Then both roads will take you there" was the intelligent reply from this super smart cat.

Indeed, if one has no plans and no direction the organization can only drift and whatever it does will always be right, having nothing to compare it with. However, for all we know the organization could be going around in circles with no progress or may even be moving backward.

Thus if an organization does not wish to follow the example of Alice's indecisiveness, then it must have advance plans on where it wants to go and then measure the progress achieved against these plans.

2.4.1 Self–assessment Self-assessment is an ongoing process of determining the current operational level of an organization on a comparative scale, measured against any of the following:

- Best in class competitors (Benchmarking),
- Own objectives (Performance),
- Business improvement opportunities, or
- Award winning requirements.

Self-Assessment process can be thought of, as an organizational health-check based on a comprehensive internal analysis of the organization's overall capability to meet customer requirements and expectations. It is undertaken by an organization to compare its own current performance level, against laid-down objectives and is a recipe for long-term success. It requires making use of the data generated regularly, which sadly, is quite often not utilized effectively. Utilization of this data helps the organization to determine the 'Relative Degree of Maturity' of its own Quality Management System. Self-assessment requires the involvement of people in the regular and systematic review of their processes and outcomes. Improving any organization's effectiveness, efficiency and responsiveness can be achieved only through the active involvement of its people in the process improvement activity.

The approach of self-assessment is quite easy to understand and simple to use. It requires questions pertaining to each major area of the system to be developed, to establish the assessment procedure. Once the questionnaire has been prepared and assessment procedure has been established, determining the organization's 'maturity level' at any point in time can easily be done, by answering the questions and evaluating ratings given, to establish the status. It is however essential to ensure that during the assessment through the use of questionnaire, every respondent's identity be kept confidential so as to get an honest feedback leading to a reliable assessment.

The approach to self-assessment given in Annex A of ISO 9004:2000, has been explained there in great detail. This explanation in the form of guidelines is simple to understand and easy to use for determining the relative degree of maturity of the QMS and opportunities for improvement.

2.4.1.1 Benefits of Self–assessment are as given below:

(i) Provides strategic direction for the organization

(ii) Presents a balanced view of the organization

(iii) Provides a valuable input to the business planning process

(iv) Enables usability at all levels of the organization

(v) Enables integration of all quality initiatives into the normal business operations

(vi) Provides a means to achieve consistency of direction and consensus on what needs to be done

(vii) Provides a powerful diagnostic tool

(viii) Enables an objective assessment against a set of criterion which is widely accepted in business circles

(ix) Enables progress to be measured over a period of time

(x) Provides an assessment based on facts

(xi) Encourages learning within the same organization as well as between different organizations

(xii) Provides opportunity to recognize outstanding levels of achievements & progress

(xiii) Provides a vital link between objectives and implementation strategies

(xiv) Provides the ability to compare performance with objectives to determine when the objectives themselves need to be raised

(xv) Provides a benchmarking opportunity

(xvi) Provides a reliable means of supplier assessment

(xvii) Provides an objective identification of the current strengths and areas of improvement by comparing the activities and results of an organization against a set of world-class corporate excellence measures

(xviii) Enables measurement of an organization's progress towards excellence

(xix) Helps focus and increase the pace of improvement initiatives

(xx) Encourages process-focused improvement activities in priority areas

(xxi) Helps prioritize and target improvements

(xxii) Helps discover overlooked strengths or areas for improvement and identify best practices

(xxiii) Provides a rigorous and structured approach for continual improvement in all activities of the business and

(xxiv) Ensures that the business improvement activities are fully integrated with the organization's strategies and plans.

2.4.2 Continual Improvement In its endeavour to be better its than competitors and to stay ahead of them, an organization needs to continually improve its performance through sustained efforts. Before looking at improvement it is necessary for the organization to learn to stabilize and maintain its achievements, which is referred to as 'Sustaining Better Performance'. The process of continual improvement has been separately discussed much more in detail further ahead.

2.4.3 Sustaining Better Performance ISO 9001:2000 in its very first line, opens the introduction with the following very significant expectation from an organization:

"The adoption of a quality management system should be a strategic decision of an organization".

Strategy basically refers to 'the art of warfare applied to the science of military planning and execution of battle field operations'. In the field of business too an organization desirous of victory needs to plan operations and execute them with military precision. Similarly, the market and competition therein, is no different from a battlefield during war, where only the fittest and wisest can be expected to survive.

Those who can understand others are merely clever
But those who can understand themselves are wise

Thus ISO 9001:2000 not only expects but demands that the QMS adoption by an organization be treated as a strategic decision by looking for business solutions using innovative strategies, for future problems. Also, if it is the intention to build and lead a customer focused, continually improving, dynamic and better performance organization it must be remembered that, "SOLUTIONS to problems of today, cannot be expected to solve problems of tomorrow". We must continually improve to stay ahead of competition and we must continuously rethink, reinvent and re-plan strategies.

The management principle of leadership plays a major role in better performance, since only an organization designed, built, sustained and improved with customer focus and superior performance as the goal can thrive and prosper. In fact in an organization a strong core strategy for achieving the vision and implementing plans helps the organization in the long term, even during periods of upheaval and recession.

To be successful, the plans need to build a structure designed to lead and manage the organization as it grows, develops and improves. This planning however is not static, but an ongoing process. Sustained better performance is based on the Top Management's ability to balance and manage the following interdependent forces:

- The need for productive conformance through rationalization of existing activities,
- The need for continual improvement of operational performance, and
- The need for growth through dynamism in strategy, processes and people.

2.5 Appreciation

Every individual or team effort made in the interest of the organization, irrespective of the outcome, must be appreciated. To raise the enthusiasm of people involved in activities that help the organisation grow they should be encouraged. This would benefit the organization itself since those who are appreciated and made enthusiastic will make efforts to give more number of suggestions leading to more improvements. The appreciation would also motivate and encourage others to come forward with their ideas.

When suggestions lead to improvement the appreciation can take many forms, such as, recognition, rewards, public praise, commendation, promotion, etc. However it is important that any effort made by people, beyond their normal work requirements for the benefit of the organization, should be recognized. The value in this appreciation is of prestige. The process of appreciation should be such that all individual efforts should result in appreciation for the individual while team performances should result in acknowledgement and appreciation for the whole group and not the prominent few. In both cases however this appreciation should act as an encouragement for all others to emulate.

2.6 Leadership in Community

A good leader is not only concerned about his people and endeavors to improve their lot, but is also concerned about others outside his organization. He tries to propagate his knowledge, for larger good by taking care of wider social issues for the benefit of others. Such visionary leaders are even prepared to volunteer their time and effort for spreading their knowledge and making available their resources for the common good of the society at large.

ISO 14000 is one such standard that such leaders can use to help organizations effectively and efficiently manage their social responsibility towards the environment and help demonstrate it by providing evidence of concern for society and commitment to legislation. A few of the benefits that accrue are as follows:

- Reduced Energy consumption
- Reduction of waste
- Reduction of risks
- Enhancement of confidence
- Development of Positive image

ISO 9001:2000 does not include the requirements specific to other management systems such as the following:

- Environmental Management
- Occupational Health and Safety Management
- Financial Management
- Risk Management

However the standard is aligned and hence compatible with these management systems.

ISO four

INVOLVEMENT OF PEOPLE

1. PEOPLE AS HUMANS

People are neither an organization's most valuable ASSET,
Nor are they its most precious RESOURCE,
They are not even valuable problem solving TOOL.
People are humans, with ambitions, dreams and expectations.
Value them for their brain power and physical skills.

Assets are 'inanimate objects bought & depreciated', Resources are 'mere inputs used & consumed' and Tools are 'mechanical implements manipulated and handled' but People are none of the above. They are Human with mental and physical capabilities and should be treated as Humans beings. They should be valued for the simple reason that they are, "a distinctive part of the organization which is capable of solving problems", leading to improvement of efficiency and enhancement of performance. A direct link exists between performance of people and the effectiveness and efficiency of the organization. Each accomplishment of the organization is the direct result of the efforts put-in by the people of the organization.

However an organization is a collective noun, since it is a team made up of many people, different from each other but with common objectives. Effective people involvement is the key of synchronized team functioning, which helps people give outputs to their maximum potential. Hence the success of the organization depends upon achieving and ensuring targeted behavioral performance of the people when working as a team. If however in any team it is felt that people need to be re-molded to suit the specific needs of the organization the change should be effected systematically through proper and planned training. The gradual rate in the change process is essential since this re-molding quite often requires that people learn new skills for which they need time. They also need considerable help, support and encouragement.

In the book 'Alice in Wonderland' the Dodo marks out a circular race-course for a 'Caucus race' with freedom given to the participants, to run and stop at will. When the race gets over and the Dodo is questioned, "Who has won?" he replies, "Every body has won and everyone must be rewarded".

Here again is an important lesson in an organizational growth race. In order to get ahead, the organization must involve as many people as possible, allowing them freedom to effect improvements at their pace and also rewarding or encouraging all of them, for their contribution, be this contribution big or small.

2. THE PEOPLE

With respect to involvement, when we say, "the people of the organization" it covers everyone right from the Chief Executive to the most humble Workman. All put together they form the team i.e. the organization. This involvement can be obtained from them by allowing them to take decisions. Obviously the decisions have to be in relation to their authority levels, but even this authority unless delegated with confidence in people would prevent them from taking decision to solve problems. People excel and rise, much above their normal levels, when confidence is reposed in them and they are given the authority to decide while their superior accepts responsibility for the decision and guides them for the future.

The Footman in the book 'Alice in Wonderland' tells Alice, "There is no use knocking on the door when I'm on the same side of the door as you". Pertinent indeed! especially for the management who should remember that the people of their organization are on the same side as they, and so working towards the same objectives. There is therefore no need for knocking on the door i.e. making a noise, rather they are to be valued for their contribution towards the organization's growth and progress. This is the only sure and positive way of exercising control over people.

Left to themselves,
people would rather do a good quality job
than a poor quality job
that is basic human nature

2.1 Satisfied People

Happy and contented people who are satisfied will always give their best output to the organization. They will take pride in their work and will gladly work towards exceeding customer expectations. This happiness comes from recognition, motivation, trust and a future in the organization. The greatest contributor to this feeling of happiness and satisfaction is the confidence people have that the organization values and encourages them and also supports them in their weak areas.

3. INVOLVEMENT APPROACH

People can contribute substantially if they feel involved. Through proper encouragement they can give-forth to their full potential. This brings us to a vital aspect of obtaining the best from people and that is "the need for adoption of a positive approach that encourages and rewards outstanding performance and thus motivates others. It thus encourages people to anticipate problems and react positively instead of merely trying to control problems or involving in firefighting".

In this scenario let us look at the way Geese fly long distances, continuously for days at end. They fly in a 'V' formation, where one of the bird is flying at the "Point" and this position of leading the formation is basically helping others. The air flowing backwards from its flapping wings generates a lift at its rear. This lift helps the two birds immediately behind to put in lesser effort and yet whose flight helps those behind and so on. If this leader bird at leading point, has to fly in this position continuously it would soon tire out. This problem is overcome by making each full-grown mature bird share this position. This help given by the leader birds to the formation in flight is rewarded by the formation. While in flight the leader birds rotate to other less difficult positions within the formation for the balance time. In-fact the group also allows the weaker birds to merely fly within the formation and not take the 'point' position at all. Thus, each bird literally benefits from the other's Physical capabilities.

Similarly in a circus, the trapeze artiste has implicit trust and faith in his partner and at the call, leaps into space knowing fully well that his partner will be where he should be, exactly at the instant when he reaches there, not a microsecond early or late. This confidence in the partner's judgment means the artiste depends upon the other's mental capabilities.

(People's involvement requires complete and willing pooling of physical and mental capabilities)

There is no denying the fact that the people who usually perform an activity, know more about the activity. They are therefore the best individuals to give information on the following:

- What will work,
- What will not work, and
- What will lead to problems.

People in general, not only do not resist but in-fact more easily accept and whole-heartedly implement ideas when they are based on their own suggestions. Thus with their involvement expensive mistakes or delay in implementation of good ideas can be avoided.

It is absolutely essential that the involvement of people is obtained through an effort towards explaining things and ensuring that they are aware of what the organization expects from them. Unless this clarity exists they would be at a loss to know how to contribute.

In the book 'Alice in Wonderland' the Gryphon asks Alice to sing a stanza of, 'You are old, father William' and she sings it all mixed-up, due to which the Gryphon is unable to understand it.

He then remarks, "What is the use of singing this stanza unless you explain it as you go along, since I'm totally confused with what you are singing".

In the same book, much earlier, when the Dodo is asked to explain about the 'Caucus Race' he remarks, "The best way to explain it, is to do it".

Indeed, both these statements are extremely logical and truthful, "Are they not?"

To sum up, it is evident that any organization must ensure clarity of understanding amongst its people and that too through practical examples.

3.1 People Involvement Requirements

The following should be borne in mind to ensure whole hearted and genuine involvement of people:

- Every person's idea should be solicited.
- There should be a mechanism to guide and direct the problem solving effort.
- People based problem solving should be a part of the system structure and discussed at suitable levels.
- Training and coaching in problem solving comprising problem identification and root-cause analysis should be given for obtaining creative solutions through involvement of all the people.
- Problem solving special teams comprising cross-organizational and cross-functional people should be used for plant-wide, department-wide and division-wide problems.

The best solution is for people to arrange their own work environments, identify problems or even non-problem improvement areas, develop solutions and implement them. This leads to ownership and pride in the work.

3.2 People Involvement Techniques

People Involvement techniques are many, some of them simple and others complex. However all encourage employees for ideas. Most popular of these are, 'Employee Surveys, Suggestion Systems and Quality Circles'. Each of these are in use, and has had varying success rate with regard to their effectiveness.

3.2.1 Employee Surveys This technique involves an annual or biannual survey consisting of distribution of a written questionnaire requesting for opinions, ideas and reaction. The survey consists of a questionnaire with the various attributes, which are to be rated on a 5-point, 7-point or 10-point scale. Space is also provided within the questionnaire for comments to be given especially in the case of extreme or negative ratings. This method involving people is quite popular for the following reasons:

- It is relatively easy and inexpensive to organize and conduct
- It collects a large amount of data covering every person and
- It helps, over a period of time, in developing trends for assessment.

This technique has the following limitations:

(i) The inputs requested have a rigid framework

(ii) The comments are expected to be short

(iii) The questions themselves are frequently biased and do not give scope for indicating total dissatisfaction, and

(iv) Delays or lack of timely actions based on feedback often lead to drop in interest.

3.2.2 Suggestion Systems This is the oldest of all techniques. This technique depends on encouraging people to submit suggestions to their supervisor or a suggestions committee. If a person's suggestion is accepted and implemented, the organization often decides to share some of the savings resulting from the implementation of the suggestion with the person responsible for it. This technique has the following advantages:

- It is relatively easy to implement
- It is a low cost method of involving people
- It allows every one an opportunity to offer a suggestion
- It shares the benefits with the originator of the idea and
- It is ongoing and not fixed in time.

This technique has the following limitations:

(i) Too few suggestions come forth

(ii) The suggestions tend to be vague and undeveloped

(iii) There is considerable delay in the submission and implementation mostly due to the effort required to develop an undeveloped idea to an implement-able level

(iv) Delay in implementation leading to delay in feedback which causes people to become disillusioned with the scheme whereby newer ideas which might have come, get delayed, and

(v) Difficulty in rewarding the originator or the developer of the idea.

3.2.3 Quality Circles This technique was developed in Japan and is quite popular in many industries. This technique consists of voluntary small groups who meet on a regular basis to discuss work-place problems. Members review data, identify problem areas, analyze possible causes and recommend solutions. Usually the group, works under a Trained Group Leader and submits their proposal to a senior manager of the organization.

Quality circles have been very successful in Japan. They have in-fact been responsible for the success of the Quality movement of Japan. This Quality Circle technique has a lot to offer and has the following advantages:

- Participation is an ongoing process,
- The members receive training and guidance,
- The members have a structured opportunity to apply this technique,
- The ideas that come forth are often fully developed and workable, and
- It helps in cost reduction, quality improvement, increased safety and improvement in the work environment.

The shortcomings of this technique are as follows:

- A lot of time is spent in meetings,
- Improvements are not as large as expected,
- Ideas pass the chain of command since they are discussed in the quality circle meetings and not with an individual's direct superior.

Whichever be the technique used, it is necessary to ensure that people involvement requirements are met through the adoption of a positive approach.

ISO

five

Process Approach

1. PROCESS APPROACH

ISO 9001:2000 requires that organizations using this standard, for establishing, documenting, implementing, maintaining and continually improving their QMS, adopt the Process Approach. This process approach is based on the belief that if any process is well-designed, controlled and managed, with the right inputs its output product is bound to be good. Process approach therefore requires the optimization of the cross-functional, interrelated activities that make up the process. It also requires a smooth overlap at 'interfaces between departments', to achieve effectiveness and efficiency. As such, process approach is a potential technique for developing an effective Quality Management System. It gives us a wonderful philosophy of treating interrelated cross-functional activities of an organization as processes.

Individual functions or departments in any organization, seldom produce a complete product without interacting with other departments. Further, when a large number of people are working together, it is not enough for people to just perform their jobs. Focusing on individual department's activities within the process can neither bring about consistency in operation nor improvement. Even within a well-meshed group of inter dependent activities of a process, each activity causes an effect on the other. Thus jobs even if well-done within their own departments, would quite often, give rise to interdepartmental problems. Thus, the inter-linkages of the various departments, at functional interfaces, would become unattended by any department. It is therefore essential for the interrelated functions to work in harmony during the value-addition process.

Process approach helps remove interdepartmental barriers through 'cross-functional' behaviour. This shift from the compartmentalized, well-defined 'departments' to the cross-functional 'processes' makes the organization more flexible and the invisible departmental walls acting as barriers crumble.

The key to successful 'Process Approach' orientation and application is 'Customer Focus'. This focus towards customer satisfaction infuses in the organization the concept of internal customer. This concept teaches the importance of treating organizations as value-adding process chains, where often concurrent or parallel activities replace sequential activities of the past. Adoption of the process approach as a very practical and easily understandable method requires the following:

- Describing the process objectives
- Specifying the resources needed
- Detailing the instructions, precautions and process operations
- Laying down operating conditions
- Spelling out the responsibilities, authorities and interrelationships
- Specifying the methods of measuring performance
- Monitoring performance
- Using feedback for correction
- Anticipating and preventing problems and
- Improving the process continually.

1.1 Comparison of Functional Approach and Process Approach

Process approach, questions the very basis of the function-based organizations, which have endured for so long and that too successfully. The functionally structured organizations have all through operated along the traditional lines and have delivered results. The question then is, 'Where is the need to change?'

Though functional approach has been in wide use and has also given results, it has been lately recognized that it gives rise to certain difficulties of over-compartmentalization, interdepartmental competition, slower communication due to bureaucracy, etc. All these are interdepartmental problems. Actually the functional approach has endured for so long merely because there was no alternative. The success of functionally operating organizations were measured against other functionally operating organizations so far.

Of late it has been recognized that, while a lot of time, money and effort is usually spent on building hierarchy, in reality the work of any organization does not flow upwards or downwards but horizontally, across the organization from one process to another. The vital linkages and relationships between these processes that have remained unaddressed till now, are recognized as the links in the chain and therefore central to effective functioning of the organization. The requirement therefore is for organizations that are flatter rather than taller and they are called 'Horizontal Organizations' with an operating structure as shown in Fig.1.

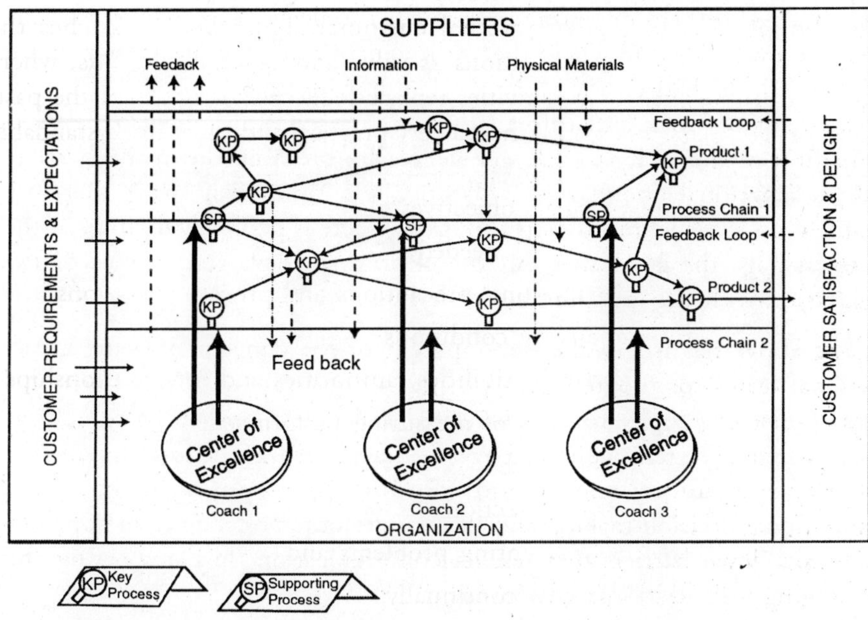

FIG. 1 *A HORIZONTAL ORGANIZATION CHART - BASED ON PROCESS APPROACH*

Adopting process approach, does not mean that the functional approach has no advantages. Both approaches have their strong points and the ideal organization would be one, which learns to balance the functional approach with the process approach. Such an approach is called the Hybrid Approach and it has a number of operational building blocks with several functional ones.

This Hybrid Approach offers the best of both the approaches, namely specialized expertise of functional approach coupled with the responsiveness of the flatter process approach.

1.1.1 Vertical Organization Traditional organizations are structured as pyramids and adopt the principle of 'need to know' with regard to communication of information. The pyramidal structure has many hierarchical positions and organizations function through, 'the flow of power and decisions' from these positions based on rules and procedures. The diverse activities within these organizations are the responsibility of different functions and each function reports to a different functional authority. This therefore gives rise to the possibility that each function pursues goals and objectives, which though individually right for the particular function, yet give rise to conflicts between functions being wrong in the overall perspective. There would therefore have to be resolution of conflicts through 'give & take' between functions for optimization.

1.1.2 Horizontal Organization Cross-functional organizational structure is a newer concept to help organizations achieve excellence. This requires a shift from a vertical structure where the work and information are managed, up and down through the various layers. The horizontal organization requires management of work and information across functions. It also requires elimination of hierarchy to a larger degree by breaking down the barriers built by functional boundaries. This does not in any way mean there are absolutely no levels within the organization. There is definitely a group at the top to manage the key issues but the effort is to have the balance of the organization with the least number of levels.

The above has led to the development of the concept of using cross-functional teams for progress and growth in organizations. Cross-functional teams consist of people from each related function coordinating to achieve common goals. The team approach by encouraging cross-functional interaction leads to better understanding and coordination, resulting in improved organizational decision-making and thereby performance. The team approach also breaks down barriers that restrict communication thus supporting and encouraging organizational development.

TABLE 5

Comparison between Vertical and Horizontal Organizational Structure

S.No.	Aspect	Organizational Structure	
		Vertical	**Horizontal**
1.	Structure	Pyramidal	Flattened
2.	Organized around	Functions	Processes
3.	People role	Tend to become specialists	Operate as team members
4.	People understanding	There is a total lack of understanding amongst the people of their role in the overall perspective	Clarity with regard to their role exists within the wider scope of the organization
5.	Availability of functional specialists	People specialists for each function get concentrated under the particular functional department	People of each function are available within each process
6.	Information flow	Flow between the functions tends to be RESTRICTED	Flow between cross-functional teams is FREE

S.No.	Aspect	Organizational Structure	
		Vertical	Horizontal
7.	Goals and Objectives	The emphasis is on each function's individually determined goals and objectives not necessarily in line with those of the organization	The emphasis is on the organizational goals and objectives under which each process determines its own aligned goals and objectives
8.	Operational smoothness	It does not encourage give and take for resolution of conflicts.	It is structured around the principle of resolving inter-functional problems especially at the process interfaces.

1.2 Difference between a Process Owner and a Coach

A process owner is like a mini-entrepreneur running his process like an organization. His responsibility is for the execution of the process and also for carrying out all or some actions of the process. He is completely and closely bound to the process being within the process itself. He is an active participant in the process, who leads from inside. His job satisfaction comes from the results he along with his people bring-about within his particular process. A process owner easily can be compared to a computer for processing data or controlling a programmable logic control.

A coach like a guide is a person educating, teaching, guiding and encouraging people for specializations and expertise. His responsibility is for mentally, physically and psychologically preparing the participants and helping them achieve their goals. He is a passive observer in the process who guides from outside. His satisfaction comes from seeing the people of his team perform and do well.

TABLE 6

Differences between Functional Approach and Process Approach

S.No.	Aspect	Functional Approach	Process Approach
1.	Focus	Functions	Customer
2.	Objective	Compliance to requirements	Customer satisfaction
3.	Organization	Hierarchical	Networked
4.	Organogram	Tall pyramial	Flat horizontal

S.No.	Aspect	Functional Approach	Process Approach
5.	Organizational Structure	Functional i.e. division of labor, hierarchy of authority and span of control	Process i.e. input-process-output, internal customer / supplier, cross-functional
6.	Hierarchy	Scalar chain of authority	Networked chain with empowerment
7.	Work flow	Does not show the flow of work	Shows how work flows horizontally across the organization
8.	Relationships	Between boss and subordinates	Between: -customers and organization -suppliers and organization -individuals in the same function -functions
9.	Operations	Across defined functional boundaries	Across identified and established process inter-linkages
10.	Work coordination	Lacks coordination across tasks, departments and functions	Well coordinated across tasks, departments and functions on account of absence of cross- functional barriers
11.	Communication	Mostly upwards or downwards	Mostly horizontal
12.	People focus	Individual task	Team work
13.	People orientation	Work for the boss	Work for the customer
14.	People Responsibility	Completing assigned tasks	Meeting performance objectives
15.	Specialists	Duplicated as they are provided for each function separately	Integrated into centers of excellence
16.	Technology	Separated into functions	Integrated within processes
17.	Pay for	- Seniority - Showing up for work - Following rules - Maintaining good relations with boss - Completing assigned tasks	- Competence and capability - Delivering results - Performance - Contributing to team results - Producing individual results

1.3 Managing through Process Approach

Organizations using the process approach require the management to take the following steps:

(i) Identify the processes: These could include design and development, marketing and sales, purchasing, product realization, distribution and delivery, etc.

(ii) Define and understand the process: Decide upon the process definition and its coverage. Understand the activities and flow, by flowcharting them. Align the process activities based on customer requirements. Determine the value adding activities and areas of no or little value addition.

(iii) Define the boundaries: Set limits within which the process will operate and specify its inputs and outputs.

(iv) Identify the sub-processes: Break it down into the basic activities.

(v) Designate a process owner: He will own, manage and improve the process. He should be knowledgeable about the process, able to influence, capable of facilitating and totally committed.

(vi) Create a partnership between user and processor: This will create a link between the chain of activities.

(vii) Understand the linkages: Understand the linkages with other processes within the organization and with its customers and suppliers.

(viii) Link parallel activities in a natural order: This helps to do simultaneous jobs and speed up the processes.

(ix) Balance Functional and Process Approach: Since most organizations are functional, adoption of the process approach shall balance the mix, of both.

(x) Train, based on the process approach: This being a new concept needs to be understood and accepted. It therefore requires a constant and persistent effort through training to reorient people.

(xi) Measure the process: This is required for assessing the current level of performance and comparing it with the required level for compliance and identifying possible areas of improvement.

(xii) Minimize reconciliation: Capture data and information at source and use it without re-entry at any other location.

(xiii) Combine jobs: This reduces lead-time and material movement.

(xiv) Manage the people: The organizational structure may have changes but the people remain the same and so they need the same motivation and fulfilment of expectations and aspirations.

(xv) Build centers of excellence: These are needed to take care of proper utilization of specialized expertise and competence by centralizing it to help support weak areas in the organizational processes.

(xvi) Improve continually: This is needed to move ahead.

(xvii) Listen to all interested parties: These interested parties consisting of customers, legislators and regulators, shareholders, suppliers and employees will provide facts and help build understanding.

2. PROCESS ORIENTATION

The orientation of organizations to processes requires that each and every action in the organization must essentially aim to add value and thus contribute to its improved performance. Thus the objective of this orientation is to remove from every process all those actions that 'do not add value' and also find ways to increase the value addition from those, which 'add value'. This is a new concept requiring complete rethinking on how this could be achieved. To get its maximum advantage, a reorientation is needed, towards constantly looking for value-addition in every activity. It also requires cutting across the traditional, function based management structure by managing along process lines.

Process Approach takes the old functional departments and reconstructs them into TWO parts which are as follows:

Processes The place where work is done and activities take place. The organizational physical skills are located here. They have merely two levels within, i.e. Owner and Contributors.

Centers of Excellence These are in-house pools of specialized knowledge and expertise available for all to share in times of need. They also have only two levels, i.e. Coach and Participant.

If you observe, one Mr. ABC who is a doctor, remains Dr. ABC all his life and is always called so. That is his designation for life. Similar is the case with a lawyer or Chartered Accountant. These people function in truly horizontal organizations. Designations are created to merely make them high-sounding and pamper individual egos. In principle, hierarchy also has the same purpose and does not help in giving results.

2.1 Process Anatomy

A Process is a systematic and planned sequence,
of cross-functional value adding activities,
performed to transform inputs into outputs,
that conform to pre-determined objectives

Thus a process always has some inputs for the needed output. The value-addition process may involve different activities, such as a series of connected actions or changes and then their verification. Any value-addition process may need some of the under mentioned inputs which on completion of the necessary action provide the required outputs. The different types of value-adding activities that take place during the processing are also given below:

2.1.1 Types of Inputs Inputs are of the following two types:

- Primary - Inputs that themselves get transformed during processing.
- Supporting - Inputs that help in the value-addition process.

2.1.2 Types of Processes The different types of processes encountered can be covered under any one or more of the following types:

- Transforming - changing in character or culture.
- Identifying - separating into smaller and more clearly defined units.
- Unifying - combining or bringing together.
- Homogenizing - creating uniformity or consistency.
- Moving - changing the placing or location.
- Holding - keep waiting in a controlled environment.
- Providing - giving or offering the requirements.

2.1.3 Types of Outputs Outputs of processes are called products, which cover both goods and services. The product could be any of the following:

(i) Goods,

(ii) Services

(iii) Goods & Services

Most often products are a combination of both Goods as well as services. It is seldom that goods do not have services attached to them.

The purpose of any process is to add value to its inputs, and, all those processes that do not serve this purpose are not true processes. Such processes are still required by the organization and continue to exist. They are merely tolerated as necessary burden on the organization. Every organization ought to look for ways and means to either eliminate or reduce such non value-adding processes.

Let us for instance consider the case of a manufacturing process wherein a product is produced by a Machine A in 5 seconds and immediately needs to be followed-up with another operation on Machine B, which takes 9 seconds. Between the two operations a time lag of 'not more than 1 second' is permitted. In such a situation, Machine A will be idle for 4 seconds for every cycle. This idling of Machine A is an obvious waste and has to be avoided. Wastages such as these are obvious and measurable but many other wasteful activities in organizations are not overlooked.

TABLE 7
Input-Process-Output (IPO)

Inputs		Processes		Outputs	
Primary	**Supporting**	**Value-adding**	**Non Value-adding**	**Goods**	**Services**
Materials Man-hour (Time)	Man Machines Methods Money Milieu (Environment) Management Mental Positive Attitude (Motivation & Morale) Messages (Information)	Transforming Unifying Homogenizing	Identifying Moving Holding Providing	Tangible, storable and transportable (Quality is Product related)	Intangible, non-storable and non-transportable. (Quality is Perception related)

For instance while a product is being inspected or shifted we do not add any value to it but still need to perform the process. Such processes are no doubt a waste and need to be avoided. However, if in these non value-adding processes a further waste occurs then, that is absolutely wrong. Such situations are 'process situations', which not only do not add value but further reduce the value of the product. These are to be treated as criminal wastes and avoided under all circumstances.

For instance the process of 'Shifting an object 2 km from point A to B by road in 30 minutes', could be done in one of the five ways given below.

(i) No Value-Addition: Start from A, follow the correct route of 2 km through heavy traffic and reach B in 30 minutes.

(ii) Negative Value-Addition: Start from A, follow a longer route of 2.5 km to avoid traffic and reach B in 30 minutes.

(iii) Negative Value-Addition: Start from A, follow a wrong route, correct after 12 minutes and return then drive fast and follow the correct route of 2 km to reach B in 42 minutes.

(iv) Negative Value-Addition: Start from A, follow the correct route of 2 km, get stuck in a traffic jam and reach B in 38 minutes.

(v) Element of Value-Addition: Start from A, follow the correct route of 2 km and smoothly travel to reach B in 25 minutes.

Thus even amongst the non value-adding activities, negative value-addition is to be essentially avoided, as this would be a criminal waste. However in situation 5 we see there is a saving of 5 minutes, and this type of saving is to be encouraged and can add an element of value to a non value-adding activity.

2.2 Boundaries and Components of Processes

Each process is generally cross-functional with its scope covering more than one department and has 'Four Hypothetical Boundaries'. The 'Initial Boundary' for convenience is shown on the left hand side, the 'Final Boundary' on the right hand side, the 'Upper Boundary' at the top and the 'Lower Boundary' at the bottom of the boxed process. These boundaries of the boxed process define the limits of the process as shown in Fig.2.

Conceptually, the inputs entering the initial boundary of a process are called its primary inputs. These inputs, are required by the process at its beginning, from its preceding processes.

Outputs leaving the final boundary of a process are called its primary outputs. These outputs that are required from the process at its end, for its succeeding processes.

Inputs entering the upper boundary of a process are its secondary inputs. They are required by the process at some intermediate stage.

Outputs leaving the lower boundary of a process are its secondary outputs. They are basically its by-products.

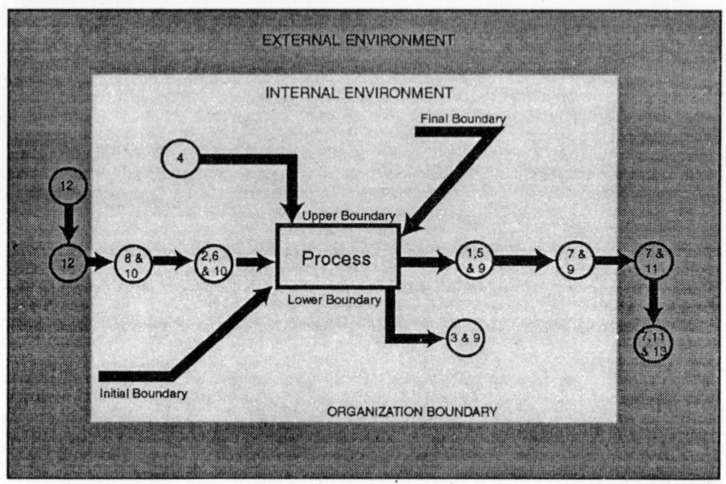

FIG. 2 *BOUNDARIES AND COMPONENTS OF A PROCESS*

It is good to distinguish and understand the difference between the following components of a process as shown in Fig.2.:

(i) **Primary Customer:** Those who get the primary outputs of a process.

(ii) **Primary Supplier:** Those who supply the primary inputs to a process.

(iii) **Secondary Customer:** Those who get the secondary outputs of a process.

(iv) **Secondary Supplier:** Those who supply the secondary inputs to a process.

(v) **Direct Customer:** The immediately subsequent receiver of the outputs of a process.

(vi) **Direct Supplier:** The immediately previous supplier of the inputs of a process.

(vii) **Indirect Customer:** All the customers subsequent to the direct customer of the process.

(viii) **Indirect Supplier:** All the suppliers previous to the direct supplier of the process.

(ix) **Internal Customer:** Those who are a part of the organization and receive the process outputs.

(x) **Internal Supplier:** Those who are a part of the organization and provide the process inputs.

(xi) **External Customer:** Those who are external to the organization and receive the process outputs.

(xii) **External Supplier:** Those who are external to the organization and provide the process inputs.

(xiii) **Ultimate Customer:** Those external customers of the organization who are the final receivers of the output of the organization.

2.3 Characteristics of Processes

a) Structural: These characteristics are concerned with the series of activities which contribute to the overall process performance. Their salient features are that they:

- Have a boundary
- Are networked
- Are flowchart-able
- Are value-adding and
- Are influenced by customer requirements.

b) Operational: These characteristics are concerned with purpose, task, control and measurement. Their special features are that they:

- Benefit from ownership by its people
- Are activity dependent
- Are focused towards the objective
- Need resources
- Require time as an important element called cycle time
- Are measurable either qualitatively or quantitatively and
- Are controllable.

c) Governing: These characteristics are concerned with those considerations that govern the processes. Their main features are that they:

- Determine how long it takes for fulfilling an order (Lead time)
- Verify if sufficient resources are available (Capacity)
- Control material availability and movement (Inventory management)
- Help produce in right quality, quantity and time (Capability assessment) and
- Help in meeting targets and improving (Performance assessment).

d) Limiting: These characteristics are concerned with the factors that cause variability. Their important features are that they:

- Have a variability
- Have an uncertainty
- Are subject to constraints and
- Are dependant.

2.3.1 Process Analysis The process approach requires description of each process and analyzing it for deficiencies, faults and weaknesses. It aims at ensuring that the processes are operationally effective and efficient when analyzed under static as well as dynamic state. As such the process ought to be designed and operated under a condition of technical completeness, correctness and consistency in relation to the objectives of the process.

The analysis of the static state of processes checks each one of them for the following:

- Technical correctness and adequacy of the process
- Correlation between the process and its objectives
- Gaps and missing links in process description
- Possible faults and likely mistakes in process description
- Ease of material and information processing and
- Convenience of information flow.

The analysis of the dynamic state of processes checks each one of them for the following:

- Equilibrium and balance
- Simplicity
- Efficiency and effectiveness
- Adaptability to change
- Improvability and
- Ability to mesh smoothly with interlinking processes.

A static system does not exist in practice and is a myth. After all, we cannot live the same moment twice as we cannot breath the same air twice or eat the same food twice. All systems and processes exist in a state of dynamism.

2.4 Classifying Processes

All processes do not have equal importance. Some processes are more important than others due to the impact they have on the organization and are normally called KEY or CORE processes. The core processes are the operational processes that result in the production of the outputs required by the external customer. These are normally the ones, which are essential to the organization's success and help it achieve its goals and objectives. Such key processes are therefore the main organizational processes and any impact on them directly affects the vital organizational operations as they are directly linked to the CRITICAL areas of the organization's activities.

SUPPORTING or OTHER processes are those that enable the core processes 'exist, operate and thrive'.

2.4.1 Characteristics of Key or Core Processes

- Have an extremely large impact on the organization.
- Are crucial to the organization's success.
- Proper performance gives the organization a competitive advantage.
- Affect the customers.
- Are multi-functional.
- Tend to be large and complex most often.
- Are the processes pertaining to the areas of specialization of the organization.

TABLE 8

Examples of a few Key and Supporting Processes

Key or Core Processes		**Supporting Processes (For both sectors)**
Manufacturing Sector	**Service Sector**	
1. Design and development 2. Marketing and Sales 3. Purchasing 4. Product realization 5. Delivery 6. Customer care and support	1. Design and development 2. Marketing and sales 3. Supplier support 4. Service realization 5. Service delivery 6. Customer care and support	1. Finance 2. Legal 3. Human resource 4. Infrastructure 5. Management 6. Information technology

2.5 Process Operation

The following rule is applied here:

The end does not justify the means and
the means are more important than the end

The management must support and encourage 'the correct way of doing jobs' and improve upon it. This no doubt requires behavioural changes but is necessary in the long run for a successful organization.

The processes SHOULD NOT FOLLOW the principle of:

" Do it Right Eventually"

The process SHOULD FOLLOW the principle of :

" Do It Right First Time, Every Time"

Ensuring complete compliance to this principle is essential so that problems are not merely corrected, but are avoided altogether. The entire emphasis therefore should be on teaching people the right way of doing their jobs, called 'Good Practices'.

"Good Practices are to Process Approach
what Good Habits are to Human Behaviour"

Inculcating good habits, no doubt takes patience, sustained effort and determination, but, once acquired they appear routine and in fact child play. They however become an extremely powerful asset for all times, as they then give us the ability to perform activities, in the correct manner, even subconsciously.

By deductive logic we can now frame a rule.

LEARN *GOOD PRACTICES*
ADOPT *THEM AS GOOD HABITS*
FOLLOW *THEM CONTINUOUSLY*
PROPAGATE *THEIR USE TO OTHERS*

2.5.1 Outsourcing of Processes Outsourcing of processes is a strategic management decision for containing and reducing costs, by purchasing complete processes from outside experts. Outsourcing done poorly can completely ruin an organization but when done properly it can help fight competition very well. Most often, the outsourcing done is for supporting processes, like training, payroll, information processing, inventory management, advertising, maintenance, legal, etc. but at times, organizations even decide to outsource key processes. However processes, which are the core competencies of an organization, that need to be guarded from competitors, are never to be outsourced. Before outsourcing, think and look ahead at the impact of the outsourcing far ahead into the future. Like it has been mentioned earlier, outsourcing is a strategic decision and neither tactical nor an operational decision.

Processes that are outsourced if done in-house, especially for support processes, tend to be costlier and non-productive as they have very little incentive to improve productivity. Outside suppliers of process realize that they have to be productive and efficient. Only by providing excellence in service with reduced costs can they continue to retain their customer. The customer can drop them and discontinue their supply anytime. Thus if 'outsourced process suppliers' want work, they must perform well and continually improve to retain customers.

If an organization at any time outsources its core competency, it is playing into the hands of the supplier who can then literally dictate terms and can itself become a competitor some time in future.

Successful outsourcing requires a large amount of,
Good judgment and management skill

Outsourcing should not be rushed into, rather the organization should move into it, very cautiously. The key areas to verify are,

- Quality
- Cost competitiveness
- Research and development capability
- Supply and delivery
- Readiness to adhere to trade secret agreements
- People

2.6 Hierarchy of Process

Every organization consists of a large number of cross-functional interlinked processes operating in harmony. Depending on the complexity of operations these bigger processes can be divided into smaller ones and further into still smaller ones. The organization therefore through the various intermediate levels can be subdivided into smaller process units. The hierarchy showing the various levels are given below:

(i) Organizational Process Chain

(ii) Macro 'Key or Supporting' Processes

(iii) Micro Processes

(iv) Activities and

(v) Tasks.

2.6.1 Organizational Process Chain The process chain begins with determination of customer requirements and expectations, goes to the external suppliers, progresses within the organization through series of internal supplier and customer relationships and finally ends with the external customer satisfaction.

External suppliers provide input products to the organizations. Within the organizations, the internal suppliers and internal customers form the value-adding process chain in a series of activities. The internal suppliers make use of resources to add value to their input product, to get outputs. These outputs are supplied to the next activity, in the process chain which therefore become their internal customers. These internal customers use the finished product of the previous activity, as their input product. They thereby themselves become internal suppliers/customers. Thus, within the organization each value-adding activity functions as both an internal supplier as well as an internal customer. Finally, the organization supplies the finished products, produced as a result of the composite value-addition activities, to external customers. An organization may have more than one process chain operating in parallel, with each such chain consisting of a number of processes operating in parallel or series.

Each value-adding activity of the process chain is like the link of a mechanical chain with the interface of every pair of activities similar to the point joining any two links of the chains. Just as smooth linkage between the links of mechanical chain reduces friction, heat and noise, similarly smooth linking of the process chain also eliminates problems.

2.6.2 Macro Processes These are the higher-level processes of the organization and are cross-functional. They have a broader base and are not confined to one department or function, but weave through many departments. These processes could belong to either "Key or Core" and "Supporting or Other" processes of the organization. 'Key Processes' have to perform well as they always have direct impact on the business. Key processes are therefore the main organizational processes and any impact on them directly affects the vital organizational operations. The key processes generally are those, which are directly linked to the CRITICAL areas of an organization's activities such as the Customer, Supplier, Design & Development, Product Realization, etc.

Every organization has to identify for itself, which processes for its activity are the 'Key Processes'. All other processes of the organization which operate in the capacity of support to the key processes shall then be called 'Supporting or Other Processes' such as maintenance, services, facilities, etc.

2.6.3 Micro Processes These processes are subsections of the macro processes and operate individually as processes with their own inputs and outputs after value-addition activities. Usually they are confined to the activities of a single function or department. These micro processes are the basic cells where the internal customer approach application brings about improvement.

2.6.4 Activities These are 'pieces of work' carried out under the micro processes and are their sub-sections consisting of a number of tasks carried out in systematic order to perform the particular piece of work.

2.6.5 Tasks These are smaller units of work under activities, which are combined together to form the resulting individual activities. Thus each activity consists of a number of tasks related to internal suppliers and internal customers.

2.7 Process Planning

Planning of process is of crucial importance since it determines, decides and governs the quality of process outputs. Any process is normally covered by certain rules and standards for guidance in the absence of which the process will fail. The design takes care of compliance and adherence to these requirements. Moreover, even though processes differ from each other, their basic requirements are the same and so planning for them has to be on similar lines.

2.8 Process Designing

Process design uses the 5 W's (What, When, Where, Why, Who) and one H (How) for arriving at the design requirements. Processes are designed initially at the 'broad macro level' and progress down to lower 'micro levels' that then can be further broken-down into activities and individual tasks.

Design requires defining the process by specifying the objectives, mapping the sequence of discrete activities to be undertaken, defining the various resources required and spelling out the process boundaries. It also lists out the physical equipment, the information required, the systematic instructions, precautions, controls needed and maintenance and measurement methods. It is extremely important not to lose sight of the limits to the capability of any process. The acceptable limits of variability should also be mentioned.

The design should also specify the 'points of transfer' and the 'points of decision-making'.

2.9 Proving the Process

After a process has been defined and designed, it has to be proved prior to implementation to ensure that the process is capable of consistently achieving and delivering desired results. This is done by verifying the results of a few trial runs and analyzing them. Once the process has been proved, it can be ensured that as long as the process is under control it will continue to deliver consistent results and conforming outputs. If at any time the outputs begin to come out as non-conforming, it can be inferred that the process is out of control. Hence quality of output can be ensured merely by control of the process.

2.10 Process Control

This activity requires maintaining an operating process in a 'state of static and dynamic balance' to continuously produce outputs confirming to stated objectives, by eliminating controllable variations. The quality of the 'product output' from the process is basically governed by the value-addition activity. This obviously means that, even when the quality of inputs to the process, are good, if the value addition or conversion activity is poor, the output quality is bound to be poor. Thus, if the process is controlled through its operating parameters, it would give consistent outputs and the product quality would remain controlled.

2.11 Process Capability

Process capability is fundamentally used in 'planning the selection' from amongst different available choices of processes. All processes have an 'inherent performance capability', which can be evaluated through analysis of data of that process. This evaluation is a valuable input for 'quality planning and subsequent operations'. In general usage, process capability is used to express the level of performance of the process. However this process capability can be determined through mathematical formulae and so is quantifiable. While evaluating process capability using formulae, it should be ensured that this evaluation is done under the normal conditions encountered in practice and not under controlled or laboratory conditions. Further, during such an evaluation, the personnel operating such processes should be the regular people.

2.12 Process Variability

All processes vary from the desired performance and this 'extent of deviation' is a measure of the variability of the processes. Even highly controlled and automated processes, have a variability. This variability is a critical input to plans. During planning the effort is to achieve the planned objective, under the actual operating conditions, despite process variability. Moreover, in any process, with time there is wear and tear, ageing and deterioration, all of which contribute to variations.

2.13 The Feedback Loop

No control activity is systematic unless a feedback loop, feeds information for continuous ongoing correction to bring back the process in line with the required objectives. A mechanism for feedback, correction, prevention and continual improvement should exist. In short a defect-free product can only be expected from a defect-free process.

2.14 Process Performance

The various measures used for assessing the performance of processes are as follows:

(i) Effectiveness: The degree to which the outcome of the process meets customer requirements.

(ii) Efficiency: The degree to which the inputs can be minimized without affecting effectiveness of the process.

(iii) Flexibility: The degree to which the process can respond to continual change with changing needs without effecting the effectiveness and efficiency.

(iv) Improvability: The degree to which the process design makes the process amenable to improvement.

(v) Excellence: A combination of all the above properties.

2.15 Process Improvement

A process however good needs to be constantly reviewed for improvement for either eliminating problems or achieving better performance by maximizing its outputs. Both require monitoring and analyzing the feedback, received from the process and its interfaces with other processes to identify possible ways to improve. This requires recognizing, accepting and attacking problems on top priority thereby increasing outputs and eliminating or reducing problems. Better still the organization must move away from merely correcting problems to preventing them. The time and effort spent will give remarkable results.

Statistical tools for analyzing feedback can be used depending upon the purpose. The tools available are both for quantitative data as well as qualitative information. The tools need not be used in isolation rather they should be used in combination for getting the best results. However all of them help in the process of decision-making.

The purpose of process improvement is to make an existing process better, cheaper and faster. It is a recognised fact that all processes ought to add value in some way or the other, else they ought to be avoided to the extent possible. This avoiding can be done by any of the following:

(i) Systematic Elimination of : Wastage, rejection, reworking, unnecessary paper-work, over-production, waiting time, transportation, inventory, defects, defectives, duplication, inspection, monitoring, reconciliation, processing, reformatting, etc.

(ii) Practical Simplification of: Forms, formats, records, instructions, procedures, communication, technology, movement, flow, processes, etc.

(iii) Methodical Combination of : Tasks, activities, jobs, procedures, teams, customers, suppliers, etc.

(iv) Mechanized Automation of: Activities that are unsafe, hazardous, unpleasant, dirty, difficult, dangerous, boring, tedious, repetitive, etc.

2.16 Corrective Actions

Actions taken within the QMS to correct incidences of 'existing quality nonconformities', by acting upon both the nonconformities as well as their causes, are called corrective actions. These nonconformities could arise out of customer complaints, audit deficiencies, purchase problems, production shortcomings, etc.

The nonconformities can therefore be classified as follows:

- Failures within the QMS relating to the product, process or system
- Complaints from the customers (internal or external)
- Complaints to suppliers (internal or external)

Each of these is considered on an individual basis and wherever appropriate, action is also taken to eliminate possibility of recurrence of similar problems in future. It is extremely important that whenever any deficiencies are encountered, they are not only thoroughly analyzed and corrected but also reported to the Top management. Moreover if the incidents are many, then there is all the more reason for in-depth trend analysis and study to arrive at the proper steps for correction and prevention.

2.17 Preventive Actions

Actions taken within the QMS to prevent incidences of 'potential non-conformities', by anticipating them in advance and taking suitable actions are called preventive actions. The following steps will provide valuable feed back. To detect and eliminate such potential problems:

(i) Service reports

(ii) Customer complaints

(iii) Inspection and test reports

(iv) Process monitoring data

(v) Audit feedback through the observations and non-conformities and

(vi) Supplier feedback and problems.

[ISO] *six*

System Approach to Management

1. SYSTEMS APPROACH

The systems approach depends on the feedback control mechanism for the effective and efficient operation of any system. Its origin lies in the principle of optimization whereby the performance of the system as a whole governs its operations and takes precedence over performance of its individual components.

When viewing the system, both the tangible and intangible resources need to be considered within its structure. Intangible resources consist of the information and the policy framework.

1.1 Traditional System Approach

The traditional system approach used by organizations in the past, for determining and establishing systems, was 'to focus on their own product, competitors' products and markets' trend. This, 'Product Focused Systems Approach' had a very limited benefit on their systems.

With the adoption of ISO 9001/9002/9003:1994 came the 'Quality System Approach for Quality Assurance', which views the system requirements based on the 20 elements. The approach aimed at controlling processes that directly affect quality. The 1994 version of the Standard was aimed to achieve customer satisfaction, by preventing non-conformity at all stages from production through to servicing. However, this 'Quality System Approach for Quality Assurance', although effective had its limitations on the insight it could provide into the system operations, thereby again limiting the effectiveness of the approach.

1.2 Improved Systems Approach

A better method of ensuring and enhancing the effectiveness and efficiency of a system, is adopted in ISO 9001:2000. This method, which is quite practical and realistic, is to treat the organization as an integrated and aligned group of interrelated, interdependent and interacting processes operating in harmony towards a common goal.

The 'System Approach to Management' aims at determining and establishing a Quality Management System that controls all business processes of the organization and their inter-linkages. While the QMS established and implemented, merely aims at controlling processes affecting quality, the systems approach goes much beyond and covers all other areas of the organization's activities.

2. SYSTEM APPROACH TO MANAGEMENT

When each process of any system is viewed in the generic 'input-process-output' pattern, it becomes comparable to similar process of every other system, (with appropriate modifications specific to the organization). Thus, the process of 'purchase' or 'sales' or 'design' at its most basic level, is the same for every system. Viewing a process in this fundamental fashion, has the advantage, that successfully used solutions applied to a process of any organization, with suitable modifications can be applied, to the same process of every other organization. This implies that even if two organizations have totally different businesses, (may be one is in the service sector and the other in manufacturing), still, 'Process Solution Superimposition' can be successfully done. Only suitable modifications specific to each business and based on each organization's individual requirements are to be made.

3. CONTROL OF INTER-LINKAGES

Everyone likes to disown inter linkages of various functions at interfaces. The interfaces if not strengthened at the links, lead to duplication of work or omission of work or even get ruptured. It is therefore important, that within a macro process, coordination and control of the interfaces is defined and maintained, at each of its micro process link-points. By doing this the link points of greatest weakness, on account of proper coordination and control would become nodal points i.e. points of minimum disturbance. In practice what happens is that proper linking not only eliminates the problems mentioned earlier but also makes the people involves at the interlinked processes appreciate each other's problems and support each other.

3.1 Feedbacks and Responsiveness

It is the feedback mechanism of any system that maintains it dynamism and progressiveness. Proper feedback looping in every system, is therefore of vital importance. Feedbacks are of the following two types:

a) Reinforcing: This is a positive type of feedback whereby the system experiences an enhancing or strengthening influence e.g. the feedback on customers helps enhance sales or strengthens product features to satisfy them.

b) Controlling: This is a negative type of feedback whereby the system experiences a balancing or correcting influence e.g. the feedback on process deficiencies helps balance necessary resources by providing the shortfalls or helps correct shortcomings.

The feedback received would serve no purpose unless it is acted upon and that too promptly. Changes based on feedback do not occur instantaneously but it is essential to recognize and accept this practical constraint of any system so that delays are within reasonable limits. Also, the influence of delays in one area of the system and its impact on another area need to be determined as they affect the dynamism of the system as a whole. Moreover, any system always contains many feedback loops, some positive and others negative. Each has a different response time. The effort should be towards OPTIMIZING the system, taking note of all the constraints.

4. SYSTEM STRATEGY

An organization's System is made-up of many processes working towards the achievement of the organization's objectives. System strategy requires to persure objectives by any of the following:

- Sub-dividing the objectives
- Identifying required actions on the subdivision and
- Allocating each subdivision to the corresponding process connected with the particular subdivision.

This 'Action by subdivision' results in each subdivision being planned for and acted upon simultaneously, thereby speeding up the achievement. Further, it helps in making the subdivisions more manageable. This is where our process approach helps, since both 'Process Approach and System Strategy' operate on the cross-functional approach and over-lap perfectly. System strategy expects the following actions from the organization for attaining these subdivided objectives:

- Determine the work to be done to implement the planned actions
- Provide the necessary resources including training and
- Distribute the above work and its responsibility.

Similar to setting objectives, the best people for setting a yardstick to evaluate the requirements for completion of allotted work by each process, are the people associated with the processes themselves.

5. BENEFITS OF SYSTEMS APPROACH

The major benefits of system approach

- Improves inter-departmental interaction,
- Brings about better understanding of constraints and capabilities of every departments.
- Leads to acceptance of the concept of internal customer, and
- Strengthens teamwork.

[ISO] seven
CONTINUAL IMPROVEMENT

1. IMPROVEMENT

George Bernard Shaw the famous English writer once said,

If you always do, what you have always done,
You will only get, what you have always gotten.

How pertinent for every situation in life! It is also true for organizations wishing to progress and grow. Improvement being the objective, the ability to do things better, is essential.

All organizations have to face the challenge of "Ever Getting Better - Forever". They need to have the ability to withstand the pressures of the market fluctuations, price wars, requirement fluctuations, shorter product life, need for cost reductions and higher quality. Only organizations performing at their peak, which are not complacent and are constantly improving can sustain and progress in the competitive global market. The planned consistent effort for improvement, which imparts the capability to survive and progress earlier referred to as 'Continuous Improvement' is now named 'Continual Improvement'.

2. COMPARISON OF CONTINUOUS AND CONTINUAL IMPROVEMENT

'Continuous' refers to any activity occurring uninterruptedly with time, in an unbroken sequence or pattern. Thus improvement when effected every moment with no break or let-up would be referred to as continuous. On a time-improvement graph it would be depicted in the form of a continuously rising straight line plot as shown in Fig. 3. This however never happens in practice, since improvement requires time, for determining the change, verifying suitability, implementing, stabilizing, assessing, monitoring, etc. This means, improvement on a continuous basis is a myth and not achievable. In view of this non-achievability of continuous improvement, ISO/TC 176 Technical Committee decided to adopt the word continual for the improvement process.

'Continual' refers to a discontinuous but repetitive activity, which can occur at irregular or regular intervals but is consistent and ongoing. Thus for continual improvement the time interval between the improvements need not be fixed and the improvements could be more pronounced at times. On the graph shown in Fig. 3., this is depicted in the form of a step-wise rise whereby the improvement is not continuous. The step heights are also not equal, indicating that the improvement is not the same each time. The horizontal portion of the step indicates that time is given for stabilization after every improvement has been incorporated. The next improvement is initiated only after the stabilization is complete.

TABLE 9

Understanding Continuous and Continual Improvement

Point on Graph	Time Interval	Improvement		Remarks
		Level Change	Type of Change	
O-0	Zero	Nil	Start	Initial Level
A-1	O-A	0-1	Continual	Small-step improvement
B-1	A-B	Nil	Continual	Stabilization (small time interval)
C-2	B-C	1-2	Continual	Another small-step improvement
D-2	C-D	Nil	Continual	Stabilization (small time interval)
E-3	D-E	2-3	Continual	Break through improvement
F-3	E-F	Nil	Continual	Stabilization (large time interval)
G-4	F-G	3-4	Continual	Another small-step improvement
H-4	G-H	Nil	Continual	Stabilization (small time interval)
H-0	O-H	0-4	CONTI – NUOUS	Continuously ascending level of improvement with no time for stabilization

Thus 'Continual Improvement' is an organization-wide process of focused and sustained incremental improvement, which could be in small or big steps. This type of improvement process being practical and feasible is more authentic and provides greater confidence to the organization, i.e. to both its people and the management. The objective of any such improvement process is to use it as a corrective mechanism to enhance the organization's performance and to use it for assuring the organisation's survival and growth.

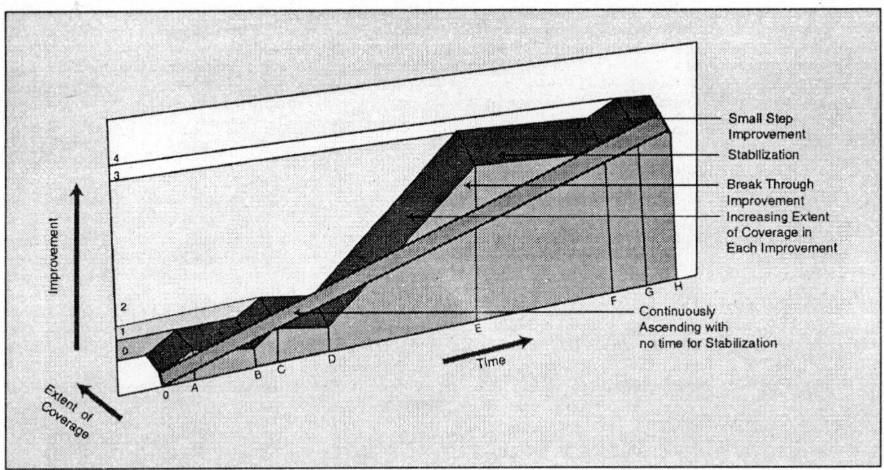

FIG. 3 *UNDERSTANDING CONTINUOUS AND CONTINUAL IMPROVEMENT*

While carrying-out continual improvements, especially in areas where improvements have already been carried out earlier, it is essential to make all efforts for also enlarging the scope of coverage every time (even if it is marginal), so as to benefit a wider area. This widening too cannot be continuous rather it would be continual.

3. MAINTENANCE AND CONTINUAL IMPROVEMENT OF THE QMS

Maintenance of the QMS is meeting requirements and fulfilling expectations by always operating at the same, predetermined performance level.

Continual Improvement of the QMS is constantly looking for ways and means to fulfil expectations by always upgrading the level of performance with time.

Small-step Improvement is the improvement process wherein the up-gradation of the level of performance is the result of small incremental steps, which are regular and constant with time almost on a daily basis. Such improvement is therefore a part of the ROUTINE CYCLE of performance of an organization. It aims at improvement in the effectiveness and efficiency of the level of performance in small steps.

Breakthrough Improvement is the improvement process where the up-gradation of the level of performance is obtained in large jumps through innovation by looking for breakthroughs widely spaced over time. Such improvement is therefore a part of the OCCASIONAL CYCLE of performance of an organization. It aims at setting newer and much higher levels of performance.

4. MAINTENANCE AND CONTINUAL IMPROVEMENT IN RELATION TO THE STANDARD

The 1994 version of ISO 9001/9002/9003 just required that the organization "establish, document, and maintain a quality system". This was a neutral approach, like telling a team to 'play and not lose the game'.

The 2000 version of ISO 9001 however requires that the organization "establish, document, implement and maintain a quality management system and continually improve its effectiveness". This is a positive and dynamic approach, like telling a team to 'play to win and also learn the opponent's strategies for winning in future too'.

5. EFFECTING CONTINUAL IMPROVEMENT

After being successful in obtaining the certificate of ISO 9001:2000 an organization can rejoice and feel pleased with its achievement. However this is, in-fact the first step in the quality journey. By getting certified for ISO 9001 the organization has merely reached the minimum level. Now the *Mantra* for progress is, "Maintain, Innovate or Improve Continually, Stabilize and Maintain once again". This cycle can be depicted as shown in Fig. 4.

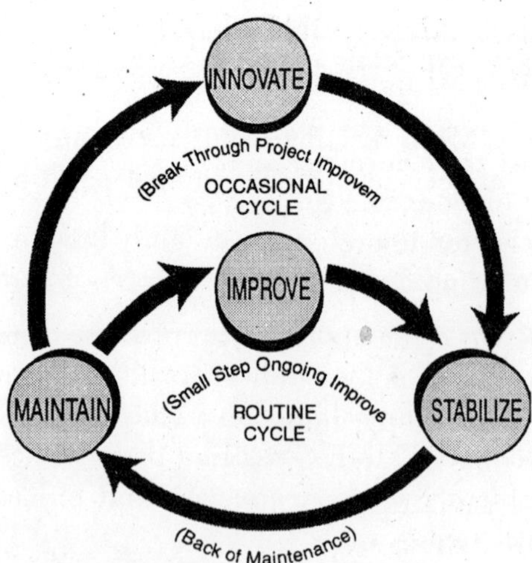

FIG. 4 *THE CONTINUAL IMPROVEMENT CYCLE*

5.1 Identifying Improvement Opportunities

The objective being Improvement of performance of the organization it is essential to identify opportunities for improvement. This can be done by:

- Carefully examining the present product, process and system to pinpoint both superfluous and problem areas,
- Questioning the affected people to get leads, and
- Bench marking against better performers.

In business when looking at performance it is not only important to improve it, but also, to sustain the current level and prevent any decline in performance. It is therefore necessary to measure the performance to establish the shortcomings and determining the means of bridging gaps.

5.1.1 Measurement

Without measurement there is no way to determine effectiveness of maintenance or improvement and hence success

Measurement is basically required to compare the improvements of the organization with the objectives to assess operational effectiveness. Thus measurement is the means of linking and tying-up all process improvement to ensure that the direction of the organizational progress is right.

It is normally said that if you can't measure any variable you can't manage that variable.

5.2 Effective Problem Solving

Effectiveness in problem solving comes from objectively scrutinizing current problem situations or measurement of current performance. Once the present level is determined a careful analysis helps identify the improvement opportunity. However we need to guard against getting misled or distracted, since things are not what they normally appear to be. Problems are many times not caused by the obvious and expected reasons. Thus to understand problems and the obstacles for improvement avoid looking at symptoms or apparent causes by maintaining complete focus on facts.

In the book 'Alice in Wonderland' The March Hare and the Mad Hatter are together and the Hatter asks Alice a riddle for which there is no answer. When told there is no answer to the riddle she remarks, "I think you might do something better with time than wasting it asking riddles with no answers". The same applies to an organization too. Do not waste time trying to solve every problem. Remember there are a few problems with no satisfactory solutions. Such problems are in-fact inevitable situations one needs to learn to live with. As an example we may like to have our competitors play a clean game but if they do not do so, the situation should be accepted as being beyond control and time need not be wasted in trying to change the competitor. Rather the organization must come to terms with the situation and take-off from there.

5.2.1 Think Positively Do not consider problems as PROBLEMS but as OPPORTUNITIES. This positive approach will itself eliminate the mental block we, as individuals have, and bring about a radical cultural change in attitude of every individual. Propagate the philosophy that if we are at level 1 and the solution of the problem can take us to level 2 then the identification of presence of the problem is a boon. The minute the problem is eliminated we are at level 2 and have improved.

5.2.2 Finding the causes Solving problems require logical analysis and focus on the causes rather than the symptoms. The symptoms should be used only to diagnose the causes. If for instance a motor fails because it is overheating while running it could be due to any of the following causes:

- The bearing could be damaged
- The cooling fan may not be rotating as its split pin is broken and has fallen
- The motor may be over loaded
- The rotor shaft may be bent or
- The input voltage may be low.

Thus, over heating is the symptom, the cause can be any of the above and the failure of the motor is the problem.

Similarly if a person is ill and has high temperature, he may have viral fever. In this case the viral fever is the cause, the high temperature is the symptom and the illness is the problem.

Use symptoms to arrive at the causes of problems

In an organization, on a particular day a machine operator within an hour of starting his work, came to the engineer and told him that his stomach was aching and wanted to consult the doctor. The engineer could have very easily signed the permission slip and allowed him to leave, putting a substitute at his stage of operation. The engineer however being diligent asked him the reason. The operator, who repeatedly operated the handle to press down on a job, told him that it was because the handle was very stiff. The engineer, neither disbelieved him nor left the matter there. He himself manned the operation and found that the handle was indeed stiff. Further, within just 5 minutes of working his stomach muscles too began to ache. He immediately had the operation stopped. He checked, and found that in the previous shift, the machine had malfunctioned and the maintenance department had carried out repairs on the machine.

On further instigation on the machine , he found out that a "setting-bolt" had been over-tightened. This diligence of the engineer not only set the problem right but also averted a bigger problem. Had the machine run on the same setting for even a full shift, it would probably have led to a major breakdown, due to seizure of few critical mating parts.

The procedure was later changed. What is pertinent is, correct analysis of the symptom, had led to the cause.

5.2.3 Investigating the causes One should not jump to a conclusion even if the possible causes for a problem are known. They have to be investigated critically. Amongst the probable causes, only some are contributory while most others are just apparent. Apparent causes are immediately visible reasons, but the contributory causes are not necessarily visible though they are the actual reasons. In the worker's stomachache problem mentioned above the apparent problem was the stiff handle whereas the actual cause was the incorrect tightening of the setting-bolt.

Sift through the causes to locate the root cause

The root causes are the most basic reasons for any problem, performance deficiency or impediments to improvement. Root cause analysis is a technique that can be used not only to solve existing problems but also to anticipate future problems.

5.2.4 Finding solutions to problems Finding solutions to problems not only requires analysis but also the ability to innovate and think of all possible options. It also necessitates considering all constraints for solving the problem. Solutions are arrived at by viewing them differently and developing new ideas through creative thinking.

In-fact only through such thinking, continual improvement is possible whereby people develop ideas that did not exist earlier.

There are many problems in existence, which can help demonstrate this aspect. The most well known problem of this type is the "Nine Dot Problem" where the aim is to 'draw only 4 straight lines to pass through all 9 dots'. The solutions are as shown in Fig. 5(a):

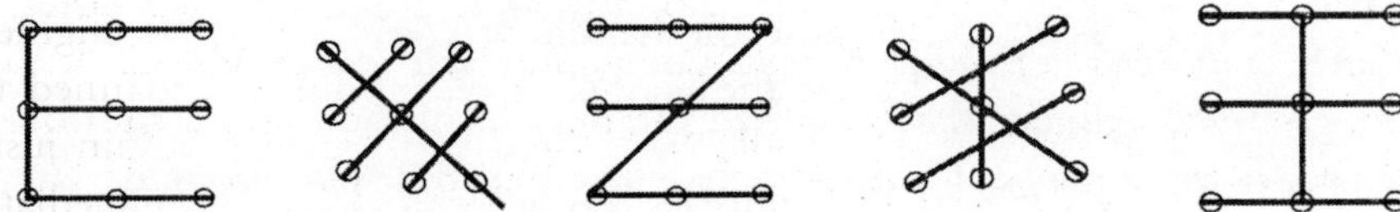

FIG. 5 (A) *ONLY 4 LINES THROUGH THE NINE DOTS*

If however, a new constraint is now added to this problem that 'each of the 4 lines must touch the other 3 lines', then the above solutions fail and only the solution as given in Fig. 5(b) complies with this added constraint:

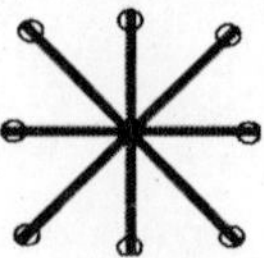

FIG. 5 (B) *ONLY 4 LINES THROUGH THE NINE DOTS WITH EACH LINE TOUCHING THE OTHER 3 LINES*

If however once again one more constraint is added that, 'all the 4 lines must be drawn in continuation without lifting up the pen even once and without drawing a line again over a line, once drawn', then even the above solution fails and the new solution emerges as given in Fig. 5(c):

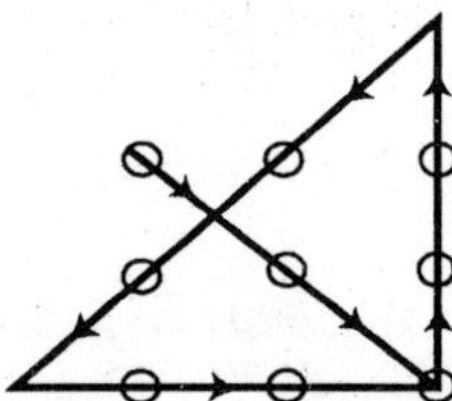

FIG 5 (C) *ONLY 4 LINES THROUGH THE NINE DOTS WITH EACH LINE TOUCHING THE OTHER 3 LINES DRAWN CONTINUOUSLY*

There is a very important lesson to be learnt from the above, i.e., 'Look at the constraints imposed once again'. At no place had the constraint implied that going out of the limits of the 9 dots is prohibited. All along, it is we, who had assumed that this constraint existed. Thus it is always we, with our closed minds and limited vision, who create the artificial boundaries and invisible barriers to miss-out on easy solutions.

Always remember,

Difficult problems generally have easy solutions

I came across an anecdote from the internet (Truth not known), which is a simple example of missing the obvious. In the early days of the space program, the astronauts reported that while trying to write in space, their pens were not writing. They tried every type of pen from the quill to the fountain pen and ball pen. Nothing worked. Huge amounts were allotted for the purpose and after considerable research a 'space compatible pen' was developed. It had a tiny gas filled cylinder that propelled the ink out of the tip at a controlled flow rate. It was a marvel for it not only worked in space but also underwater. It was wonderful to have solved such a difficult problem even if at a high cost.

There are two versions to the subsequent part of this episode (again truth not known):

(i) Years later, the cosmonauts were asked about their solution to this problem, to know how the difficulty was over come for them. They replied that they had used pencils.

(ii) A schoolboy who later visited the space station and heard of this problem innocently inquired, why a pencil was not used.

Whatever be the facts, it is evident that the obvious had been missed.

This difficult problem indeed had a simple solution.

Open your mind, widen your vision and THINK AT A TANGENT !!!

5.2.5 Implementing Problem Solutions The remedial solutions once identified should be implemented in such a way that the solution is permanent and the problem does not recur. All actions necessary to close the corrective action loop ought to be ensured. No problem is ever trivial, and so must have the same level of corrective effort.

5.2.6 Follow Through Corrective actions or improvements once implemented must be followed-up to ensure that no new problems occur and the action has set in correctly. It is like the trial of a 'newly tailored suit' taken after stitching to remove the wrinkles and ensure a perfect fit. In process improvements too, the changes made mostly need fine-tuning. At times, after an improvement is made during operation, it may be realized that a particular factor was not considered while making the change and in-fact this additional factor has necessitated reversion to the earlier method or process. All this arises from the follow through and so it forms an important part of the improvement process.

6. GENERIC IMPROVEMENT TARGETS

In business when looking at performance it is not only important to try to improve it, but also to sustain the current level and further in-fact prevent any decline in performance. It is therefore necessary to measure performance so as to establish the shortcoming to determine the means of bridging the gap. The main reasons for the measurement need are as follows:

- To ensure that customer requirements have been met
- To be able to set new targets for performance
- To improve quality
- To exceed expectations
- To ensure customer focus

- To ensure best practices
- To meet promises and commitments
- To reduce costs
- To increase effectiveness and efficiency
- To ensure satisfactory level of training
- To improve capacity utilization
- To optimize resource utilization
- To reduce time required to carry out the same operation
- To eliminate the obstacles in the way of smooth performance

7. CONTINUAL IMPROVEMENT METHODS

ISO 9004:2000 the consistent pair to ISO 9001:2000 clearly states the following two fundamental methods of effecting continual improvement:

(i) Break-through project improvement method, and

(ii) Small-step ongoing improvement method.

These two methods are like the "The hare and the tortoise" of the fable. Only in this case both are winners. Break-through project is the HARE method, which looks for fast improvements in big leaps, also with larger breaks in-between. The small-step ongoing improvement is the TORTOISE method, which looks for slow but steady improvements in small steps, and has very small or almost no breaks, in-between. Both methods are useful and have their own advantages. Therefore, the organization should continually make use of both methods for effecting improvements, by constantly making use of the tortoise method to remain dynamic and being on the look out for making use of the hare method for surging ahead in spurts.

Success does not happen over night and so aiming for a 100% improvement, company-wide is neither realistic nor practical. Focus therefore should be on incremental improvements in vital areas. Even a modest 2 to 3% improvement over a long period of time can add up to a significant value and keep the competition at bay. Moreover, this small-step improvement is extremely cost effective. In the meantime the organization must also be on the lookout for possible improvement avenues in vital areas, by seeking likely opportunities for break-through, and then exploit them in a planned manner.

The entire improvement effort should be concentrated only on the 'vital processes'. This stress on the vital processes ensures that the improvements actually benefit the organization, where it matters. It should be remembered that, processes that are being systematically managed and monitored would already be efficient and any further improvement in them would give genuine benefits to the organization.

7.1 Break-through Project Improvement

Break-through project improvement consists of achieving radical improvements through focused and systematic exploitation of 'potential opportunities' by applying ingenuous ideas to effect quantum jumps.

This method is used for bringing about an improvement by normally comparing the existing level of performance with 'competitors performance data' or 'desired objectives' or 'market requirements'. Break-through however requires looking at opportunities, by breaking away from conventions and taking quantum leaps through unconventional, parallel or tangential thinking. This type of improvement takes time and needs a lot of planning, provision of resources, technology and innovative approach to help surge beyond competition in a tremendous leap.

This method being mostly technology driven thrives on the following:

- Rapidly expanding markets
- Consumer orientation in mass-produced products
- Abundant and low cost resources
- A belief that success with innovations can off-set sluggish performance in traditional operations
- A management, which is more concerned about increasing sales than about reducing costs.

7.2 Small-step Ongoing Improvement

Small-step ongoing improvement consists of incremental improvement in small-steps of high frequency short cycles, which appear to have little impact when viewed in isolation but which cumulatively over a period of time make significant contributions for performance enhancement.

This method is often used by the people at the operational level for improving performance in their own work-areas. This requires "doing little things, little better, every time" thereby setting higher standards for the next effort. This type of improvement is effected by constantly studying the existing problems causing variations followed by identifying their causes, controlling them and finding better solutions thereby bring about a gradual, steady and continual improvement in their area of work. This leads to improvement in performance over a period of time. Progress is not brought by a breakthrough but is incremental in nature and involves a high proportion of small-steps. So it is this method which generally becomes the backbone of the organization's progress.

This method thrives in any situation when there is:

- Sharp increase in the costs of materials, energy and labor
- Overcapacity of production facilities
- Increased market competition among companies in saturated or dwindling markets
- Changing consumer values and more exacting quality requirements
- A need to introduce new products more rapidly
- A need to lower the breakeven point.

TABLE 10

Comparison between Small-step and Break-through Methods

No.	Criteria	Small-step Ongoing Improvement	Break-through Project Improvements
1.	Method	Tortoise	Hare
2.	Increments	In small step	In big steps
3.	Nature of change	Continual	Intermittent
4.	Rate of Change	Gradual but constant	Steep but irregular
5.	Reason of Change	Due to a systematic set-up in the organization	Due to initiative by the set-up of the organization
6.	People Involvement	Everybody is involved	Only those who have been selected are involved
7.	Efforts	Group	Individual
8.	Idea implementation	Requires conventional know-how	Requires technological break-through
9.	Relies upon	People	Technology
10.	Financial Investment	Little Required	Considerable requirement
11.	Impact	Long-term	Short-term
12.	Applicability	For existing products	For both existing & new products
13.	Targets	Consolidation of existing market	Consolidation of existing & entry into new markets
14.	Achieves	Improvement or cost reduction	New or different offering
15.	Requires	Problem identification, analysis and solving through attention to detail	Innovative thinking, risk taking and rapid action to enter the market

8. GUIDELINES FOR MANAGING CONTINUAL IMPROVEMENT PROJECTS

The major guidelines for managing continual improvement projects are given below

(i) Pick a tool you understand
(ii) Pick a project which is easy and where success seems assured
(iii) Involve people from all related areas
(iv) Train the team in the tools being applied
(v) Record existing processes and record changes
(vi) Ensure project is completed and regularly audited
(vii) Maintain the new methods
(viii) Publish benefits and
(ix) Acknowledge progress and benefits.

ISO

eight

Factual Approach to Decision-Making

1. FACTS FOR DECISION-MAKING

Facts are the raw material for decision-making

All of us tend to work at times by intuition and of-course past experience, but even this type of decision-making is based on facts, where the available options depend on facts and only the selection from these is done by intuition or experience. If facts are just not used and decisions are based entirely on assumptions or hunches, we are not solving the problem, but creating further problems for ourselves. Thus, if problems are to be solved, then facts ought to be the fundamental basis for all decision-making. Even more, when the decisions are concerned with complex situations within an organization, with a lot at stake. In such situations, if decisions are supported by facts, there would be greater confidence and support from all concerned, ensuring success.

In our struggle to constantly produce consistent outputs and effect improvements, facts become extremely precious inputs for decisions. Only by knowing our 'Product Quality Level' (both external as well as internal) do we get the reference level against which the current quality can be judged. The measurement of quality level, through comparison with the previous level helps determine the status and take decisions.

TABLE 11

Steps Facilitating Understanding for Future Decisions

No.	Quality Level	Current Status	Decision
1.	Lower than earlier	Quality Declined	Take corrective actions
2.	Same as earlier	Quality Maintained	Take improvement actions
3.	Higher than earlier	Quality Improved	Take further improvement action

1.1 What is a fact?

Talk in general terms and
You will have people hearing you out.
Talk facts, giving details with specifics and
You will have people leaning forward to listen.

A truthful set of data that can be used as evidence, is a fact. Within an organization a lot of data is generated. Collection of data utilizes valuable time, effort and resource. It is therefore necessary to avoid getting confused or misled, by irrelevant and unnecessary data. Data collected should be truthful, correct and relevant to the purpose. After proper collection, data should be understood carefully, before it could be used as a fact. It should also be remembered that both 'a negative as well as a positive fact' is useful, as long as it is truthful, since both give us information. Facts therefore are extremely important, for providing a true and comprehensive picture of any situation, activity or process.

A truthful set of data makes-up a fact

In the book 'Alice in Wonderland' the White Rabbit is asked to present evidence of the Knave's guilt, which requires him to read from a parchment with some verses written on it. The King pronounces the prisoner guilty even though it is unsigned because he feels that not signing itself is an indication of guilt. However our intelligent heroine of the story Alice discovers it is not in the prisoner's writing and stands up for him. Thus we observe that the analytical assumption of the King even though logical was proved wrong while the fact was right by itself.

The facts we observe form the only basis of evidence.

1.2 Determining Facts

In determining facts it is necessary that the data collected is correct, useable and needed. Hence while collecting data the following questions should be clearly answered:

- What is our objective?
- Why are we collecting the data?
- What type of data is required?

This leads us to the logical sequence in determining facts, which should be to:

- Establish the objective of collecting data
- Determine the type of data required by the objective

- Collect relevant data
- Separate disputable data
- Remove any biases
- Arrive at unbiased and undisputable neutral truthful data i.e. facts
- Establish relationships among the facts for factual approach.

1.3 Using logic

Logic basically means correct reasoning through proper correlation of facts, whereby out of all the available data the facts stand out and all other alternatives are eliminated. It depends upon rational thinking, which requires sifting through the available information to separate-out the factual certainties. These facts can then be used to arrive at a conclusion.

Logic is useful even for tackling uncertain conditions. In such a situation the various possibilities are listed and their logical consequences are established. This in turn would help in knowing the likely occurrences.

In either case, once the above are known adequate precautions to counter them in the form of plans can be produced. Since the best-laid plans too can backfire, a contingency back-up for their failures can be made in advance using logic.

Logic however is a tool, and like every other tool, would be of no use unless its application is correct..

2. FACTUAL APPROACH

Most processes are made up of multiple sets of activities, where each set has a different effect on the process. While studying basic facts from such different sources, if each set of facts is viewed by itself, it will tell us a different story. If we view facts of different sources in isolation, then even though each set of facts is right in itself, it would lead us to erroneous actions when used for decision making. This is because within the cross-functional processes, facts are viewed as a whole and it gives us a true picture of the process. This is called the factual approach and is a powerful decision-making tool for solving problems, besides maintaining and improving the quality.

Factual approach requires viewing related facts, in combination

3. DECISION MAKING

Make proactive and reflective decision, not reactive and reflexive decision

Decision-making is the process of comparatively assessing the various options for selecting the most suitable solution. Thus the steps involved in this decision-making process are as follows:

- Identify the problem and locate its critical aspects
- Define the solution requirements to be reached
- Balance the present conditions and future requirements
- Analyze the problem
- Determine the necessary and relevant data
- Screen the data to isolate the facts from assumptions
- Develop possible solutions
- Select the best solution (even if it be maintenance of status quo) for the purpose
- Implement the solution
- Maintain the modified solution in operation
- Verify operational effectiveness and
- Based on the feedback either continue the operation or re-modify the solution for implementation and reassessment.

3.1 Personal Capabilities Affecting Decision Making

The personal capabilities affecting decision making are given as under

- Skill in identifying problems
- Capability of understanding the problem
- Analytical capacity to get useful information from facts
- Deductive ability to arrive at solutions
- Ability to get decisions implemented
- Monitoring tenacity
- Capability of understanding the feedback
- Ability to retract from a decision or correct an incorrect decision.

4. STATISTICS IN OUR DAILY LIVES

The science of statistics is not difficult to understand. Even in our daily lives, we use statistics without realizing it.

(i) The lady in the kitchen who checks just three to four grains of rice, and declares the rice cooked or otherwise uses random samples to assess a lot.

(ii) The person who fills 40 liters of petrol and confidently says it will last him 620 km is going by his car's average petrol consumption, based on past performance data.

(iii) Each individual's routine of 'daily activities' follows a pattern, as in a flowchart.

(iv) During purchase of groceries at the shop the prices of each item are compared with different brands to decide on the purchase. This is an example of the development of a complex comparative matrix, that too in our minds.

(v) When the cricketer repeatedly bowls the same line and length through out the day, he is exhibiting control of process capability.

(vi) The scooter mechanic, even though a small boy, zeros onto the cause of the malfunction, by using the cause-effect principle, and that too mentally.

(vii) The child, checking the mix of hot and cold water, before bathing is ensuring that the temperature measurement is within his acceptable control limits.

There is no end to such examples. Many more can be cited and they are all cases of common day use of statistics without the user realizing it.

5. STATISTICS IN BUSINESS

There is a general apprehension, that a high level of mathematics is required for using and understanding statistical tools for analysis. This is a myth. With the availability of calculators and computers, difficulty of mathematical calculations is no longer an issue. The only thing needed to understand them is logical thinking. Many people feel, that tools are useful only for engineering industries. Actually, this is not true. As already seen we use it in our daily lives too. Statistics is therefore useful for all types of businesses, both in the manufacturing and the service sectors. Statistics explains the cause-effect phenomenon as follows:

Every effect often has a number of causes.
These causes contribute to deviations.
The deviations produce this effect.

It is pertinent that, of the many causes for an effect, only a few causes are the major contributors to deviations. These causes can be easily identified, studied and controlled using simple statistical tools. Thus, the use of statistical tools for studying facts, to arrive at scientifically made decisions, lends credibility to the decisions.

The tools of statistics are therefore a key for developing a scientific fact-based approach on decision-making. The need is to use the tools, not just for solving technical problems, but to use them for decision-making by evaluating processes and procedures.

5.1 Statistical Tools

A large number of Statistical tools being available, the dilemma is to decide, 'what tool to use and for what purpose'. The degree of success is largely dependent upon the selection of the right tool. It is therefore necessary to be clear on the purpose of applying the tool. It could be to determine the solution to a problem or to verify the scope of improvement. Once the purpose is clear the selection can be made from amongst the different tools available for such a use. It should be remembered that, only if the right tool is used the solution determined would give permanent benefits. (Please also see Appendix C for further information on Statistical Tools).

ISO nine

Mutually Beneficial Supplier Relationships

1. SUPPORTING SUPPLIERS

Involvement and complete support of the suppliers are as important as involvement of our own people

In any process operating in a closed loop, the output is input dependent. An organization also operates as a closed loop system. Incoming material quality therefore determines the quality of the output in a big way. Suppliers as such, have an extremely important role to play in the organization's quest for effective and efficient operations, to achieve customer satisfaction. All organizations are suppliers as well as customers, and so play a 'dual role'. They can therefore easily understand both, the problems of a supplier as well as the importance of meeting customer requirements.

An organization is a customer for its suppliers, and so must be satisfied by these suppliers. This requires the supplier to determine the organization's requirements, so as to meet them satisfactorily. Rather than wait for this to happen, the organization should on its own, feed this information to the suppliers. Providing the information in advance will make the job of their suppliers easy. Once the suppliers are aware of the needs and expectations they will be able to align themselves, with the organizations requirements. Thus volunteering the information and helping the suppliers will mutually benefit both the suppliers and the organization.

2. ESTABLISHING RELATIONSHIPS

As a first step for deriving mutual benefits it is essential to ensure that the suppliers get increased business. This increase in business is logically possible only if, the organization consciously and systematically recognizes, acknowledges and encourages the good and potential suppliers. Selection of the good few by giving them the preferred status will motivate the suppliers and strengthen the relationship with them.

It is essential to identify the suppliers' capabilities and understand their limitations for which the following need to be determined:

- Do they share similar principles and values as the organization?
- Do they value their people?
- Do they have a quality orientation?
- Are they receptive to positive change?
- Is a long-term partnership with them feasible?

This approach will make it possible for the organization to identify the areas where they can be of help to their suppliers, who can then take it up from there, with their own innovation and continual improvement.

Suppliers and customers big or small
mutual benefits concern all

3. SUPPLIER

Traditionally the word 'supplier' was used to define people external to the organization who sell their products to the organization. Today it is used more broadly to include even the people working within the organization, who internally supply any product for value addition through processing.

Supplier is any one whose product becomes the receiver's input

3.1 External Suppliers

These are suppliers who are not a part of the organization and whose products become the organization's inputs. They are basically resource suppliers.

3.2 Internal Suppliers

These suppliers are a part of the organization as they supply in-process product intermediates, as inputs to the subsequent stages. Thus, each stage of activity within the organization, which supplies its outputs, for further value addition, to the next stage can be called the internal supplier to the next stage.

4. OUTSOURCING VS. IN-SOURCING

Outsourcing as per the dictionary means, 'to obtain by contract a component, assembly, process or service from an outside source' while In-sourcing means, 'to produce a component, assembly, process or service internally'.

The decision to outsource is basically a strategic decision with far reaching implications and consequences. It needs the organization to make a judicious decision in this regard after fully understanding it. The decision to outsource can be applied to every process or area of activity of an organization be it purchasing, design, research, production, assembly, engineering, warehousing, communication, transportation, distribution, delivery, marketing, sales, human resource, pay roll, information technology, canteen and cafeteria, security, etc. The decision to outsource leads to success when it is based upon an accurate analytical assessment by the organization.

In Purchase Management terminology '**Contracting-out**' is not the same as '**Outsourcing**'. They differ in the following ways:

(i) Contracting-out is short-term while outsourcing is for longer durations.

(ii) The Contractors merely provide the process as a standard product unlike the outsourced process who customize the process requirements to those of the organization.

(iii) In a Contract, the organization uses external resources where as, in outsourcing it also transfers its internal operations including the staff, to the concerned process provider.

(iv) Contracting-out is merely a formal customer-supplier relationship, while outsourcing is a partnership.

(v) Contracting-out is an operational or tactical decision while outsourcing is a strategic decision.

Note:

(i) **Strategic management** relates to long term planning for a period of five to ten years ahead. This establishes direction and priorities for the organization. This provides a statement of 'where the organization wants to go' and is related to its vision, mission, goals and objectives.

(ii) **Tactical management** relates to short term planning for one to three years into the future. This is concerned with how the organization will arrive, 'where it wants to go'. It is linked with the plans and budgets.

(iii) **Operational management** relates to immediate ends in view with duration of even less than one year. This sets out the specific actions to be undertaken concerning operations of limited importance and brief duration.

Section

III

Understanding the Standard

ISO

ten

Understanding PDCA Improvement Cycle

1. WHOSE CONCEPT IS PDCA?

Use of PDCA cycle as a Quality improvement tool, was devised and suggested by Dr. William Edwards Deming, born in Iowa, USA in October 1900. He received his Ph.D. in mathematical physics from Yale University. He studied under Mr. R.A. Fisher and was also influenced by Dr. Walter Shewhart, both of whom were statisticians. During 1941, he lectured American industrialists and engineers on the methods for improving productivity and reducing scrap. His ideas however did not get much support or following in America. Later, after the war ended he was invited to Japan to lecture there. In 1950, his speech to the CEOs of 100 industrial leaders followed by another lecture to 400 in 1951, made the Japanese adopt his ideas, widely. Adoption of his ideas and implementation of techniques caused the Japanese to lead the world in quality. In recognition of his contribution to the success of their quality movement, the Japanese honored him with the second order of the Sacred Treasure, one of Japan's most distinguished awards. Subsequently, in his honor they have also instituted a quality award called the Deming Prize.

It was Deming who gave the world this concept of breaking down any activity into four fundamental steps of Plan-Do-Check-Act and then carrying out that activity using this cycle repeatedly. In this PDCA cycle shown in Fig. 6., during the process of ACT for correcting the process based on the feedback from CHECK, Deming advised concentration on the removal of assignable causes for problems, rather than chance causes.

In order to make the cycle capable of assuring continuous improvement, Deming propounded that the cycle be applied repeatedly in the execution of any activity for ensuring consistency and reliability. Further, during every repetition, an attempt was to be made to raise the level for the process of PLAN, based on the feedback received from CHECK to bring about improvement. Thus at the end of each ACT the level of PLAN process would be higher than the previous level.

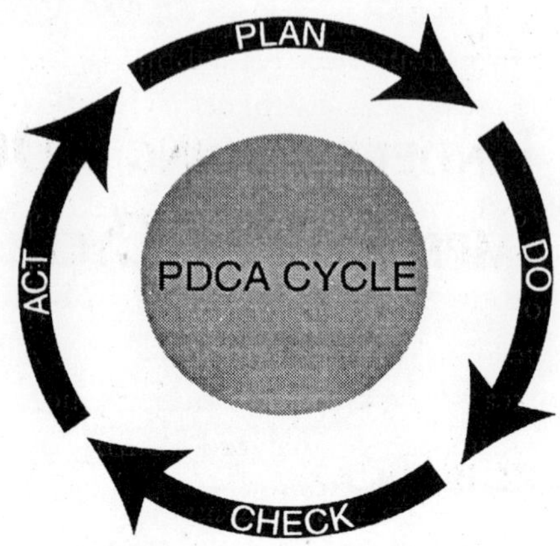

FIG. 6 *DEMING'S PDCA CYCLE*

The purpose of PDCA therefore, is not just to correct deviations from the standards, but to effect improvements by anticipating defects and preventing them from recurring by continually revising the standard set.

Later another Quality Guru, Dr. Joseph M. Juran, stated that PDCA should not be viewed as a flat cycle but like an ever-rising spiral. This concept is therefore, sometimes called, 'Juran Spiral' requiring that the PDCA cycle be repeated frequently and after every improvement, reviewed for further improvement.

2. PLAN-DO-CHECK-ACT IMPROVEMENT CYCLE

The "Plan-Do-Check-Act Improvement Cycle", is different from the other improvement methods, which depend upon ideas and inspiration. Ideas can only be random and so the improvements are also irregular. The PDCA is a systematic and organized process, in which the activities follow a set cyclic pattern consisting of planning, implementing, verifying and taking corrective actions. This cycle can be applied to any type of activity for developing, implementing and improving its effectiveness. Every improvement made leads to the establishment of a better method, which is again challenged for determining a still better method leading to continual improvement.

The key words of this cycle are explained below:

(i) Plan - This is the most important process for which responsibility has been assigned to the top management. If the plans are themselves inadequate, all subsequent actions are bound to take the wrong direction. If however the plans are clear and well-laid, activities are bound to be methodical and efficient.

The first step in the planning process therefore, is to establish objectives. Once the objectives are defined, determining the strategy, processes and tools necessary for achieving the results need to be decided and systematically worked out.

(ii) Do - This is the phase of actual implementation of the plans. This requires proper understanding and communication of the plans. All necessary resources are also required to be made available for this process.

(iii) Check - This is the process of monitoring and measuring performance. The results obtained are analyzed and compared against the plans to determine the extent of achievement of the planned results. At this stage it also becomes known if the plans themselves were satisfactory or deficient and whether they need to be revised.

(iv) Act - This is the process of utilizing the feedback from the check process and acting on it to improve performance. It is important not only to correct the symptoms but also the causes. The sure path to success lies in the removal of the causes and not the symptoms.

(v) Improvement - This basically requires the bridging of the gap between, 'what is desired' and 'what is achieved' as shown in Fig. 7. Further at no point of time any standard or level of performance should be considered as final. Each standard set is to be challenged and a better one sought.

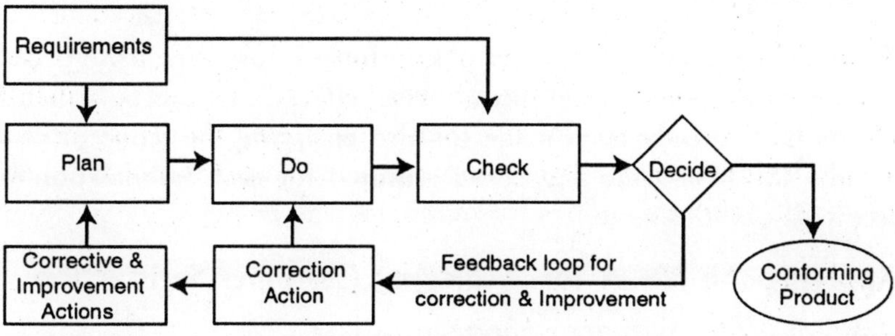

FIG. 7 *PDCA IMPROVEMENT CYCLE APPLIED TO A GENERIC PROCESS*

3. STABILIZATION, AN ADDITIONAL REQUIREMENT OF PDCA IMPROVEMENT CYCLE

The PDCA cycle is not meaningful unless any improvement effected is stabilized and maintained for a while to gain confidence, so that the achievement has become sustainable and can now be treated as the current level. Very often after an improvement is effected it is observed that the subsequent stabilization takes place at a level slightly lower than the initial level achieved, during the improvement process as shown in Fig. 8.

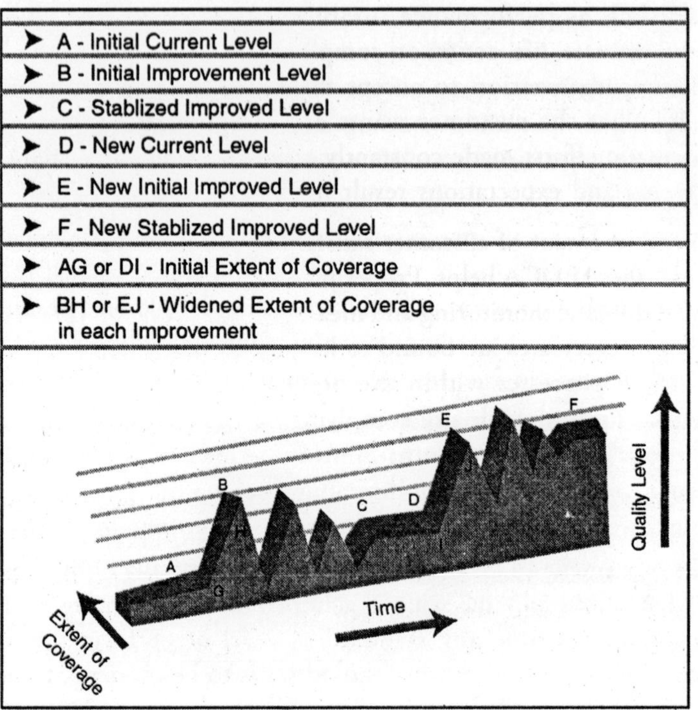

Fig. 8 *Stabilization of Processes During PDCA*

While carrying out stabilization of continual improvements, especially in areas where improvements have already been effected, it is to be remembered that efforts have already been made for also enlarging the scope of coverage continually. Thus the time and effort required for each stabilization would not necessarily be the same.

3.3 Applying the PDCA for Achieving Customer Satisfaction

The very purpose of ISO 9001:2000 is two fold:

- Product consistency in meeting customer and regulatory requirements
- Enhancement of customer satisfaction through continual improvement.

The first requirement is achievable through the 'PDCA Cycle' and the second requirement through the 'PDCA Spiral'. Thus, a combination of the cycle and spiral, which is called the 'PDCA Improvement Cycle', helps achieve both the purposes.

Customers always expect the quality level of the product delivered to them to be improved regularly. This expectation could be with regard to any attribute such as performance, usability, service, reliability, safety, cost-reduction, features, life, action on complaint, etc. Whatever be the expectation, it is for the organization to accept the challenge and constantly strive to determine what the customer wants and make improvements. Methodical and systematic efforts made constantly to achieve and in fact exceeding these requirements and expectations result in customer satisfaction.

The achievement of customer satisfaction has to be attempted proactively and this is where PDCA helps. Proper planning, implementation and execution of plans, systematic monitoring and measurement, proper feedback and prompt correction in every area are bound to lead to success. The PDCA cycle can be applied to all processes within the organization to ensure enhancement of customer satisfaction while still complying with the organization's own policies and also regulatory requirements.

It is in fact not sufficient to just target customer satisfaction. The organization should target achievement of customer delight by giving them products that exceed their expectation. This is what brings back old customers for repeat business and also adds new customers.

eleven
THE TWIST-RING TOOL

1. WHAT IS THE TWIST-RING TOOL?

The Twist-Ring Tool is a simple, yet powerful 'Tool of Analogy' for very effectively demonstrating, the "Dynamics of the PDCA in Action". This twist-ring is well-known in mathematical science. However the use of this ring as a tool of analysis and its explanation has been developed by the author to demonstrate the improvement process in a dynamic state using the PDCA Cycle.

2. HOW TO MAKE THE TWIST-RING TOOL?

Take a strip of paper about one centimeter wide and about 40 to 45 centimeters long. Write 'Plan, Do, Check, Act' on one face of the paper, spacing it out as shown in Fig. 9. Also, draw an upward pointing arrow after each word. Now turnover the strip as shown in figure below ensuring the top edge of the strip goes down and the bottom edge comes up. However, ensure that while turning over, the left side of the strip continues to remain on the left and the right side on the right. Once again write 'Plan, Do, Check, Act' and draw arrows as earlier, on the strip maintaining gaps as before.

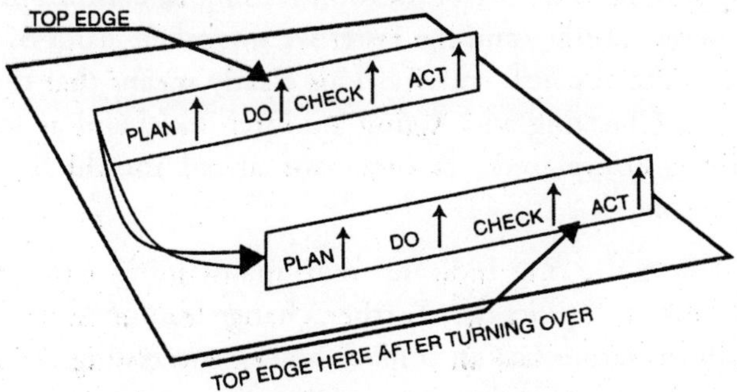

FIG. 9 *GETTING THE TWIST-RING STRIPS READY*

Now bring the two ends together, give half a twist to the right hand end of the strip and stick the ends together. The strip will form a ring with a twist as shown in Fig. 10. This is the TWIST-RING TOOL and it is ready for your use.

This twist-ring when studied closely will surprisingly reveal that it has just one continuous edge and only one surface. This may appear strange but is true.

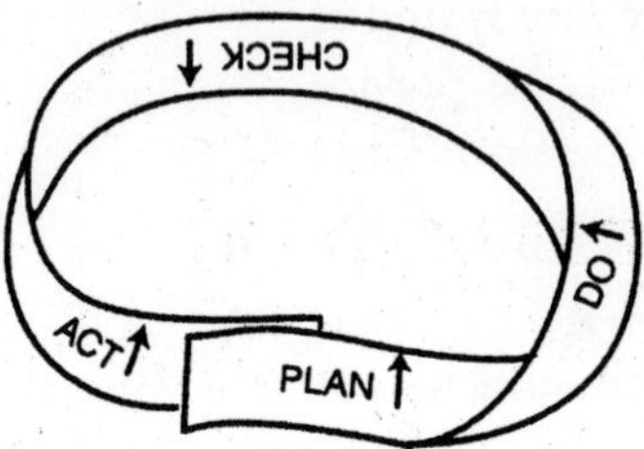

FIG. 10 *THE TWIST-RING TOOL*

3. TOOL OF ANALOGY

The twist-ring tool gets its power from the half twist given to one end before sticking the two ends together. Every time in our analogy it is this "Twist In The Ring" which would have a different role and help us understand the PDCA in its dynamic state.

3.1 Twist represents 'Transition'

In the ring, as we try to 'shift' (overcome) the 'twist' (transition) across any activity on the 'ring' (process) to 'smoothen' (improve) the 'present location' (present status) on the 'ring' (process) this twist keeps 'moving' (activity) ahead to the 'next location' (future status) of the activity further down. (Note if you make too small a ring, this effect would not be seen properly and the twist would appear at an incorrect location leading to confusion). We observe that the twist never vanishes and the faster we smoothen it out over an activity, the faster it moves to the next activity. This clearly means that the activities of Planning, Doing, Checking and Acting are interlinked and as soon as any of these activities is completed, its successor ahead should be immediately attended and so on.

The TWIST in the ring indicates that 'maintaining a transitory state of change' is essential in all processes. Further, change leading to the improvement being transitory in nature has an impact on the succeeding activities making it necessary for dynamism in improvements and to ensure smooth operations within the processes.

3.2 Twist represents 'Improvement'

While shifting ahead the 'twist' (improvement) in the ring, we observe the arrows drawn by us are pointing upwards on the face near to us and downward on the rear face. The lower edge of the ring in front represents the present level of performance while the upper edge represents the improved level of the organization. Thus, the improved level achieved earlier repeatedly keeps becoming the present level when the twists shifted forward. Next looking at the back face of the activity one would see the arrow tip there pointing to the bottom edge confirming that the previous improved level is now the present level at the bottom edge of the front face. This present level has to be improved again to go to the top so as to be on the top of competition.

What was discussed above is a macro process. At the micro level, one would observe that any process such as PLAN, DO, CHECK or ACT written on the two faces of the strip experiences a cyclical up (on the front face) and down (on the back face) during the twist smoothening. This means that each micro process during the transition undergoes improvement from the previous level by reaching a higher level, which then becomes the target.

3.3 Connectivity of Internal and External Environment

On a similar ring write 'Plan for Internal Customer, Do for Internal Customer, Check for Internal Customer, Act for Internal Customer' on one face of the paper, spacing it out as before. Now on the flip side write 'Plan for External Customer, Do for External Customer, Check for External Customer, Act for External Customer' spacing it out as before. Now stick the two ends together but do not forget to give half a twist to one end of the strip before joining them.

The inside of the ring represents the internal environment/customer and the outside represents the external environment/customer of the organization. This is a good tool to demonstrate that Planning, Doing, Checking and Acting when done for the internal environment/customer is actually being done for the external environment/customer also.

3.4 Twist Represents Lack of Clarity

Take a pair of scissors and cut the ring, 'along the center line of the width' right round the ring. The arrows drawn by us earlier would be cut across and hence would be like trying to separate the improved level from the current level. But, surprisingly the strip does not get cut into two rings as expected instead we once again get one bigger ring, thereby indicating that the improved level always depends on the present level reached and that both are linked. The parted ring would now have more twists than the earlier ring. This means if the organization tries to improve without taking cognizance of the present state it will lead to more twists. (lack of clarity)

Thus we observe that this TWIST-RING is a powerful tool to demonstrate any process of change leading to improvement. There is no end to the way the twist can be viewed to represent the dynamics of process improvement through the PDCA Cycle.

Even the change over from ISO 9001 / 9002 / 9003:1994 to ISO 9001:2000 is a twist-ring smoothening process.

ISO

twelve

DIFFERENCES BETWEEN ISO 9001:1994 AND ISO 9001:2000

The 2000 version of ISO 9001 has undergone major changes and for understanding these it is best to compare the two versions to establish the differences between them. The following Table 12 makes the necessary comparison.

TABLE 12

Comparison of ISO 9001:1994 and ISO 9001:2000

No.	Requirement	ISO 9001:1994	ISO 9001:2000
1.	System Model	Quality assurance model	Quality assurance and customer satisfaction model
2.	System Requirement	The quality system to be established documented, and maintained	The quality management system to be established, documented, implemented, maintained and continually improved
3.	System Structure	Based on 'Discrete Elements' identified in the standard	Based on the more logical 'Plan-Do-Check-Act improvement cycle'
4.	System Design Basis	20 elements	8 quality management principles
5.	System Orientation	Conformance to 'Specified Contractual Requirements'	Conformance to 'Customer and Regulatory Requirements' supported by continual improvement

No.	Requirement	ISO 9001:1994	ISO 9001:2000
6.	System Purpose	Achieving customer satisfaction through maintenance of the quality system with stress on prevention of non-conformities	- Achieving and enhancing customer satisfaction through continual improvement - demonstrating ability to consistently provide products that meet customer and applicable regulatory requirements
7.	System Terminology	Seller – sub-contractor Processor – supplier Buyer – customer	Seller – supplier Processor – organization Buyer – customer
8.	System Focus	Contractual requirements based on - Accepting specified requirements, resolving differences and ensuring capability - Making amendments when required	Customer satisfaction based on - Stated needs - Implied needs - Expectations - Regulatory and statutory requirements - Unspecified requirements considered important by the organization
9.	System Exclusions	Not permitted but taken care in the three standards where the scope of each is different ISO 9001 complete from design to supply including installation and servicing ISO 9002 only for established designs ISO 9003 only for final inspection and test	Permits exclusions only limited to requirements relating to product realization under clause 7 of the standard. These exclusions are permitted depending upon the nature of the organization and its product, with the condition that these exclusions should not affect the organization's ability or responsibility to comply with customer and applicable regulatory requirements
10.	Guiding Standard	ISO 9004-1:1994 was only a guide to the standard	ISO 9004:2000 also guides but acts as a "Consistent Pair" by complementing the standard

No.	Requirement	ISO 9001:1994	ISO 9001:2000
11.	Approach	"Functional Approach" Based on control of 'activity / function dependent departments' already identified by this standard	"Process Approach" based on identification and control of interacting and interdependent processes, their inter-linkages and inter-faces
12.	Business concerns	Customer and the organization	All interested parties
13.	Improvement Target	Improvement of the quality system based on its performance	"Continual Improvement" of the effectiveness of the QMS based on the quality policy, quality objectives, audit results, analysis of data, corrective and preventive actions and management reviews
14.	Mandatory Documents (Level 1 Documents)	- Quality policy - Quality objectives - Quality system manual - Quality plans	- Quality policy - Quality objectives - QMS manual - Process Inter-relationship diagram - Quality plans
15.	Mandatory Documented Procedures (Level 2 Documents)	- Contract review - Control and verification of design - Document and data control - Purchase - Control of customer supplied product - Product identification and traceability (optional) - Process control - Inspection and testing - Control and calibration of inspection, measuring and test equipment - Inspection and test status - Control of non-conforming products - Corrective actions - Preventive actions	-Document control -Control of quality records -Internal quality audit -Control of non-conformity -Corrective actions -Preventive actions

No.	Requirement	ISO 9001:1994	ISO 9001:2000
		-Handling, storage, packaging, preservation & delivery -Control of quality records -Internal quality audit -Training -Servicing -Statistical techniques	-Document control -Control of quality records -Internal quality audit -Control of non-conformity -Corrective actions -Preventive actions
16.	**Quality Policy**	To show commitment to quality	To show evidence of commitment to development, implementation and continual improvement of the QMS
17.	Quality Objectives	To be defined and documented	-To be established in measurable terms at relevant functions and levels -To be consistent with quality policy -To be improvement oriented -To be reviewed periodically for up-grading them when required
18.	Top Management Responsibility	Limited involvement and responsibility	Greatly increased involvement and responsibility requiring demonstration of commitment to development and improvement of QMS, adherence to regulatory requirements and setting measurable dynamic objectives
19.	Management Representative's Responsibility and Authority	-Ensuring "Quality System" is established, implemented and maintained	-Ensuring "QMS Processes" are established, implemented and maintained

No.	Requirement	ISO 9001:1994	ISO 9001:2000
			-Ensuring promotion of awareness of customer requirements within the organization
20.	Customer Focus	Limited only to the extent of meeting customer requirements	Wide and hence customer focus as an essential requirement has been addressed specifically
21.	Customer Satisfaction	"Achievement" through prevention of non-conformities	"Enhancement" through - Effective application of system - Assurance of conformity - Continual improvement
22.	Customer Perception	No such requirement	Monitoring and measurement to be done
23.	Customer Communication	No direct and specific reference	Effective arrangements shall be determined and implemented
24.	Internal Communication	No stated requirement	Top management is responsible for ensuring that processes of internal communication within the organization are - Established - Used in actual practice
25.	Requirement of Resources	Limited to identifying and providing all resources including trained manpower	To determine, provide, effectively manage, utilize, preserve and continually improve the resources of manpower, materials, infrastructure, work- environment and information needed for ensuring customer satisfaction
26.	Human Resource requirements	Only limited to the extent of - Education, training and / or experience	To comply with requirements of - Competence, awareness and training

No.	Requirement	ISO 9001:1994	ISO 9001:2000
		- Use of qualified personnel for special processes	- Knowledge of their role and contribution for the achievement of the objectives - Maintain records of education, training, skills and experience
27.	Analysis of data	No direct and specific reference	Analysis with regard to - Customer satisfaction - Product conformity - Characteristics and trends of processes including opportunities for preventive actions - Suppliers Related
28.	Statistical Techniques	Limited use of the techniques based on identification of their need for controlling process capability and product characteristics	To be used for analysis and improvement of product, process and QMS
29.	Management Review	To be carried out at defined intervals, for ensuring continuing suitability and effectiveness	To be carried out at planned intervals, using the defined inputs for obtaining the required outputs, to ensure adequacy and to assess further opportunities for improvement, changes to the QMS, the quality policy and the quality objectives
30.	Performance Assessment	Indirect reference to performance of the quality system only under the responsibility of management representative	Through self-assessment for establishing the current level and determining improvement opportunities
31.	Control of Records	For "Quality records"	For "All QMS related records"
32.	Compatibility with other Management System Standards	Not aligned	Aligned with ISO 14001:1996

[ISO] *thirteen*

Understanding ISO 9001:2000 Requirements

1. INTRODUCTION

The primary goal of any organization is to ensure it complies with the requirements specified by customers and regulatory bodies, as well as those additional requirements deemed necessary by the organization itself for its existence. Further every organization desires to be, not only profitable and competitive, but also better than the best, in its own field. To assist organizations move towards their goals, this standard has laid down certain requirements. These requirements help organizations to establish, document, implement, maintain and continually improve their Quality Management System as a mandate for certification in accordance with ISO 9001:2000.

This standard has been logically broken-up inline with the 'Plan-Do-Check-Act Cycle'. The clauses have been further divided into sub-clauses specifying the various requirements for each. An understanding of the various clauses of this standard would therefore help in their proper use, for ensuring success of the QMS.

Each clause or sub-clause has therefore been taken up separately and explained. Refer ISO 9001:2000 and read each clause or sub-clause of the standard before reading the relevant explanation for ease of correlation. The sequence and numbering of the clauses and sub clauses in this chapter have been deliberately retained and reproduced exactly as per the standard to facilitate one-to-one correspondence.

ISO 9001:2000 aims at customer satisfaction through quality assurance and is supported by another standard, ISO 9004:2000 to give guidance in understanding the standard. The aim of this ISO 9004 however is to help organizations in performance improvement. The two standards together form a consistent pair and ISO 9004:2000 should definitely be read for better understanding and guidance. Thus,

ISO 9001:2000 aims at providing EFFECTIVENESS to the QMS,

ISÓ 9004:2000 aims at providing EFFICIENCY to the QMS.

These standards in combination would lead to EXCELLENCE in the QMS.

ISO 9004:2000 is no doubt a wonderful guidance document and should be used to the fullest extent possible. It is however NOT a guide for the implementation of ISO 9001:2000, and its use is not mandatory for organizations adopting ISO 9001:2000.

4. QUALITY MANAGEMENT SYSTEM

4.1 General requirements

The purpose of the clause to ensure that the organization adopts the process approach to establish, document, implement and maintain its QMS and continually improves its effectiveness in accordance with the requirements of this international standard.

What does the clause mean? In order to comply with the requirements of this standard–the organization is expected to:

(i) Establish the QMS,

(ii) Document the entire QMS,

(iii) Carry out effective implementation and maintenance of QMS.

(iv) Attempt continual improvement of QMS with regard to its effectiveness to maintain it dynamic and progressive,

(v) Identify processes required for effective functioning of the QMS. These processes should be directly related to the following areas of the organization:

a) Management activities,

b) Provision of resources,

c) Product realization, and

d) Measurement.

(vi) Determine interactions amongst identified processes and place them sequentially according to their operational requirements,

(vii) Identify the key process as the central process and establish its inter-linkage with other processes, with special emphasis on the identification of the interfaces and controls at these points,

(viii) Establish the method of effective operation and control of these processes,

(ix) Establish the operating and control parameters for these processes

(x) Determine and provide the various resources including information, required by the processes for their operation and monitoring are provided

(xi) Ensure the processes are monitored and measured, with the results of the measurement being suitably analyzed to assess each process,

(xii) Take all actions necessary for achieving the planned results

(xiii) Ensure continual improvement of the processes is endeavoured and all actions necessary for achieving this objective are determined and pursued

(xiv) Whenever outsourcing of processes affecting product conformity to requirements is done, ensure these processes are suitably controlled. The basic requirement is that the organization ought to build and encourage competencies, which are critical to its success and develop these, and at the same time prepare to outsource non-critical activities or processes

(xv) Specify the type, methods and extent of control on the outsourced processes.

4.2 Documentation Requirements

4.2.1 General

The purpose of the clause ensure than the organization documents and maintains the mandatory requirements of QMS.

What does the clause mean? The organization is expected to:

(i) Prepare the QMS documentation depending upon requirements of the organization in any type of convenient medium such as on paper or in computer

(ii) Document the quality policy,

(iii) Document the quality objectives at the organizational and at lower levels,

(iv) Document the QMS manual,

(v) Establish and then document the mandatory procedures, given below:

- a) Procedure for control of documents,
- b) Procedure for control of quality records,
- c) Procedure for internal audit,
- d) Procedure for control of non-conforming product,

e) Procedure for corrective action, and

f) Procedure for preventive action.

(vi) Implement and maintain these documented procedures

(vii) Document other operating procedures which may be required

(viii) Maintain the records required by the standard, and

(ix) Use any form or medium such as paper, magnetic tape or disk, electronic or computer disk, photographs, master samples, etc. to maintain the documents.

4.2.2 Quality Manual

The purpose of the clause To ensure that the QMS manual, is established and maintained by the organization as per the requirements of this standard.

What does the clause mean? The organization should establish and maintain a QMS Manual, which should essentially include the following:

(i) The scope of areas of activities of the organization covered by the manual,

(ii) Details of any exclusions and their logical justification. These exclusions are from requirements covered under clause 7 of the standard. The most likely exclusions are as follows:

a) Design,

b) Customer property,

c) Product traceability, and

d) Outsourced processes.

(iii) Cross-reference to documented procedures, required by the established QMS, for the relevant clause or sub-clause of the standard:

a) Mandatory procedures, and

b) Mandatory records.

(iv) Description of the interaction between the identified processes of the QMS.

4.2.3 Control of Documents

The purpose of the clause To ensure that the organization essentially controls all QMS documentation.

What does the clause mean? The purpose of this clause is to make it clear that, control of all QMS related documents are mandatory, so that only correct version of documents are used and no unauthorized changes are made to them. This clause requires the following:

(i) The controls to be exercised on various documents of the QMS shall be defined and documented in a Procedure

(ii) All the documents before issue to the user shall be verified, reviewed and approved for adequacy by the designated authority

(iii) Whenever changes to documents are necessary, they shall be reviewed and only then updated. All these changed documents shall once again go through the process of verification, review and re-approval

(iv) All documents shall be uniquely identified by an identification system, which shall facilitate the identifying of the number of changes and the current revision status of the document

(v) The entire documentation has been created for the simple purpose of ensuring that, at each place of use, the user has a reference document for guidance in case of a doubt. This clause therefore requires that a system should be established and documented to explain how the relevant version of the applicable document shall be made available at each place of use

(vi) The documents shall be maintained perfectly legible and neat for ease of readability, without which the very purpose of documentation is lost. If the user is unable to read what is written then the document is useless. Also a system should be put into operation, to readily identify each document through a unique numbering system to make access, use, traceability, retrieval, etc. quite easy

(vii) External documents to the organization but of vital importance to the organization shall be controlled to ensure availability of the correct version of the document and its usage, as advised by the originator. They shall be identified within the system with the organization's own identification method for proper reference. Moreover these documents shall be made available only to those who need them by controlling their distribution

(viii) All obsolete documents shall be withdrawn through a control mechanism to prevent their use even unintentionally. Many organizations prefer to retain a copy of the obsolete documents for knowledge and future reference. Such documents shall be properly identified by suitable means, to prevent mix-up and to enable them to be accessed whenever required.

4.2.4 Control of Records

The purpose of the clause To ensure that the organization essentially controls all the QMS records.

What does the clause mean?

(i) The organization ought to have the capability to demonstrate through objective evidence, the conformity of the QMS to the requirements of the standard and its effective operation. Records are to be used to establish and maintain them.

(ii) The records should be maintained perfectly legible and neat for ease of readability, without which their very purpose is lost. They are basically a source of data to be used for improvement and if the user is unable to read what is written then the record becomes useless.

(iii) The system should be put into operation, to readily identify each record through a unique numbering system to make access, use, traceability, retrieval, etc. easy.

(iv) The controls on the various records of the QMS to be exercised, shall be established and documented in a procedure to make it easy to identify, store, protect, retrieve, maintain, retain and dispose them.

5. MANAGEMENT RESPONSIBILITY

5.1 Management Commitment

The purpose of the clause To advise the top management, that they need to demonstrate their commitment to the establishment, implementation and continual improvement of the QMS.

What does the clause mean? Greatly increased involvement of the top management consisting of responsibility for the Quality Management System on the following:

(i) Provide evidence of commitment for development, implementation and continual improvement of the effectiveness of the QMS,

(ii) Communicate within the organization the importance of meeting customer, statutory and regulatory requirements,

(iii) Establish and document quality policy,

(iv) Establishing organizational level as well as lower level quality objectives consistent with the quality policy,

(v) Ensure planning is done for meeting the QMS requirements and quality objectives,

(vi) Ensure the system is dynamic, but changes when made are preplanned and then implemented,

(vii) Review the QMS at planned intervals through management reviews to ensure its continuing suitability, adequacy and effectiveness, and

(viii) Ensure availability of all necessary resources.

Note : Statutory requirements relate to 'written laws, acts or rules' enacted by legislative bodies, judiciary or institutions of state . However regulatory requirements relate to 'principles or rules of usage' applied for bringing into conformity with accepted procedures or norms of behavior. For instance, in India, while driving on the road 'keep to the left' is a statutory requirement, whereas 'keep to your lanes' is a regulatory requirement.

5.2 Customer Focus

The purpose of the clause To ensure that the entire organizational focus is on determining and meeting the customer requirements.

What does the clause mean? The emphasis of this standard being on Customer Satisfaction, in this clause, it specifically addresses Customer focus, the first of the 8 QMS Principles. Simply stated, the standard expects the organization to:

a) Understand the importance attached to this requirement of the standard due to which its responsibility has been given to the top management of the organization,

b) Determine the customer requirements,

c) Meet these requirements, and

d) Work towards enhancing customer satisfaction.

5.3 Quality Policy

The purpose of the clause To ensure that the top management establishes and propagates a dynamic quality policy.

What does the clause mean? This is the most important feature of the QMS as it sets the framework of the system and gives direction to the organization. This is the responsibility of the top management. The requirements in this regard are as follows:

a) To state, document and endorse the quality policy,

b) To ensure the policy is in line with the purpose of the organization and over-all corporate policy and is not a broad sweeping statement, which just sounds good, such as, "We shall strive for excellence",

c) To have a policy that is inspiring (not insipid) to the people, so that they have an inner urge to perform better,

d) To demonstrate commitment towards compliance and continual improvement of the QMS,

e) To ensure that the Quality objectives are covered under the framework of the Quality Policy,

f) Merely communicating the policy to the employees is not enough hence also to ensure that it is understood by all of them, and

g) To keep the policy dynamic and review it for possible improvement.

5.4 Planning

5.4.1 Quality Objectives

The purpose of the clause To ensure that the top management establishes measurable and dynamic quality objectives.

What does the clause mean? Once again the top management has been made responsible for this important requirement of ensuring the establishment of the quality objectives:

(i) The quality objectives established should cover those required by the organization for achieving its quality related goals for the product, processes and system,

(ii) The quality objectives are to be established not only at the organizational level but also at the relevant lower levels, in line with the overall objectives of the organization,

(iii) It is extremely important to ensure that vague statements are not included in the quality objectives that are established. Infact all quality objectives should be stated in measurable terms where the progress can easily be measured and monitored, and

(iv) The established quality objectives should be consistent with the quality policy of the organization.

5.4.2 Quality Management System Planning

The purpose of the clause To ensure required planning is done for maintaining and effecting changes to the QMS.

What does the clause mean?

(i) Recognize that QMS planning is primarily the top management responsibility,

(ii) Even when this planning is done by others, there is no scope for the top management to resort to 'responsibility evasion by using the excuse that this has been delegated',

(iii) The purpose of planning is clearly stated, which is to meet the requirements given in Clause 4.1 of the standard, and

(iv) Changes whenever made should not touch upon the QMS but upon the operational aspects i.e. QMS is not to be diluted during the operational changes.

5.5 Responsibility, Authority and Communication

5.5.1 Responsibility and Authority

The purpose of the clause To ensure the responsibilities and authorities are defined and communicated within the organization.

What does the clause mean? The standard has widened its coverage by increasing the type of people of the organization whose responsibility and authority need to be defined i.e. laid down precisely. The earlier standard only covered those persons whose work directly affected quality whereas this standard does not impose any such condition and so expects the responsibility and authority of all the people of the organization to be defined. It is therefore for the organization to justify if someone's responsibility and authority definition is omitted.

It also expects this responsibility and authority to be communicated within the organization and clearly understood by everyone.

5.5.2 Management Representative

The purpose of the clause To ensure that a management representative is appointed from among the members of the management.

What does the clause mean?

(i) The Management Representative (MR) is a pivotally important person within the QMS and a key figure for all ISO related activities. The appointment of the MR should be done by the top management, and he should be a person selected from amongst members of the organization's management.

(ii) The responsibility and authority of the MR should flow from the top management.

(iii) The MR should ensure that all processes needed for the QMS are established, implemented and maintained.

(iv) He should also ensure that the performance of the QMS after assessment is communicated to the top management.

(v) All information related to the need for improvement in the QMS should also be communicated to the top management.

(vi) It is for the MR to ensure that the customer requirements that have been determined are communicated within the organization, and people are fully aware of these.

(vii) Liason with all external agencies on matters related to the QMS can also be done by the MR although it is not mandatory for this responsibility to be given to him.

5.5.3 Internal Communication

The purpose of the clause To ensure that appropriate communication processes are established, and that communication takes place within the organization.

What does the clause mean? The top management has been given the responsibility that,

(i) They ensure establishment of appropriate processes consisting of the channels, means, methods, etc. for communication within the organization, amongst its people,

(ii) The processes established are not only laid down on paper but also used, and

(iii) The communication with regard to the effectiveness of the QMS occurs.

5.6 Management Review

5.6.1 General

The purpose of the clause To ensure that the QMS of the organization is regularly reviewed by the top management.

What does the clause mean?

(i) The top management is expected to review the QMS at planned intervals. The earlier version required the review to be done at defined intervals, which means that the interval between reviews was to be defined and adhered to. The present standard however gives the organization a greater flexibility whereby the top management may change the interval, planned for review whenever required based on feedback.

(ii) The reviews are expected to establish whether the QMS that has been implemented continues to be suitable, adequate and effective or it needs to be changed.

(iii) The need for change when determined should also look at the need to change the quality policy and the quality objectives.

(iv) The basic purpose of establishing the QMS is to use it as a tool for improvements. Thus the review ought to determine and assess all opportunities available for effecting improvements without diluting standards.

(v) Records of management reviews are to be essentially maintained.

5.6.2 Review Inputs

The purpose of the clause To ensure that all required inputs for review that have been specified are considered during the review.

What does the clause mean? The management review is an extremely important mechanism of assessment and control by the top management of an organization. The standard has specified the areas of the QMS, from which information regarding their functioning, performance and feedback should be essentially studied, discussed and acted upon during each management review. These areas have been listed in the standard as, 'review inputs'. The organization is at liberty to review any other area if needed, but the mentioned areas must necessarily be reviewed. Further, it should be possible for the organization to demonstrate through documentary evidence, that regular reviews in these areas are carried-out. The areas specified are:

(i) All types of feedback and information generated during any type of audit of the organization.

(ii) Any kind of feedback received from the customer irrespective of whether it is a complaint, requirement, expectation, suggestion, viewpoint, opinion or even feeling.

(iii) Complete data and problems relating to the performance of processes and conformity of the product.

(iv) The status of any corrective or preventive actions taken, especially with regard to the difficulties encountered and also the successes. This may also include information on the level of implementation for the actions initiated, with emphasis on the additional requirements for ensuring their success.

(v) During every review obviously some decisions would be taken. The subsequent review should study actions on the previous decisions to assess the extent of implementation by determining the follow-up actions taken.

(vi) Every organization's QMS is expected to be dynamic and on the constant lookout for bringing about changes in improving, strengthening, simply reversing or correcting a previous decision regarding the product, process or system, and

(vii) The most important aspect of the QMS is the sustained, continual improvement effort. Here, all the improvement related information i.e. regarding improvements already in progress, as well as the new improvement opportunities identified, must be discussed.

5.6.3 Review Outputs

The purpose of the clause To ensure that the review outputs of the 'management reviews' include decisions regarding all the listed areas.

What does the clause mean? The purpose of the review being maintenance, correction and improvement of performance, this standard specifies the outputs the organization should determine during the review. The outputs listed comprise decisions and actions needed on the following:

(i) The actions required for the improvement of the QMS and its processes.

(ii) The actions needed for improvement of the product with regard to customer requirements, and

(iii) The provisional resources required for which the top management must initiate action.

6. RESOURCE MANAGEMENT

6.1 Provision of Resources

The purpose of the clause To ensure that the organization determines and provides all the needed resources.

What does the clause mean? No organization can function successfully or its employees deliver satisfactory results, unless all the appropriate and necessary resources are provided in required quantities. These resources could be financial resources, information resources, input resources, plant and machinery resources, technology resources, monitoring and measurement resources, manpower resources, etc. These resources form the inputs to the various value-adding processes of the organization.

The standard requires that the organization should determine and provide the needed resources well in time, for achieving the following objectives:

(i) To implement and maintain the QMS,

(ii) To continually improve the effectiveness of the QMS, and

(iii) To enhance customer satisfaction by meeting their requirements.

6.2 Human Resources

6.2.1 General

The purpose of the clause To ensure that personnel in the organization whose work affects product quality are allotted jobs based on their competence.

What does the clause mean? The people employed by the organization, especially those who carry out work that affects the quality of the product, should be competent. Producing poor quality and blaming the incompetence of the people is not accepted as an excuse by the QMS. It is for the management to assess people capability and allocate work based on their competence if poor quality output results, either the employee has made a mistake that needs to be corrected or the management is at fault for having assessed the competence wrongly.

The assessment of competence has to be based on the appropriateness of the employee's education, training, skill and experience. This means all critical jobs that affect the quality of the product should have a 'job requirement definition'.

6.2.2 Competence, Awareness and Training

The purpose of the clause To ensure that suitably skilled personnel with necessary competence and training are assigned jobs for quality outputs.

What does the clause mean? It is for the organization to ensure the competence, awareness and training of its employees. The organization is required to take the following actions:

(i) Determine the competence requirements of the jobs being done which affect the quality of the product.

(ii) Having determined the competence requirements of the various jobs, the organization should assess the competence of its people and then assign jobs based on people's competence in relation to job requirements. In all cases where there is a mismatch between people competence and job requirements the organization must provide the necessary training or arrange to provide training so that the job requirements are fully met.

(iii) Having trained the people the organization should also determine whether the training has been effective or not. If needed the employees may be re-trained.

(iv) Each employee should have his individual identity and not merely be, a cog in the wheel with no knowledge of the importance of his work. Each employee should be made aware of the significance, relevance and importance of his work. They all should also know how their work affects the product quality and how it contributes to the achievement of the quality objectives of the organization.

(v) The organization should maintain proper records of the employees' education, training, skills and experience.

Note: Make use of 'IS/ISO 10015:1999 Indian Standard - Guidelines for Training for further understanding this requirement. Also make use of the standard to define, design, plan, provide, evaluate, monitor and improve the training process.

6.3 Infrastructure

The purpose of the clause To ensure that the organization provides suitable infrastructure necessary for achieving conformity of product with the requirements

What does the clause mean? The standard requires that the organization has to determine whatever infrastructure is needed to achieve product conformity. Having determined the requirements, they must then be provided consistently and maintained. In the absence of this basic infrastructure neither the processes can operate methodically nor can people function satisfactorily.

The infrastructure that is to be acted upon consists of the following:

(i) The building, workspace and associated utilities.

(ii) The process equipment i.e. the machinery & associated equipment, tools, jigs, fixtures, testing and measuring equipment, procedures, methods, data, control parameters, etc.

(iii) The supporting services i.e. transport, communication equipment, library services, etc.

6.4 Work Environment

The purpose of the clause To create working conditions which are conducive for optimizing performance of the people.

What does the clause mean? The work environment refers to factors such as workplace layout, facilities, ergonomics, social environment amongst the people, comfortable and safe working conditions, cleanliness and hygiene, control of pollution, etc.

In short it is a combination of the physical and human environment.

7. PRODUCT REALIZATION

7.1 Planning of Product Realization

The purpose of the clause To ensure that planning covers all aspects of process development, quality objectives, resource mobilization, documentation, etc.

What does the clause mean? Product realization is the process of transforming the inputs by adding value to them to get the required outputs. This product realization can succeed, only if an organization plans adequately for this vital process. Product realization is a macro process made up of numerous micro processes. Each one of these micro processes should be planned for and then developed by establishing their requirements and controls. All these processes needed for product realization ought to be planned and then developed into a smooth and synchronized system to make them more systematic and result oriented. While carrying out this planning for product realization it should be ensured that the plans are in line with the requirements of all other processes and they do not contradict each other. During the planning of product realization, the organization should determine the following:

(i) The quality objectives related to product realization,

(ii) The product requirements determined from all sources,

(iii) The need to establish processes and documents,

(iv) The need to provide resources specific to the product,

(v) The required verification, validation, monitoring, inspection and test activities specific to the product,

(vi) The criteria for product acceptance, and

(vii) The records needed to provide evidence that both, 'the realization processes and resulting products' meet all requirements.

This planning will obviously result in an output for use by the organization. The organization must ensure that the output is in a form suitable for the organization's method of operations. For instance the organization may make use of flowcharts, tabular forms, lists, etc., either on paper or in the electronic media.

7.2 Customer Related Processes

7.2.1 Determination of Requirements Related to the Product

The purpose of the clause To ensure that the organization determines the customer related requirements of the product.

What does the clause mean? The product that an organization produces for the customers assumes extreme importance as this is the very justification and the basis for the existence of the organization. It is therefore necessary for the organization to determine the various requirements to be met by their product, to the fullest extent possible hence the organization should as certain:

a) All specified requirements of the customers, relating to the product, its packaging, delivery, after sale service, etc., and set time bound targets

b) All unstated requirements of the customer, which although not stated but are necessary for the specified or intended use, to which the product is applied.

c) All statutory and regulatory requirements applicable to the product during its lifecycle from manufacture to disposal at the end of its life, and

d) Any other additional requirements even though not mentioned by either the customer or the regulating authorities but still felt necessary by the organization based on its own judgment and experience.

7.2.2 Review of Requirements Related to the Product

The purpose of the clause To ensure that the organization reviews all the product-related requirements prior to supply commitment to the customer.

What does the clause mean? The organization is expected to review all the requirements related to their product prior to making any commitment to the Customer. This commitment regarding the product could take any form such as, submission of tenders, acceptance of contract or orders, acceptance of changes to contracts 'or' orders, etc. This review shall ensure the following:

a. The customer's requirement and the statutory requirements in relation to the product are clearly defined and understood by both parties with no scope for any doubt 'or' ambiguity.

b. Contracts 'or' orders are accepted based on review after assessing capacity, capability and readiness to execute it. However, situations arise where changes become necessary due to:

   (i) Customer request,

   (ii) Changes in statutory policies, or

   (iii) Any other reason.

   Any such deviation from the accepted contract 'or' order ought to be resolved immediately, ensuring capacity, capability and readiness under the changed conditions.

c. Every review must essentially assess and ensure that the conditions accepted under any order 'or' contract are acceptable to the organization. It is also ensured that the organization has the capability and capacity to meet the defined requirements.

All reviews shall be documented to ensure availability of unambiguous information regarding the decisions taken. Further, any action becoming necessary on account of the original or altered decisions shall also be documented.

Numerous instances exists where, customer requirements are not provided by the customers. In such cases it is for the organization to determine the requirements, obtain confirmation from the customer and finalise them.

In case the requirements are changed either in the beginning or during the course of the execution of the contract 'or' order, an immediate action for review, followed by amendment to the necessary documents shall be taken. This is to ensure that the concerned personnel are aware of the changes, so that they can incorporate them in their subsequent operations.

7.2.3 Customer Communication

The purpose of the clause To ensure that the organization determines and implements effective methods of communication with the customer to get complete and reliable timely feedback from the customer.

What does the clause mean? The organization is expected to determine the means and arrangements that ought to be established for ensuring effective communication with the customer. Later on these means and arrangements should be implemented. The communication that takes place should ensure the following:

a) Complete information regarding the product to be supplied is determined.

b) Whenever any enquiry is received from a customer regarding a product, it should be studied properly by the organization. Proper communication should then be established with the customer seeking full details and clarifications with regard to their requirements. Orders for supply should be accepted and decisions communicated to customers only after all clarifications are obtained and ambiguities if any resolved. Order accepted by the organization are finalized after, carefully collecting the complete information from the customers and ensuring that all doubtful issues are resolved. Later, even during the course of the execution of an order, if an amendment becomes necessary, either because it is required by the customer or found essential by the organization, it should be approved and accepted both by the organization and the customer. This is further recorded in proof of the acceptance and approval.

c) Proper communication is established with the customer to elicit feedback of every kind that could be used to improve the existing product or plan for newer products. Customer complaints are to be given the highest priority and communication in this regard should get full support.

7.3 DESIGN AND DEVELOPMENT

7.3.1 Design and Development Planning

The purpose of the clause To ensure that the design and development of the product is planned and controlled by the organization.

What does the clause mean?

(i) The standard requires the design and development activity of the organization to commence by first undertaking the preparation of plans for the design and development of each product. These designs are also to be controlled to ensure that they do not undergo any unauthorized changes and yet remain dynamic.

(ii) For ensuring consistency in the process of designing and developing its products, the organization during the planning process, should determine and list the various stages through which the design and development activities are required to pass.

(iii) For each stage identified, the method of review, verification and validation for the design should be determined and specified.

(iv) The planning process must include decisions, and delegation of responsibility and authority required for successfully carrying out the design and development activity.

(v) Design and development being an activity requiring the contribution and active involvement of different groups of people, there is a need for effective communication between those involved and an unambiguous definition and assignment of responsibility for the activities.

(vi) Finally, all the planning done in relation to the designing and development activity shall be appropriately updated through proper documentation during the progress of the design and development itself.

7.3.2 Design and Development Inputs

The purpose of the clause To ensure that all required inputs for product design and development are, determined and documented.

What does the clause mean? Design and development are to be based on requirements and hence these requirements form the basis for determining the inputs to design. All such information shall be recorded and carefully maintained for re-verification, whenever required. The inputs to be determined and recorded are:

a. The functional and performance requirements expected from the product.

b. All the requirements of statutory and regulatory nature, that become applicable to the product in its entire life cycle.

c. Information on previous designs which could be of relevance, help and use.

d. Other unspecified requirements which are essential for design and development of the Product.

After-the inputs have been defined they should be reviewed for adequacy and if necessary, changes be made to ensure that they are complete and sufficient. Ambiguous and conflicting requirements shall be resolved to align all the inputs.

7.3.3 Design and Development Outputs

The purpose of the clause To ensure that the design and development outputs are in a form that makes it possible to verify them against the inputs.

What does the clause mean? The outputs of design and development, which determine the desired product output shall be prepared and provided in a manner which makes it possible to verify these outputs based on the inputs. All such outputs which define the product have to be approved prior to release. These outputs shall have the following features:

a) Meet the input requirements for the design and development,

b) Act as a base for providing adequate and appropriate information for purchase, production and servicing the product,

c) Clearly specify the acceptance criteria, and

d) Specify those parameters or characteristics of the product, which are to be ensured for safe and proper use of the product.

7.3.4 Design and Development Review

The purpose of the clause To ensure that design and development is systematically reviewed at appropriate stages as per plan.

What does the clause mean? The planning done for the design and development ought to be provided for constant and systematic real time reviews of progress, at regular intervals. Suitable stages are identified and established at which such reviews in accordance with the plan can be carried out and then these reviews should actually be performed. The purpose of these reviews should be to evaluate the following:

a) Whether the design and development being carried out at the stage where the verification is done has progressed as desired and whether it shall be capable of meeting specified requirements.

b) Whether changes or modifications that become necessary due to problems encountered, are actually incorporated. The modifications should target corrections, to align the plan in line with the desired requirements.

During all such reviews, participants of each function under review, should be available to give feedback and all information required pertaining to the function.

These reviews and actions arising on account of the reviews should be properly documented.

7.3.5 Design and Development Verification

The purpose of the clause To ensure that planned verifications of design and development outputs are done to check if they meet the input requirements.

What does the clause mean? Planning facilitates verification of the progress of design and development, and so, this verification should be performed as per the plan. The purpose of this verification should be to determine and thereby ensure that the design and development out-puts meet the input requirements. Records of all such verifications should be maintained. Any actions arising out of the verifications should also be recorded and maintained.

7.3.6 Design and Development Validation

The purpose of the clause To ensure that a planned validation of design and development is carried-out to check whether the product designed and developed meets the requirements.

What does the clause mean? The validation of design and development should be made in accordance with the planned arrangements ensuring the product that has been designed and developed is capable of meeting the desired requirements. Results of validation should be assessed based on input and out-put characteristics. Records of the results of validation and all necessary actions should be maintained.

7.3.7 Control of Design and Development Changes

The purpose of the clause To ensure that all changes to design and development are controlled.

What does the clause mean? Any change made to the design and development already done, is a valuable information and hence the standard requires such a change to be identified and recorded. Further every change has to be reviewed, verified, validated and approved prior to implementation into the design.

While carrying out review of the design and development changes, the review process should not only evaluate every change but also its impact and effect on the related parts and components. This review should also take into consideration the effect of the change on the products already supplied to the customer. All review records of changes and all necessary actions taken should be recorded.

7.4 Purchasing

7.4.1 Purchasing Process

The purpose of the clause To ensure that the purchased products conform to specified purchase requirements.

What does the clause mean? The purchasing process determines not only the quality of inputs but also their timely receipt in correct quantities and at the correct place of use. The organization is therefore expected to strictly ensure that the purchased products completely comply with the specified and expected purchase requirements.

It is not essential that the same level and extent of control be applied to all purchase products. The criticality and importance of the purchased product and its effect on the subsequent product realization 'or' the final product shall be the basis for deciding upon the extent of control on the supplier.

The organization ought to evaluate and select suppliers based on their ability to supply the product in accordance with the organization's requirements. The organization should therefore fix its own criteria for selection, evaluation and re-evaluation of suppliers. For products, which have a larger impact on the organization's work, greater control ought to be exercised while for products where the impact is marginal a more relaxed control can be exercised.

Records of the results of evaluation and any necessary action arising out of the evaluation shall be maintained.

7.4.2 Purchasing Information

The purpose of the clause To ensure that the supplier of product is given complete and unambiguous information for the purchase.

What does the clause mean? No purchase can be made unless complete information for affecting the purchase is made available to the supplier. This therefore, is a very important requirement, for which the organization is expected to describe the product in the purchase information provided, by giving the following details:

a) Specification of the product to be purchased,
b) Requirement for inspection, testing and approval,
c) Inspection, testing and approval procedures, processes and equipment needed,
d) Requirements for qualification of personnel where human expertise is the item being purchased, and
e) The QMS requirements that shall apply to the supplier and the product.

Adequate and detailed information shall be prepared but made available to the supplier only after ensuring it for correctness. This is to prevent unnecessary communications at a later date.

7.4.3 Verification of Purchased Product

The purpose of the clause To ensure that the purchased products meet specified purchase requirements.

What does the clause mean? Unless the product purchased is verified, prior to use for correctness and compliance with requirements, it could lead to problems. The organization is therefore expected to establish and implement inspection 'or' other activities, which are necessary to ensure that whichever product is purchased it meets the specified purchase requirements and the user is confident of this activity.

A number of times the organization or its customer decides to perform verification at the product supplier's premises. In such a case the organization is expected to state the following in the purchase information given to the supplier:

a) The intended verification arrangement, and
b) The methods by which the product shall be released after the verification.

7.5 Production and Service Provision

7.5.1 Control of Production and Service Provision

The purpose of the clause To ensure that the production and service of the organization is controlled.

What does the clause mean? The entire production and servicing activity of the organization should be planned and controlled. The control to be exercised could be as follows:

a) Ensure availability of necessary and complete information to the user, with regard to the product characteristics.

b) Provide work instructions for all activities that make the processes free from dependence on people who 'have or control' this information. Thus any qualified individual with little guidance using the work instructions could perform the activity.

c) Ensure availability of suitable equipment for appropriate use.

d) Ensure availability of appropriate monitoring and measuring devices and their correct usage.

e) Ensure the implementation of monitoring and measurement processes and techniques.

f) Ensure the implementation of release, delivery and post delivery activities.

7.5.2 Validation of Processes for Production and Service Provision

The purpose of the clause To ensure that all special processes of the organization are validated to qualify the operational parameters.

What does the clause mean? A number of processes normally referred to, as 'special processes' exist in an organization, wherein the resulting output from the process cannot be monitored or measured subsequent to the process. In these special processes the deficiencies of their outputs are not immediately identifiable or verifiable and become apparent only after the product is put to use 'or' the service is delivered. All such processes are to be validated for production and service proficiency.

The object of validation is to demonstrate the ability of these special processes to achieve planned results repeatedly by controlling the process, based on determined parameters. The organization therefore has to establish the following:

a) Define the criteria for review and approval of special processes,

b) Approve the requirement of the equipment and qualification of personnel, who would perform these processes,

c) Specify the special methods and procedures adopted for controlling the process,

d) Specify the type of records and the information to be monitored for control, and

e) Specify the procedure to be adopted for re-validating a process already validated.

7.5.3 Identification and Traceability

The purpose of the clause To ensure that identification and traceability is maintained wherever required for the product.

What does the clause mean? This requirement is optional in nature and left to the organization's discretion. The organization, through the entire process of product realization, is expected to,

1) Identify the product by any convenient means, which is suitable for the purpose and is also foolproof.
2) Identify the status of the product, with respect to monitoring and measurement carried out on it at each stage, as it progresses through the process.
3) Maintain the traceability if required for the product, through a system of unique identification for each of the inputs by controlling and recording all the relevant details pertaining to traceability.

It is not essential to compulsorily mark the product, for ensuring its identification and traceability in the product realization process. The existing practice in many industries is to maintain identification and traceability merely by the configuration or location of the product and this method is acceptable as per the standard.

Configuration refers to the functional and physical characteristics of a product as defined in the technical documents and achieved on the product. Configuration management however refers to those activities that help in the identification, control, monitoring and auditing of the product configuration.

7.5.4 Customer Property

The purpose of the clause To ensure control, safe custody, proper use and appropriate accounting and reporting of customer property.

What does the clause mean? Many a time, customers give their supplier free issue products, for either use or incorporation in the finished product being supplied to them. These products supplied by the customers continue to belong to them and so are termed Customer Property. With regard to this customer property, the organization is expected to:

(i) Exercise complete care with these product as long as they are in their control or are being used by them,

(ii) Identify, protect and safeguard these products,

(iii) Report to the customer regarding loss, damage and unsuitability for use if it occurs, and

(iv) Maintain records of the stocks, utilization, receipts, damages, loss and unsuitability.

7.5.5 Preservation of Product

The purpose of the clause To ensure that the conformity of the product is preserved during internal processing and delivery up to the intended destination.

What does the clause mean? The organization is expected to preserve the product with safe handling, packaging, storing and protection. The purpose of this preservation is to ensure that the product continues to conform to requirements during the entire process of internal processing through delivery right up to the required destination. This preservation not only applies to the finished product but also to the constituent parts of the product.

7.6 Control of Monitoring and Measuring Devices

The purpose of the clause To ensure that the monitoring and measuring is done, to provide valid evidence of product conformity to the requirements.

What does the clause mean? In order to provide evidence of conformity of the product to the determined requirements the organization is expected to:

a) determine the monitoring and measurement to be done, and

b) determine the monitoring and measurement devices needed.

The organization is expected to establish the processes needed for ensuring that monitoring and measurement:

a) Can be carried out satisfactorily, and

b) Is actually carried out inline with requirements.

In order to ensure validity of the results of measurements, the organization is expected to take the following actions with regard to the measuring equipment:

(i) Calibration or verification at specified intervals or prior to use, to measurement standards traceable to national or international level. If no such standards for calibration exist the basis used for calibration or verification ought to be recorded,

(ii) Adjustment or readjustment as necessary.

(iii) Unique identification for each equipment, to facilitate determination of the calibration status of each.

(iv) Safeguard the original settings done during calibration, changing which would change the validity of the calibration and make the measurements invalid, and

(v) Protect them from damage and deterioration during the process of handling, maintenance and storage.

Further, whenever the equipment are found to be non-conforming the organization must have a method and mechanism to assess and record the previous measurements to ascertain their validity. In such a case the organization shall also take the needed corrective actions on the defective measuring equipment. Since this defective equipment has been in use, it is quite likely that some non-conforming products may have been found to conform to requirements due to equipment error. The organization ought to take appropriate actions to identify and isolate such non-conforming products by making an additional check. Even if the product has left the premises of the organization or has reached the customer, the organization has to have a positive attitude and take proactive actions to detect the non-conforming products and withdraw it for correcting the product supplied to the customer.

The results of all calibrations and verifications done on the measuring equipment must be maintained in the form of records.

These days computer software is used for many monitoring and measurement applications. In such a case the software itself ought to be initially tested for its ability to carry out the required check prior to use. At frequent intervals its suitability too should be assessed and ensured.

8. MEASUREMENT, ANALYSIS AND IMPROVEMENT

8.1 General

The purpose of the clause To plan and implement assessment of performance of the organization with regard to

a) product and QMS conformity, and

b) scope for continually improving the effectiveness of the QMS.

What does the clause mean? The organization is expected to

(i) Plan how each of the monitoring, measurement, analysis and improvement are to be done.

(ii) Implement the monitoring, measurement, analysis and improvement processes as per plans.

(iii) Decide upon the methods (including identifying the appropriate statistical techniques suitable for the purpose) that should be used for monitoring, measurement, analysis and improvement when it is carried out.

(iv) Determine and decide upon the extent of use of the methods identified for the monitoring, measurement, analysis and improvement processes.

This planning and implementation is done to have the capability to:

a) Demonstrate that the products at every stage conform to the requirements,

b) Ensure that the QMS conforms to the planned and implemented requirements, and

c) Continually improve the effectiveness of the QMS by gradually bring up its level, over a period of time.

8.2 Monitoring and Measurement

8.2.1 Customer Satisfaction

The purpose of the clause To determine what the customers perceive, has been the organization's success in meeting requirements.

What does the clause mean? The very purpose of this standard is to ensure customer satisfaction and so the organization is expected to:

(i) Measure and monitor the success of the organization with regard to customer satisfaction.

(ii) Organize facility for collecting information on customer's perceptions about the organization to monitor customer satisfaction.

(iii) Determine the method that shall be used to collect this information.

(iv) Decide upon the method by which the information collected shall be used for assessment.

(v) Determine the success of the organization in meeting the customer requirements and more than that, determining what the customers perceive about this success.

8.2.2 Internal Audit

The purpose of the clause to determine whether the QMS

- conforms to planned arrangements,
- conforms to the requirements as per this standard, and
- conforms to the requirements fixed by the organization itself for the established QMS.

What does the clause mean? In order to achieve its purpose the organization is expected to,

(i) Plan to carry out internal audits based on the status and importance of the area to be audited as well as the results of the previous audit,

(ii) Define the responsibility and requirements for planning, conducting, reporting and maintaining the results of audits,

(iii) Plan and define the criteria, scope, frequency, intervals and method of the internal audits,

(iv) Define the method of selection of auditors by ensuring that none of the auditors audit their own work,

(v) Conduct the internal audits at the planned intervals,

(vi) Ensure objectivity and impartiality in the audits carried out,

(vii) Ensure that actions are taken without undue delay to eliminate non-conformities and their causes, and this responsibility shall rest with the management responsible for the area audited,

(viii) Ensure that verification of the actions taken are done as a part of the follow-up activities, and

(ix) Document all results of the verifications done.

8.2.3 Monitoring and Measurement of Processes

The purpose of the clause To assess the performance of these identified processes under the QMS with regard to their effectiveness and efficiency.

What does the clause mean? The organization is expected to:

(i) Apply suitable methods for monitoring or (where applicable) measurement of the QMS processes.

(ii) Ensure the methods applied demonstrate the ability of the processes to achieve planned results.

(iii) Ensure conformity of the product through correction or corrective actions whenever planned results are not achieved.

8.2.4 Monitoring and Measurement of Product

The purpose of the clause To assess the conformance of the product to specified requirements.

What does the clause mean?

The organization is expected to:

(i) Plan the monitoring and measurement required on the product.

(ii) Verify whether the product requirements have been met through monitoring and measuring of the characteristics of the product.

(iii) Ensure the verification is done at appropriate stages of the product realization process in accordance with the planned arrangements.

(iv) Maintain evidence of conformity of the product compared to the acceptance criteria in the form of records.

(v) Ensure that all such records indicate the person(s) authorizing the release of the product.

(vi) Ensure that the product release and service delivery are permitted only after all planned arrangements of monitoring and measurement have been completed.

(vii) Ensure deviation from the planned arrangements for product release and delivery service are allowed only after approval by the relevant authority or where applicable, by the customer.

8.3 Control of Nonconforming Product

The purpose of the clause To ensure that products, which do not conform to requirements, are identified and controlled to prevent unintended use or delivery.

What does the clause mean? All nonconforming products shall be dealt with in the following ways:

a) Initially action should be taken to eliminate the detected nonconformity.

b) Next the necessary authorization of the relevant authority or (where applicable) the customer should be obtained for any concessions. This authorization should permit use, release or acceptance depending on the decision taken.

c) Finally actions to prevent the original intended use or application of these nonconforming products should be taken.

To control the nonconforming products the organization is expected to:

(i) Have a method for identifying and controlling products, which do not meet product requirements so that even unintentionally they cannot be used or delivered.

(ii) Have a procedure specifying the control methodology and also indicating who would be responsible for dealing with the nonconforming products identified.

(iii) Maintain records regarding the nature of nonconformity and any subsequent actions taken. These records should include details of any concession obtained from the specified requirements along with the details of the authority, which has permitted the concession.

(iv) Re-verify the products that were non conforming and have been corrected, to ensure conformity to requirements.

(v) Take actions appropriate to the actual or potential effect of any non-conformity in the product detected after delivery or use has started.

8.4 Analysis of Data

The purpose of the clause To have a method for determining the type of analysis suitable for each data, collecting relevant data and finally analyzing the data collected from various sources for the following reasons:

a) To demonstrate the suitability and effectiveness of the quality management system and

b) To evaluate where and how continual improvement of the 'effectiveness of the QMS' can be made.

What does the clause mean? the organization is expected to

(i) Have a system for determining, collecting and analyzing appropriate data to demonstrate the suitability and effectiveness of the quality management system.

(ii) Utilize all data generated within the organization as a result of monitoring and measurement as also the data received from other relevant sources.

(iii) Have a method to evaluate where and how continual improvement of the 'effectiveness of the QMS' can be made.

(iv) Identify the specific areas for which analysis of data must provide information to assess the success in performance. These areas are:

   a) Customer satisfaction,

   b) Conformity of product to the requirements,

   c) Characteristics and trends of processes and products including opportunities for preventive action, and

   d) Suppliers data.

8.5 Improvement

8.5.1 Continual Improvement

The purpose of the clause To constantly strive for and achieve, enhancement of the effectiveness of the quality management system.

What does the clause mean? The organization is expected to plan for, promote and practise continual improvement for which it should make use of the following:

(i) The quality policy—as a tool to prove to its people the management's complete support to continual improvement and hence seek their whole hearted commitment,

(ii) The quality objectives—to show them the targets to be achieved,

(iii) The audit results—to demonstrate to them the present level and the areas of weakness and the shortcomings in them,

(iv) The analysis of data—to show them where, which area can be strengthened, for which aspect and how this can be done,

(v) The corrective actions—-to determine the extent, areas and nature of deviation as also the correct-ability of these deviations,

(vi) The preventive actions—to show those areas where problems could have arisen but have been controlled and likely problems prevented, and

(vii) The management reviews—to assess the performance of the QMS and take note of and act upon the decisions taken.

8.5.2 Corrective Action

The purpose of the clause To correct nonconformities and eliminate their causes so as to prevent recurrence.

What does the clause mean? The organization is expected to:

(i) Take appropriate actions to eliminate the root-cause of non-conformities to prevent their recurrence. The actions ought to be appropriate to the effect of the non-conformity, which means that if the impact of a non-conformity observed is marginal and that too in an insignificant area the effort spent in setting it right could be minimal but should the impact or significance of the non-conformity be large, it ought to get the highest priority.

(ii) The procedure for established corrective actions should be documented and should define the requirements for:

a) Reviewing non-conformities (including customer complaints),

b) Determining the causes of non-conformities,

c) Evaluating the need for action to ensure that non-conformities do not recur,

d) Determining and implementing action needed,

e) Maintaining records of the results of action taken, and

f) Reviewing the corrective action taken.

8.5.3 Preventive Action

The purpose of the clause To eliminate the cause of potential non-conformities thereby preventing their occurrence.

What does the clause mean?

The organization is expected to

(i) Take appropriate actions to eliminate the root-cause of potential non-conformities so as to prevent their occurrence. The actions ought to be appropriate to the effect of the potential non-conformity, which means that if the impact of any non-conformity is likely to be marginal and that too in an insignificant area, the effort spent in preventing it, could be proportionately reduced.

(ii) The procedure for preventive actions established should be documented and should define the requirements for:

a) Determining potential non-conformities and their causes,

b) Evaluating the need for action to prevent occurrence of non-conformities,

c) Determining and implementing the actions needed,

d) Maintaining records of results for the action taken, and

e) Reviewing preventive action taken.

Section

IV

Using the Standard

ISO

fourteen

The QMS Documentation Requirements

1. DOCUMENT VS. DOCUMENTATION

The word 'Document' refers to, "the written, printed or drawn piece of record in any form (on paper or in computer) that provides information or evidence" such as an instruction, a procedure, a drawing, etc.

'Documentation' however refers to, "the collection of particular type of documents compiled as a set" such as the QMS manual, QMS procedures, work instructions, maintenance instructions, calibration instructions, inspection instructions, etc.

2. FEATURES OF QMS DOCUMENTATION

QMS Documentation can be more effective and easily usable, only if it has the following features:

- It is in line with the quality objectives of the organization.
- It is simple, understandable, easy to use and realistic.
- It is readily available and well-understood.
- It is easily changeable
- It is provided for suitable data collection where needed.
- It is verifiable for adequacy and compliance in practice to ISO.

It is appropriately interlinked as 'References', from each level to the lower levels through suitable cross-referencing. In fact it is for this purpose that a document numbering system needs to be developed for the entire QMS documentation.

3. BENEFITS OF DOCUMENTATION

- It formalizes the way people do their daily jobs.
- It specifies the acceptable practices.
- It makes available vital feedback needed for effecting improvements.
- It standardizes practices so that they are not people dependent.
- It brings about a consistency in all work and hence in management too.
- It provides a reference for assessing the degree of compliance in practice.
- It helps in training.
- It helps provide evidence of the availability of a QMS that conforms to and functions as per ISO 9001:2000.
- It provides a two-way communication channel between the policies and the activities of the organization.
- It helps in finding deficiencies in the product, process and system.

4. DESIGN OF THE DOCUMENTATION

The prime reason for designing the documentation properly is not the obvious reason of making it more attractive, but to make it clearer, more accessible and easily usable. A badly designed and structured documentation will lead to frustration and so people will try to avoid using it. However, a well-designed documentation will encourage use and help people solve their problems. Therefore if the design is done well it will make the structure of the information clearer and understandable. Proper design makes the documentation better for the users in the following ways:

(i) It makes the information readily accessible,

(ii) It makes the documentation legible, and

(iii) It makes the information easily understandable.

5. STRUCTURE OF THE DOCUMENTATION

A standard structure should be used for the QMS documentation whether it be, the QMS manual, the QMS procedures or the instructions. The following is a typical structure, which should be put together as a single set:

Cover Page: The first page of the document usually contains the following:

(i) The title of the documentation

(ii) The number of the Standard and year, and

(iii) The name and address of the organization

(See Cover Page of the Sample Manual and Procedures given in Chapter 19, 20 and 21)

Contents Page: This normally contain the following:

(i) The serial number

(ii) Each document's unique document number

(iii) Name of the document

(iv) Number of pages in the document

(See 'Contents Page' of the sample manual and procedures given in chapter 19, 20 and 21)

Amendment Data Record: This should list the following:

1) The serial number
2) Each document's unique document number
3) Name of the document
4) Page number of document changed
5) Issue number and issue date
6) Page revision number and page revision date, and
7) Nature of change/amendment during revision

(See 'Amendment Data Page' of the sample manual and procedures given in chapter 19, 20 and 21)

Section Identification Pages: Each section should start on a fresh page and tabbed index pages or different colored pages should be used before start of each new section to make it stand out. This would also help people go straight to the section they wish to use directly. This would contain the following:

(i) The section number

(ii) Section name

(See 'Section Identification Page' of the sample manual given in chapter 19)

Document Pages: These pages are the actual documents required by the QMS and contain the main text covering the manual documents, procedures and instructions. They contain

1) The relevant ISO 9001 clause number to which the document relates
2) Each document's unique document number
3) Name of the document
4) The main text, and
5) Number of pages in the document

(See 'Document Pages' of the sample manual and procedures given in chapter 19, 20 and 21)

Index Pages: These pages are not essential to have but may be included if felt necessary. They figure at the end of the documentation and contain the names of specific topics in the actual documents and their exact page number location. These pages are extremely tedious and time consuming to make. An index is useful to access information quickly. A computer may be used for indexing the topics. These pages contain:

(i) Name of specific topics

(ii) Page reference of location

(See 'Index Pages' of this book)

6. BINDING OF THE DOCUMENTATION

The documents should be put together such that they are easy to use yet easy to remove, replace and update the pages. The best method therefore is to have them in the form of a file. They should be in the standard A4 format. For ease of identification, adopt different colored files for different types of documentation.

Example: QMS manual - Red
QMS mandatory procedures - Dark blue
QMS optional procedures - Dark green
QMS work instructions - Brown
QMS inspection instructions - Grey
QMS maintenance instructions - Yellow
QMS calibration instructions - Black
QMS specifications - Orange
QMS controlled lists - Light blue

7. FORMAT OF THE DOCUMENTS

The format of the pages, as far as possible should, remain the same for all documents. The format should normally contain the following (See the sample documents provided in Chapter 19, 20 and 21 for understanding the format of documents better):

(i) Name of the organization: Each page of the documentation should bear the name and/or the logo of the organization.

(ii) Title of the document: The title itself should reflect, 'the nature of contents' of the document for ease of use.

(iii) Document number: As per the document numbering system adopted, each document must be given its unique number for ease of identification and cross-referencing.

(iv) Numbering of pages: Each document may have one or more pages. The pages should be numbered giving the page number followed by the number of pages in that particular document. For example a document may have 7 pages of which page number 5 would be numbered as, "Page 5 of 7" and page number seven as "Page 7 of 7". This ensures that when a page gets revised, replaced, substituted or even a new page gets added to the document the entire numbering does not get affected. However, more importantly the user of the document knows how many pages the document contains and cannot miss a page during use.

(v) Issue number and issue date: Each document must bear the issue number and the date of issue on it. In the beginning the issue number of the document stands at '1' and the Issue Date is 'the date on which the particular document has been issued'.

(vi) Page revision number and page revision date: At the time of the issue of the first set of documents their revision number is '0' and the revision date is 'Nil'. However as and when the document is changed or revised or amended the revision number gets incremented by one and the revision date is the 'date on which the document has undergone a revision'. However the issue number and issue date remains unchanged. After a specific number of revisions (could be any thing from 10 to 100 or even more depending on the frequency of changes) the issue number gets incremented by one and the issue date is also changed to 'the date on which the change has occurred'. Simultaneously the revision number is brought back to '0' on the document and the Revision Date is also changed to 'Nil'.

(vii) Purpose: This should be explicitly stated to make the reason for using the document clear to the user.

(viii) Scope: This describes the processes covered, their users, inputs and outputs to which the particular document is applicable.

(ix) Responsibility: This is a very important requirement that must be essentially specified for each document. This clear assignment of responsibility ensures proper use of documents and completion of all tasks as per requirements. In case more than one individual is assigned responsibility there should be clear definition of who has the primary responsibility for the proper application of the document.

(x) Definitions: All special terms, technical terms and abbreviations (including those used within the organization and well-known internally) should be formally defined in simple language for greater clarity.

(xi) Description: This is the main body of the document, which contains the main substance of the document. It may contain as much matter as required and may contain many paragraphs.

(xii) References: These are related documents which are required by the main document for:

a) Explaining or clarifying certain points

b) Providing information

c) Avoiding explanations within the document

d) Referring to certain ready-made documents of external or internal origin, and

e) Cross-referring to documents lower or higher in the hierarchy of the QMS.

(xiii) Appendices or annexures: These are supporting documents that are given a distinct identity but are attached to the main document on account of:

a) The frequent need of the supporting document's information, and

b) The ease of use due to the availability of the supporting document's information.

(xiv) Name and signature of reviewing authority: This is a vital requirement since all documents before use ought to be reviewed for suitability, adequacy and acceptability.

(xv) Name and signature of approving authority: This is also a vital requirement as no document is to be used unless it has been approved to demonstrate the clearance for use by the approving authority.

8. HIERARCHY OF QMS DOCUMENTATION

ISO 9001:2000 explicitly states, "The organization shall establish, document, implement and maintain a quality management system and - - - " which means that documentation of the QMS is an essential requirement. This documentation basically requires creating, maintaining, preserving and improving the entire ISO related information in written, printed or computer generated fashion.

The QMS documentation has a hierarchy consisting of 4 levels of documents linked to ISO 9001:2000 as shown below:

Hierarchy	Documentation
Level 0	ISO 9001:2000
Level 1	a) Vision statement b) Quality policy c) Organizational quality objectives d) QMS manual e) Process relationship diagrams
Level 2	QMS procedures
Level 3	Instructions for planning, operation and control of, work, inspection, maintenance, calibration, plans, schedules, specifications, drawings, lists, etc.
Level 4	Records, forms, formats, labels, tags, tally sheets, etc.

Note: ISO 9001 does not specify the documentation level, in which the 'Organizational Quality Objectives' should figure. It is for the organizations to decide this, but in order to give them the highest importance, many organizations place this document either in the manual or with the procedures.

The above mentioned is the most basic and the bare minimum hierarchy, but in bigger organizations there can be more than one level. Under each level there could be a corporate manual, a divisional manual, a departmental manual, etc.

The common fear of ISO 9001:2000, is due to the misconception that it leads to massive increase in documentation is unfounded. The standard's requirement for mandatory documentation is advised only in those areas where their absence would have an adverse effect on quality. Thus the extent of the QMS documentation can differ from one organization to another based on the following:

(i) Size of the organization

(ii) Type of activity

(iii) Complexity of the processes

(iv) Interaction of the processes with each other, and

(v) Competence of the personnel for whom the documentation has been prepared

8.1 Vision Statement

The 'Vision' is a statement expressing the top management's dream and perception, regarding where they would like the organization to be, sometime in the future. This therefore states the ambitious level of the organization to be reached in a time period, which could be even ten years ahead or more. It generates a feeling of pride, excitement and satisfaction in targeting it.

Vision, an imaginative aspiration of the future,
is opportunistic and extremely challenging
but believable and achievable

This statement is short, crisp and to the point. It should as far as possible not consist of more than 15 words. We have already learnt that:

An organization is based on a vision. Its policies, procedures, systems of operation and practices are all supported in balance by the vision. When the vision is successfully achieved, the organization advances; when the vision fails, the organization goes down.

Vision therefore, is what makes an organization. Without a vision an organization can exist and may even survive, but its progress will come only from high aims.

8.2 Quality Policy

The quality policy is an inspiring statement of the management's undertaking regarding the course of actions the organization is to adopt, to realize the Vision. The policy statement exhibits the top management's clear commitment to the following:

a) Customer satisfaction through the process of consistently fulfilling customer requirements and exceeding the expectations
b) Value for people of the organization and their welfare coupled with concern for all those people on whom the organization's activities have a direct or indirect impact
c) Continual improvement through culture and systematic effort towards this purpose through anticipation, and
d) Unity of goals of all interested parties with concern for their interests.

This statement however sincere and emphatic would fail unless it is propagated, understood, implemented, maintained and improved.

8.3 Quality Objectives

The fulfilment of the top management's vision and realization of the quality policy requires the identification of the primary goals based on which the quality objectives are established. While the quality policy is a reflection of the primary goals, the quality objectives are the operational level targets to be reached. These objectives, act as the organization's own reference standard against which, they can measure and assess their own performance. The quality objectives are significant since their presence has an impact on performance improvement, both at the organizational level as well as the lower levels within the organization.

8.4 QMS Manual

This is the apex documentation of any QMS, which guides and directs all quality related activities of the organization. Basically it exhibits to all interested parties, what the organization's position is on the various quality requirements, why they must be applied, how to interpret and use each of them, who is responsible for the various aspects and which link document to use to tackle issues related to specific requirements. Its main features are as follows:

1) The quality policy and quality objectives of the organization are included in this document. In order to exhibit 'Total commitment and support of the Chief Executive of the organization', the quality policy should be signed by him.
2) It is general in nature, more at policy level giving an overview of the QMS but unambiguously linking with each requirement of ISO 9001:2000. In effect it sums up as a customized ISO 9001, exclusively tailored to the organization specific needs.
3) It explains in brief, simple and easy to understand terms how each requirement, under each clause of ISO 9001:2000, has been addressed within the organization's QMS.
4) It is normally structured in line with the clauses and requirements of the international standard, although it is not necessary to do this. This method only helps ensure, complete conformity and compliance to the standard in the same logical sequence. Since the manual has to be cross-referable to the standard, adoption of one-to-one correspondence approach between the clauses makes auditing, revising and updating easier.
5) It links each requirement of the standard with the next level of documentation given in the form of procedures. In effect it provides the essential foundation on which procedures are built.
6) It is a document that can be provided to customers or potential customers on request to demonstrate the system capability and commitment to quality of the organization.
7) It provides considerable insight into the primary functions of the organization and how these functions are managed and controlled.

Note:

1. If the QMS manual has been made well, it can be used as a training document rather than using the ISO 9001:2000.
2. The manual concerns the internal people, customers, assessors and the suppliers.
3. Refer and make use of ISO 10013:1995 'Guidelines for Developing Quality Manuals' while preparing the QMS manual.

8.5 Process Relationship Diagrams

The standard requires that the organization identifies and analyzes all its processes, which invariably are cross-functional and multi-departmental. These processes should be then classified into "Key or Core Processes" and "Supporting or Other Processes". It is preferable to call the processes as 'Supporting Processes'. Let every individual feel his process is important and has a role to play. If people feel their process is, just a secondary process of lesser significance they would lose interest.

'Key Processes' are defined as those processes which are directly related to the customers, supplier, design and development or product realization. All other processes are defined as 'Supporting Processes'.

Having identified and classified the processes, each process should then be depicted diagrammatically for its inter-relationship with other key and supporting processes. These 'Process Relationship Diagrams' are required to help the organization function, based on the process approach for effective and efficient performance. Within each process the interacting internal activity chain, should also be documented as a 'Process Flow Chart', for showing sequences, inputs, outputs, inter-linkages, control points and scope for improvement.

8.6 QMS Procedures

This document is the basic operating document that specifies the particular order and manner of performing an activity. It describes what to do, who to do, when to do, where to do, why to do and how to do with regard to the activities. While the Manual is concept based, the procedures are activity based. They therefore translate into practice the requirements of the QMS manual to fulfil ISO requirements.

The Procedures therefore cover the following with regard to the activities:

1) Area of use
2) Purpose of the activity

3) Scope of the activity
4) Responsibility
5) Method
6) Physical inputs
7) Control measures required
8) Required documentation and
9) Reference to related instructions and formats.

The procedures can be classified if required as under:

1) Mandatory level procedures, and
2) Optional or other necessary procedures.

OR

1) System level procedures,
2) Operational level procedures, and
3) Process level procedures.

It is for the organization to decide how to classify their procedure. Unless the classification helps in control of operations, do not make unnecessary classification just for the name sake.

Note: Many a time customers request an organization to send them a copy of their QMS manual for their review and records. There is no bar in sending them a copy rather there is the advantage of providing them confidence in the organization's system by exhibiting adequacy of the QMS Manual. However, ensure that this copy is an, 'Uncontrolled Copy'. Never give copies of the documented QMS Procedures to outsiders including customers. They are an organization's internal documents and a customer cannot demand copies of these to be given to them. All that the organization can give, if requested and needed, is a copy of the list of procedures in use.

8.7 Instructions

These describe how any job should be performed. They consist of a detailed set of sequential and easy to understand steps that must be followed for performing jobs. They are meant to provide clear understanding of the job and thereby ensure continuity of work even when personnel change.

They give directions for performing any type of work, process-activity, operation, maintenance, test, inspection, calibration, etc. They may be in the form of written instructions, flow-charts, diagrams, reports, tables, reference samples, specifications, codes of practices, check lists, technical and legal documents, etc.

They should preferably be documented by the users themselves and in addition to English, should also be, in vernacular, for ease of understanding.

Note: While QMS procedures are multi-activity instructions, Instructions are single activity instructions, listing out the various tasks falling within the activity. In a small organization, instructions can be merged with the QMS procedures, if desired.

8.8 Records, Forms, Formats

These documents are basically generated while collecting data for evaluation and assessment of products, process and system to ascertain compliance with requirements. They also help in ensuring traceability and effecting improvements in the current level of performance. These documents are also used as objective evidence to demonstrate conformity of the QMS to the various requirements of the standard. They include files, records, forms and formats and can be available and stored in any medium i.e. paper or computer.

The records are used to provide the following information regarding the QMS

- The current status of the QMS
- Supplier performance
- Personnel data
- Process data
- Product details
- Customer satisfaction or dissatisfaction
- Corrective and preventive actions and
- The extent to which the quality objectives have been achieved

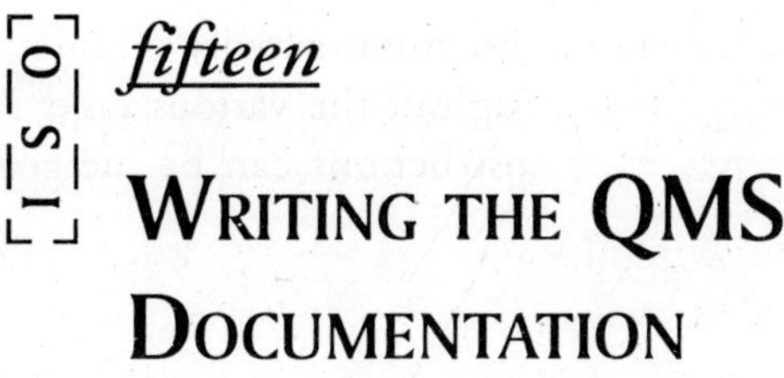

fifteen
WRITING THE QMS DOCUMENTATION

1. WRITING THE DOCUMENTATION

Not everything can be documented

In writing the QMS documentation it should be borne in mind that the documentation is to be used by four types of users with different levels of technical and organizational knowledge as shown in Fig. 11. Therefore it is necessary to write in simple terms for ease of the user, as the documentation is basically for them. However, as many terms of the ISO related vocabulary are to be made use of. The organization's users should learn to understand these terms and use them. For this, it is essential to explain these 'terms or special concepts related to ISO' within the documentation itself. An useful ISO document, 'Guidelines for quality management system documentation,' which under preparation may be referred for guidance as soon as it is available and even the documentation already prepared and in use ought to be reviewed for improvement based on it.

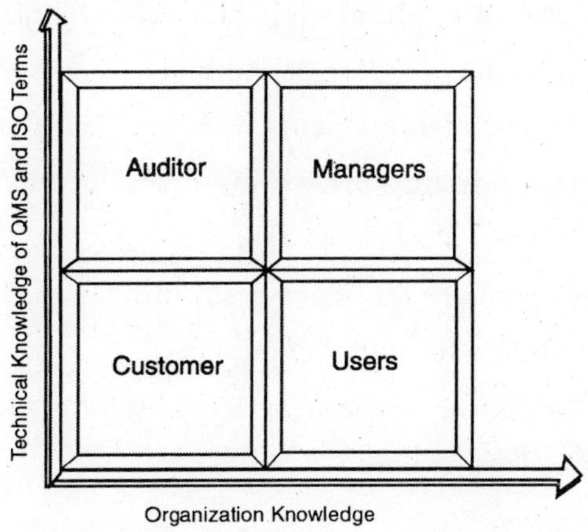

FIG. 11 *MATRIX OF ORGANIZATION AND ISO RELATED KNOWLEDGE*

1.1 Rules for Writing the Documentation

(i) Use common words as far as possible.

(ii) Write simple and short sentences.

(iii) Explain technical terms or concepts by means of footnotes or explanation, after the term is used, or through a glossary.

(iv) Do not try to write like an essay, where we use different word every time for the same thing. Use the same word repeatedly without any hesitation in the interest of clarity and to prevent confusion.

(v) Use direct speech in place of indirect and active voice in place of passive.

(vi) Use lists and tables as far as possible.

(vii) Match practice and documentation.

1.2 Steps in Writing the Documentation

The documentation is the output of the organization for its own use and so everybody should be involved with it. However, 'one person or a group of persons' should be assigned the responsibility for the preparation of the documentation in the following order:

(i) Collect all existing quality related documents and list them

(ii) Identify all processes and divide them into 'Key' and 'Supporting' processes

(iii) Draw flow charts of each Process

(iv) Draw process inter-relationship diagrams

(v) Examine the interfaces of processes

(vi) Identify areas of duplication or omission of work

(vii) Decide upon the contents of the body

(viii) Ensure all QMS requirements have been addressed

(ix) Allocate responsibility for writing draft documents

(x) Document the critical areas first

(xi) Secondly document the easy ones to fully cover the remaining areas

(xii) Circulate the drafts to get comments

(xiii) Edit the drafts for correctness, reliability and simplicity

(xiv) Prepare final manuscript

(xv) Get it reviewed

(xvi) Obtain authorization for its use

(xvii) Monitor use of the documents for a period of time and correct where- ever required

(xviii) Print and distribute as per distribution procedure

2. WRITING THE QUALITY POLICY

The quality policy should be, just a single page document, easily understandable and simple. In writing the policy, word it any way and include any point you wish, but ensure that the quality policy never contradicts any statutory requirements and is also in line with other policies of the top management.

The quality policy being an extremely critical component of the QMS, must have the approval of the top management, even if it has been written and worded by someone else. This approval has to be exhibited by the top management, through endorsement, by signing it and also putting the date.

It is important to write the quality policy such that, when it is read it must give a feeling that the organization is sincere in what it says and is committed to this statement. In other words, it should give the readers a sense of security and confidence in the organization's systems. It must also deliver a message of support, concern, trust and commitment to the employees.

In short, the quality policy ought to publicly set-forth the organization's commitment to quality through:

(i) Fulfilling and exceeding customer requirements and expectations,

(ii) Value of its people,

(iii) Coordinated and cohesive team-work,

(iv) Culture for continual improvement through anticipation and attention to detail, and

(v) Concern for all affected parties.

3. WRITING THE QUALITY OBJECTIVES

Establishing the primary quality goals of the organization, by extracting them from the quality policy, is the first step in the planning carried out for achieving customer satisfaction. The following are a few typical primary goals:

- To ensure customer satisfaction and to strive for customer delight
- To improve effectiveness and efficiency

- To ensure that with passage of time the level of performance does not drop but is maintained equal to or better than competitors' level (Relative Improvement)
- To continually improve performance with time (Absolute Improvement)
- To have means of measuring and comparing own performance
- To provide a framework for formulation of strategies and policies
- To have a basis for acquiring, allocating and utilizing resources and
- To provide clarity regarding the direction of the organization.

Only after knowing the primary goals can the quality objectives be set and the means of achieving them, be decided. The fixing of measurable quality objectives and in fact, their very existence, has a significant impact on performance improvement, both at the organization level as well as the lower levels within the organization. These quality objectives, act as the organization's own reference standard, against which, they can measure and assess their own performance. The quality objectives should not be fixed very high but should be attainable, however they should not be low either. Keep them out of reach and at a respectable level. These quality objectives should be set in measurable terms normally on a scale of 1-5, 1-10, or 1-100.

3.1 Criteria of Fixing Objectives

The basic criteria on which any organization fixes its objectives are as follows:

- Determine the purpose.
- Pursue optimization of overall and not individual performance.
- Include all activities.
- Achieve cost-effectiveness.
- Target all-round benefits.
- Ensure flexibility for easy upgrade.
- Keep them simple, understandable and clear.
- Set to achievable levels.
- Ensure they are practical.
- Establish scale of impact and importance.
- Verify current laws and regulatory requirements.
- Determine concerns of interested parties.
- Identify difficulties, limitations and constraints with respect to technology and capability.

3.2 Hierarchy of Objectives

The quality objectives determined and written down should be established not only for the organization as a whole, but also for the lower levels within. The hierarchy for these could be as follows:

(i) Organizational level quality objectives

(ii) Process level quality objectives

(iii) Department level quality objectives, and

(iv) Activity level quality objectives

When the quality objectives are established for different levels within the organization, in line with their requirements and are aligned with the established organization level quality objectives, they help each level indirectly in contributing towards the achievement of the organization level quality objectives. They also ensure that each level in its area of work is aware of the current needs of the organization and systematically reviews them at regular periodicity to change for the future.

3.3 Typical Objectives

- Increase customer satisfaction
- Reduce customer complaints
- Increase productivity in terms of right first time, every time
- Reduce wastage, rework and rejection
- Better supplier relations and performance
- Improve delivery
- Reduce consumption of inputs
- Improve time response
- Enhance training to all levels
- Increase growth
- Maximization of returns on investment
- Reduce variability
- Reduce personnel turnover
- Adoption of continual improvement
- Increase safety awareness
- Increase environmental awareness
- Improve markets, and
- Scientific decision making

3.4 Steps in Setting Measurable Values to Quality Objectives

(i) Considering the purpose of the organization to align with the objectives.

(ii) Determine the objectives.

(iii) List the numerical measures of the objectives.

(iv) Specify priority of the objective attributes.

(v) Determine time period and rate for attaining the objectives.

(vi) Set the measurable level to be reached.

(vii) Specify the method of measurement and comparison.

(viii) Specify the 'mandatory or minimum level' and 'desirable or maximum level'.

4. WRITING THE QMS MANUAL

The manual should be the output of everyone who is connected to it and for whom it is relevant. However, in practice the manual is relevant to every department and every process. Then, should everyone be involved? The answer is an obvious NO.

Select a 'Documentation committee' just like your 'Implementation committee'. Have knowledgeable representatives from each department and prepare a draft. Have at the most 3 persons responsible to actually write out the draft based on the information provided by the members of this 'Documentation committee'. This draft can then be reviewed and polished.

The following steps would help in writing the QMS manual:

(i) Collect a copy of all quality related documents and list them.

(ii) Open a separate file for each clause of the standard and put the collected documents in the relevant file for the clause under which they fit.

(iii) List the various processes, with their sequence, interaction and application in the organization.

(iv) Classify the processes into 'Key Processes' and 'Supporting Processes'.

(v) Study and analyze each key process and establish its purpose and depict diagrammatically its inter-relationship with other key and supporting processes.

(vi) Within each process, document the interacting internal activity chain in the form of a 'Process Flow Chart', for showing sequences, inputs, outputs, inter-linkages, control points and scope for improvement.

(vii) Specify the criteria and methods being used for the operation and control of processes.

(viii) List the outsourced processes and the type and methods of control that are being exercised on them.

(ix) List out the resources required and information necessary for the operation and monitoring of processes.

(x) Review the above process related documents and identify duplications and omissions.

(xi) Decide the contents relevant to each clause.

(xii) Prepare the draft ensuring that all requirements of the standard are addressed adequately and appropriately.

(xiii) Circulate the draft among all staff-members, soliciting comments.

(xiv) Edit ruthlessly for corrections and alignment with the requirements of the standard.

(xv) Ensure simplicity and clarity.

(xvi) Rewrite the corrected manual.

(xvii) Study it in use and once again correct for problems.

4.1 Preparing Diagrams for Process Relationships

1) A separate diagram shall be prepared for each key process, which shall be made the 'Central Key Process' of the diagram.
2) All other 'Related' key and supporting processes shall be identified and located around the central key process on the diagram.
3) The central key process shall be linked to all the related processes using continuous lines for material flow and dotted lines for information flow.
4) Arrow heads shall be marked to show direction of flow for both materials as well as information.
5) Along each line, details of the corresponding material or information flowing along the line interlinking processes, shall be written for the relevant line.
6) Draw the feedback loops showing the information that is being relayed back to help the central key process as also the corrective actions for the process.

4.2 Preparing Diagrams for Macro Processes

Preparing a graphical representation in the form of flowcharts builds a thorough understanding of the process. The effective way of drawing these charts is to proceed along the following lines:

(i) Take a large sheet of paper.

(ii) Identify and state the process.

(iii) Write the macro process name on top of the paper.

(iv) Define and write the purpose.

(v) Specify and write the scope.

(vi) Define and write the process boundaries.

(vii) List and write the names of functional groups involved, in sequence.

(viii) Enlist the appropriate human resource for the process.

(ix) Decide upon the name of the process owner, champion, facilitator, coach or whatever name by which the leader of the process is called and write it on the paper.

(x) Collect existing flowcharts, procedures, etc.

(xi) Write the following on separate post-it TM stickers so that they can be easily shifted around.

  a) The starting point of the process

  b) The final output of the process and

  c) The names of each-sub-process.

(xii) Paste the stickers in sequence on the sheet of paper

(xiii) Draw arrows from the starting point through the sub processes to the final output

(xiv) Control the extent of details in the flowchart in relation to the purpose

(xv) Review and revise to correct inaccuracies

4.3 Preparing Diagrams for Micro Processes

The sub-processes of the macro processes are called micro processes. These micro process charts would have more details than the major processes given on the top row of the chart and include the detailed listing regarding the people, materials, tools, equipment, time, suppliers, customers and other information below each element. It is more a tabular form of chart than a flow diagram.

5. WRITING THE QMS PROCEDURES

Writing of these documents should be done at the actual user's level. They should be written by any manager, foreman, supervisor, staff, operative, etc. who actually need and use them. It is quite possible that some people at these levels may not be able to write properly due to poor 'power of expression'. Ensure that the subject matter is their output and get it written for them with accuracy.

Use a standard format for all procedures and number them. Use simple language with small sentences. Endeavor to write whatever the actual existing procedures are and how they help the organization in fulfilling the requirements of the standard, in relation to the particular clause under which the procedure fits in. Having done this, now look for loopholes, weak areas, incorrect practices, etc. This will give control over the procedures without making them much different from actual practice, thereby minimizing imposition of new unnecessary changes to practice.

The exercise should definitely be used to:

(i) Document existing procedures accurately
(ii) Reflect on existing practices
(iii) Determine better ways of doing the same job
(iv) Make all round improvements, and
(v) Ensure implementation of decisions

The following steps would help in writing the QMS procedures:

(i) Identify the purpose of the procedure
(ii) Ensure its need
(iii) Determine if it can be clubbed with some other procedure to reduce paperwork
(iv) Define the scope
(v) Collect information regarding the existing practice
(vi) Write the way the actual practice exists
(vii) Compare with the requirements of the standard
(viii) Correct wherever necessary
(ix) Prepare the draft
(x) Obtain comments
(xi) Incorporate changes, and
(xii) Review and obtain authorization to use the procedure.

6. WRITING INSTRUCTIONS

Write the instructions in simply worded, easy to follow numbered steps. Use terms that the users are conversant with, even if in actual practice a more appropriate term exists. If you wish to correct the user and teach them the better term, use both terms for some time and then eliminate the common usage term, through a document change procedure. Do not hesitate to use drawings, diagrams, pictures, samples, etc. for explaining workmanship criterion. Also list all the equipment, tools, gauges, instruments, etc. that the user is supposed to handle.

The rule is simple.

Write the instruction in the same sequence of steps
As the job ought to be performed

7. WRITING RECORDS

Prepare the blank formats, forms and records to be filled by making the least number of changes to the existing records. Only if absolutely necessary make a change, and then also try to keep it as close as possible to the old format.

For both old as well as new records, the format must be designed to collect complete and unambiguous data.

Formats, forms and records are written by the people within the organization to record any information or data obtained during the course of their day-to-day work. These records are the objective evidence of the organization and so must be accurate, legible, complete and up-to-date. Only approved copies of formats should be used within the organization.

ISO

sixteen

Documentation List for ISO 9001:2000

1. MANUAL AND PROCEDURE DOCUMENTS

The fact that ISO 9001:2000 has only listed 6 mandatory procedures is not a coincidence but a deliberate attempt to permit organizations, to take their own decisions on what their system demands as necessary to be documented. This freedom has been given so that organizations adopt a more 'Common Sense Approach' to documentation. Organizations should take advantage of this relaxation and only document to the extent necessary. However, this relaxation does not mean that even necessary documents required by an organization can be ignored and can be dispensed with. Those documents needed by the organization for its own operations obviously have to be documented for operational effectiveness and efficiency. The list of procedures that any organization uses therefore is not imposed, but left to the discretion of the organization.

The list given below in Table 13 has therefore been deliberately made detailed and exhaustive to help organizations understand and then decide upon their documentation. The **'mandatory procedures given in bold to highlight them'** of course still remain only 6 in number. (Sample documents of the 6 mandatory procedures along with a few procedures for new requirements have been given in Chapter 20 for the convenience of readers.)

TABLE 13

List of Level 1 and Level 2 Documents

Cl. No.	Level 1 QMS Manual	Level 2 QMS Procedures
4.1	1) QMS requirements – general 2) List of processes, with their sequence, interaction and application in the organization 3) List of outsourced processes 4) Criteria and methods for operation and control of processes 5) List of resources required and information necessary for the operation and monitoring of processes	(i) Procedure for identifying processes needed and their sequence and interaction (ii) Procedure for classifying processes into key and supporting processes (iii) Procedure for process approach (iv) Procedure for determining criteria and methods for operation and control of processes (v) Procedure for providing resources and information to support and monitor the processes (vi) Procedure for monitoring, measuring and analyzing the processes (vii) Procedure for implementing and continually improving processes (viii) Procedure for outsourcing processes (ix) Procedure for control of outsourced processes
4.2.1	(i) Documentation requirements – general (ii) Quality Policy (iii) Quality Objectives (iv) QMS Manual documents	-------
4.2.2	(i) QMS Manual (ii) Scope of the QMS (iii) List of exclusions with justification (iv) Description of interaction between identified processes	(i) Procedure for establishment, maintenance and review of the QMS Manual (ii) Procedure for preparing and maintaining QMS Procedures (iii) Procedure for preparing and maintaining quality plans

Cl. No.	Level 1 QMS Manual	Level 2 QMS Procedures
4.2.3	Control of documents	(i) Procedure for document control (ii) Procedure for approval of documents (iii) Procedure for review, updation and re-approval of documents (iv) Procedure for identifying change and revision status of documents (v) Procedure for document changes (vi) Procedure for legibility and identification of documents (vii) Procedure for identification and control of external origin documents (viii) Procedure for identification, control and use of obsolete documents (ix) Procedure for document indexing
4.2.4	Control of records	(i) Procedure for control of records (ii) Procedure for legibility of records (iii) Procedure for identification of records (iv) Procedure for storage, protection and retrieval of records (v) Procedure for retention time of records (vi) Procedure for disposition of records
5.1	Management • commitment	(i) Procedure for demonstrating Top Management commitment (ii) Procedure for effecting Top Management communication within organization
5.2	Customer focus	(i) Procedure for determining customer requirements (ii) Procedure for meeting customer requirements
5.3	Quality Policy	(i) Procedure for establishing the quality policy (ii) Procedure for communicating the quality policy (iii) Procedure for reviewing the quality policy

Cl. No.	Level 1 QMS Manual	Level 2 QMS Procedures
5.4.1	Quality Objectives	(i) Procedure for establishing the quality objectives at various levels (ii) Procedure for reviewing the quality objectives (iii) Procedure for measuring and comparing achievements with quality objectives
5.4.2	QMS planning	(i) Procedure for QMS Planning (ii) Procedure for assessing need for changes to the QMS (iii) Procedure for effecting changes in the QMS
5.5.1	Responsibility and Authority	(i) Procedure for assigning responsibility and authority (ii) Procedure for communicating responsibility and authority (iii) Procedure for preparing and maintaining job descriptions
5.5.2	Management representative	Procedure for promoting awareness of customer requirements
5.5.3	Internal communication	Procedure for establishing and ensuring internal communication
5.6.1	Management Review—general	Procedure for management review
5.6.2	Review inputs	Procedure for compiling inputs for management review
5.6.3	Review outputs	Procedure for deciding and acting on management review outputs
6.1	Provision of resources	(i) Procedure for planning for resources (ii) Procedure for determining and providing resources
6.2.1	Human resources—general	Procedure for assessing competence of personnel

Cl. No.	Level 1 QMS Manual	Level 2 QMS Procedures
6.2.2	Competence, awareness and training	(i) Procedure for identifying work, affecting product quality (ii) Procedure for ensuring competence of people (iii) Procedure for assigning jobs to people (iv) Procedure for planning, identifying needs and imparting training (v) Procedure for reviewing training, based on feedback (vi) Procedure for achieving quality objectives
6.3	Infrastructure	(i) Procedure for determining, providing and maintaining the building, workspace and associated utilities (ii) Procedure for determining, providing and maintaining the process equipment (iii) Procedure for determining, providing and maintaining the supporting services
6.4	Work environment	(i) Procedure for determining and managing work environment
7.1	Planning of product realization	(i) Procedure for planning and development of product realization processes (ii) Procedure for establishing processes, documents and resources for product (iii) Procedure for verification, validation, monitoring, inspection and testing of products (iv) Procedure for determining product acceptance criteria
7.2.1	Determination of customer requirements related to product	(i) Procedure for determining customer requirements (ii) Procedure for determining unstated customer requirements (iii) Procedure for determining statutory and regulatory requirements (iv) Procedure for determining additional requirements felt necessary by the organization

Cl. No.	Level 1 QMS Manual	Level 2 QMS Procedures
7.2.2	Review of customer requirements related to product	(i) Procedure for reviewing and amending product requirements (ii) Procedure for communicating changes to customer requirements
7.2.3	Customer communication	Procedure for customer communication
7.3.1	Design and development planning	(i) Procedure for design and development planning (ii) Procedure for allocation of work for design and development (iii) Procedure for determining the design and development stages (iv) Procedure for management of the technical interfaces for design and development
7.3.2	Design and development inputs	(i) Procedure for determination of design and development inputs (ii) Procedure for review of design and development inputs
7.3.3	Design and development outputs	(i) Procedure for establishing design and development output requirements (ii) Procedure for approval of design and development outputs
7.3.4	Design and development review	(i) Procedure for planning of design and development review (ii) Procedure for review of design and development outputs
7.3.5	Design and development verification	1) Procedure for design and development verification planning 2) Procedure for design and development verification
7.3.6	Design and development validation	(i) Procedure for planning of design and development validation (ii) Procedure for design and development validation
7.3.7	Control of design and development	(i) Procedure for identification of design and development changes (ii) Procedure for review, verification, validation and approval of design and development changes

Cl. No.	Level 1 QMS Manual	Level 2 QMS Procedures
7.4.1	Purchasing process	(i) Procedure for purchasing (ii) Procedure for evaluation, selection and re-evaluation of suppliers (iii) Procedure for assessment of suppliers (iv) Procedure for preparation and maintenance of assessed supplier list
7.4.2	Purchasing information	(i) Procedure for specifying purchase information (ii) Procedure for communicating purchasing information (iii) Procedure for preparation, review and approval of purchase documents
7.4.3	Verification of purchased product	(i) Procedure for verification of purchased product after receipt (ii) Procedure for quarantine areas for the purchased product (iii) Procedure for verification and release of purchased product at suppliers premises (iv) Procedure for verification and release of purchased product by organization's customer
7.5.1	Control of production and service provision	(i) Procedure for production planning (ii) Procedure for service planning (iii) Procedure for production process control (iv) Procedure for service process control (v) Procedure for tool design (vi) Procedure for qualification of tools, jigs and fixtures
7.5.2	Validation of processes for production and service provision	(i) Procedure for qualification and validation of special processes (ii) Procedure for review, approval and revalidation of special processes
7.5.3	Identification and trace ability	(i) Procedure for product identification (ii) Procedure for product status identification (iii) Procedure for product traceability

Cl. No.	Level 1 QMS Manual	Level 2 QMS Procedures
7.5.4	Customer property	(i) Procedure for identification, verification, protection and safeguard of customer property (ii) Procedure for accounting and reporting customer property details
7.5.5	Preservation of product	Procedure for preservation of the product or its parts
7.6	Control of monitoring and measuring devices	(i) Procedure for determining the monitoring and measurement to be undertaken (ii) Procedure for determining the monitoring and measurement devices required (iii) Procedure for establishing processes for carrying out the monitoring and measurement required (iv) Procedure for identification and regular calibration of the monitoring and measuring devices (v) Procedure for specifying and maintaining the monitoring and measurement controlled environment (vi) Procedure for safeguard of the adjustments of monitoring and measuring devices (vii) Procedure for protection of monitoring and measuring devices during handling, maintenance and storage (viii) Procedure for actions when monitoring and measuring devices are found to be out of limits (ix) Procedure for confirming ability of software to satisfy monitoring and measurement requirements
8.1	Measurement, analysis and improvement – general	(i) Procedure for planning the monitoring, measurement, analysis and improvement of processes (ii) Procedure for implementing the monitoring, measurement, analysis and improvement of processes

Cl. No.	Level 1 QMS Manual	Level 2 QMS Procedures
8.2.1	Customer satisfaction	(i) Procedure for customer satisfaction assessment (ii) Procedure for determining customer perception regarding the organization's success in meeting requirements (iii) Procedure for analysis of customer perception data (iv) Procedure for using the customer perception feedback
8.2.2	**Internal audit**	(i) **Procedure for planning of Internal Audits** (ii) **Procedure for conducting Internal Audits** (iii) **Procedure for reporting on the Internal Audit results** (iv) **Procedure for corrective actions on the Internal Audit results** (v) **Procedure for follow-up Audit**
8.2.3	Monitoring and measurement of processes	(i) Procedure for ascertaining achievement of planned results through monitoring and measuring of QMS processes (ii) Procedure for implementing corrective actions and improvement of QMS processes
8.2.4	Monitoring and measurement of product	(i) Procedure for planning monitoring and measurement of the product (ii) Procedure for monitoring and measuring characteristics of the product (iii) Procedure for workmanship criteria (iv) Procedure for inspection and release of the product

Cl. No.	Level 1 QMS Manual	Level 2 QMS Procedures
8.3	**Control of non-conforming product**	**(i) Procedure for identification and control of non-conforming product** **(ii) Procedure for review and disposition of non- conforming product** **(iii) Procedure for evaluation of non-conforming product** **(iv) Procedure for re-verification of corrected non- conforming product** **(v) Procedure for dealing with non-conforming product detected after delivery to customer**
8.4	Analysis of data	(i) Procedure for determination, collection and analysis of customer satisfaction data (ii) Procedure for determination, collection and analysis of product conformity data (iii) Procedure for determination, collection and analysis of data relating to characteristics and trends of processes and product (iv) Procedure for determination, collection and analysis of suppliers related data (v) Procedure for evaluating scope and assessing opportunities for continual improvement
8.5.1	Continual improvement	Procedure for planning and managing continual improvement
8.5.2	Corrective actions	**(i) Procedure for dealing with customer complaints** **(ii) Procedure for product recall and replacement** **(iii) Procedure for determining the cause of non-conformities** **(iv) Procedure for evaluating non-conformities** **(v) Procedure for eliminating the cause of non-conformities** **(vi) Procedure for reviewing corrective actions**

Cl. No.	Level 1 QMS Manual	Level 2 QMS Procedures
8.5.3	**Preventive actions**	**(i) Procedure for determining the cause of potential non-conformities** **(ii) Procedure for evaluating potential non-conformities** **(iii) Procedure for eliminating the cause of potential non-conformities** **(iv) Procedure for reviewing preventive actions**

(i) An organization should figure out where each of its level 3 and level 4 documents that have been taken under control, fit and accordingly refer and locate them, in the QMS documentation.

(ii) An organization may wish to combine some procedures under a single heading to reduce the number of procedures to keep them at a manageable level. For instance the list given above gives the following nine separate procedures for clause '4.2.3 Control of documents' of the standard. The organization may, in the place of these procedures once again listed below, decide to have a single 'Procedure for document control'

- Procedure for document control
- Procedure for approval of documents
- Procedure for review, updation and re-approval of documents
- Procedure for identifying change and revision status of documents
- Procedure for document changes
- Procedure for legibility and identification of documents
- Procedure for identification and control of external origin documents
- Procedure for identification, control and use of obsolete documents and
- Procedure for document indexing

OR

While applying the requirements of clause '7.3.1 Design and development planning' the organization may decide to replace the four procedures listed below and decide to have a single 'Procedure for design and development planning'.

- Procedure for design and development planning
- Procedure for allocation of work for design and development

- Procedure for determining the design and development stages and
- Procedure for management of the technical interfaces for design and development.

OR

The organization may even combine all the 16 procedures for the 7 clauses for design and development under 7.3.1, 7.3.2, 7.3.3, 7.3.4, 7.3.5, 7.3.6 and 7.3.7 and decide to have a single 'Procedure for design and development'.

All these are completely acceptable, as long as the various requirements of the relevant clause of the ISO have been properly addressed and documented in the single combined procedure.

2.0 Mandatory records

ISO 9001 requires organizations to have the capability to demonstrate the existence of a QMS complying with its requirements. It is for this purpose that the standard necessarily requires the organization to maintain the following mandatory records:

TABLE 14

Mandatory records (Level 4 documents)

S.No.	Clause No.	Name of the record
1.	4.1	Record for control of outsourced processes
2.	4.2.3	Record for control of documents
3.	5.6.1	Record for management review
4.	6.2.2	Records of education, training, skills and experience
5.	7.1	Records for providing evidence that product realization processes and resulting product meet requirements
6.	7.2.2	Record for review of customer requirements and actions needed
7.	7.3.2	Record of product input requirements for design and development
8.	7.3.4	Record of design and development reviews
9.	7.3.5	Record of design and development verification
10.	7.3.6	Record of design and development validation
11.	7.3.7	Record of design and development changes
12.	7.4.1	Record of supplier evaluation results and necessary actions
13.	7.5.2	Record of validation of processes

S.No.	Clause No.	Name of the record
14.	7.5.4	Record for control and use of customer property
15.	7.6	Record for calibration and verification of monitoring and measuring devices
16.	8.2.1	Record for customer satisfaction and dissatisfaction
17.	8.2.2	Record for internal audit
18.	8.2.4	Records for providing evidence of conformity of product with acceptance criteria
19.	8.3	Record of nature of non-conformity and subsequent actions
20.	8.5.2	Record of results of corrective actions
21.	8.5.3	Record of results of preventive actions

ISO

seventeen

Applying ISO 9001:2000 to 'Your Organization'

1. GENERAL

ISO 9001:2000 requires organizations to establish, document, implement, maintain and continually improve the effectiveness of their QMS. This therefore requires the organization to study and understand the standard and consciously decide to adopt this quality management framework for better performance. Since 'managing the organization well', is the job of the top management, the standard demands discipline and total commitment from them.

The special features of the standard are as follows:

(i) The ISO 9001:2000 has maintained dynamism and responsiveness to the changing needs of the market. Whereas many organizations have failed to be market responsive, the International Organization for Standardization through the changes in ISO 9001 during the past and 'especially this version' exhibited that it is totally market driven.

(ii) It continues to propagate a formal management system for quality, to ensure the achievement, maintenance and enhancement of customer satisfaction.

(iii) The standard has become very 'user-friendly' by breaking up the requirements into a logical cycle of PDCA and adopting general usage terms such as supplier, organization and customer.

(iv) There has been elimination of confusion by combining 9001, 9002 and 9003:1994. There had existed lack of clarity in the minds of non-professionals, regarding the difference in the three models and they doubted whether one model was superior to the other. This standard is now applicable to all types of organization, which were earlier covered under three different heads.

(v) There has been a simplification and improved structuring of the standard.

(vi) The efforts and time invested by the users of ISO 9001:1994 does not go waste but gets used by reorientation of the 'System Design Basis' from the '20 Elements of PDCA'.

(vii) There has been inclusion of an important requirement i.e. expecting the organization to be concerned regarding 'benefit of all interested parties' and not merely the 'customer and the organization itself'.

2. APPLYING AND USING ISO 9001:2000

Applying ISO 9001:2000 to an organization therefore requires a deliberate, disciplined and committed effort towards formally establishing, documenting, implementing, maintaining and continually improving the effectiveness of the organization's QMS.

The meaning of each of the actions required is as follows:

Establish Determine and formally create the QMS as per ISO requirements.

Document Prepare written documents for the established QMS and then record facts as evidence.

Implement Put the QMS into action for achieving compliance to ISO requirements.

Maintain Retain in proper or good condition the organization for preventing its down-slide.

Continually Improve Constantly strive to improve on the existing levels by moving ahead, 'in small but regular improvement steps'.

Those organizations which desires to adopt ISO 9001:2000 and put it into practice, often speculate on how to apply this standard to their particular industry. There are two types of such organizations, one a group of those who are already certified as per the 1994 version of the standard and are in the TRANSITION phase while the other group is of those who are planning to adopt this standard for the first time and are the NEW ASPIRANTS. In either case the work of applying and using the standard, has to be a planned, systematic and disciplined exercise.

Organizations in the TRANSITION phase with a quality system as per ISO 9001/9002/9003:1994 should remember the following:

(i) ISO 9001, ISO 9002 & ISO 9003:1994 will become obsolete once the 2000 version of the standard is adopted.

(ii) The present cut-off date for change-over is 31 December 2003 by ISO and 31 December 2002 by most of the certifying bodies. This difference has been maintained for keeping provision of re-assessment wherever required.

(iii) Many consultants advise against redoing the documentation but just taking care of the additions and changes of the new standard. IT IS STRONGLY ADVISED NOT TO DO THIS. One will never be able to fully realign the system in a systematic manner. IT IS BEST TO REWRITE THE DOCUMENTS ALLOVER AGAIN. It just requires about a month's effort, but in the long run it would benefit the organization by keeping the documentation exactly in line with ISO 9001:2000.

Organizations that figure in the group of NEW ASPIRANTS without a certified quality system as per ISO 9001/9002/9003:1994 should follow all steps listed below and the cut-off date constraint does not apply to them.

3. SEQUENCE OF STEPS FOR APPLYING THE STANDARD

The following is the sequence of steps that any organization needs to go through for applying and utilizing the standard. Bear in mind that, all these steps may not apply to all organizations. It is for the organization to determine the applicable steps:

1) **Ensure that the top management understands all the requirements:** The entire project of adopting the QMS as per ISO 9001:2000 will not even take-off unless the top Management understands all requirements, their own responsibilities and the need for their commitment. They must therefore, in the very beginning voluntarily undergo an orientation course to develop the right attitude or at least the organization's consultant must explain the standard and its requirements to them.

2) **Obtain top management commitment:** The implementation cannot proceed without the top management commitment and whole-hearted support. It should be ensured, and if the support is missing or partially, it only means they need further explanation, and training for eliciting commitment. This commitment has to be exhibited by the top management by actively supporting and not merely speaking of support or overriding / ignoring the entire exercise. They should in-fact review progress and ensure availability of all necessary resources.

3) **Determine expenditure involved:** The organization functions for profits or at-least it should get other benefits. Without some benefit no organization would go for an expenditure of the type that is required for this work. It is

wise to set up a system, which can measure the benefits e.g. benefits due to waste reduction, improved output, improved performance, etc.

4) **Select a consultant:** It is better to take the help of a qualified consultant even if expertise exists in-house. This is to ensure that you get the advantage of the wide and varied exposure and experience of the consultant. Further the consultant would follow a time bound schedule to fulfil his obligation at the earliest. Unlike this, an insider who may have other responsibilities can temporarily get diverted, if some other urgent work has to be done. It should be made sure that the consultant has specialist skills in the interpretation of the standard and also understands the specifics of your industry. Working without a consultant's guidance can prove to be a false economy. Use the consultant to guide but let the documentation be done by the people of the organization. Please ensure the consultant remains available to clear doubts of the top management and helps in training the employees and carrying out audits.

Remember, consultants are of two types - 'the experts' and 'the facilitator'. The expert can give all required specialist advice using his storehouse of vast experience gathered over many years. The facilitator while being knowledgeable is more a counsellor and will only guide. The organization must be clear about the type of consultant they wish to engage.

5) **Involve the employees:** The employees must be fully briefed well in advance regarding the distinct advantages of this major step, so that they feel motivated and involved. Only through the whole-hearted contribution of the employees, can the organization succeed. Their being made aware of the development, and kept informed of the progress is therefore of utmost importance. At the initial stage itself the consultant should normally be introduced to the employees so that they get to know him and avail his services as and when required.

6) **Set-up the implementation team:** The entire project should be assigned to an implementation team composed of representatives of all key processes and a few supporting processes. This group along with the help of the consultant will interpret the standard and correlate the QMS requirements to the organization's needs. They will allot responsibility for drafting the QMS documentation to concerned competent people and also for monitoring progress and report on problems encountered for remedial actions.

7) **Assess current level of existing QMS:** Every organization however small or big would definitely be having some kind of a quality management system. This needs to be determined and compared with requirements to look for areas of deficiency. Having identified the areas and the deficiencies, the task to strengthen them becomes quite easy.

8) **Create an implementation plan:** The task at hand at this stage is to plan how the implementation exercise should be carried out, who are the people who should be assigned this responsibility and finally how the system requirements established and documented should be put into action.

9) **Provide training:** The ISO appears to be documentation dependent but is actually people dependent. This means the people ought to understand the standard, its requirements, the organization's plans and the management's directions to effectively function towards the QMS. The people therefore need to be suitably oriented and trained.

10) **Decide the method of supplier approval:** The most time consuming task is the listing of existing suppliers, their assessment and approval. This requirement however is essential for the satisfactory functioning of the QMS. But, before embarking on this task it is necessary to decide regarding the method of assessment and approval of their performance.

11) **Decide upon the method of incoming product inspection:** Deciding upon the inspection of the purchased product, for ensuring its quality is the next task, wherein the method of verification and the acceptance criteria need to be specified. After these are decided it is also necessary to communicate this to the suppliers so that they become aware of the requirements and are able to meet them before effecting supplies. The method of communicating these requirements to the suppliers should therefore be decided.

12) **Decide upon the scope & exclusions:** The scope refers to the coverage of the QMS with regard to the activities of the organization. Unless there is clarity in the scope of coverage it would lead to confusion and lack of coordinated effort. The exclusions are necessary to know which parts of the standard are not applicable to the activities of the organization.

13) **Identify, list & sequence the processes:** The organization needs to be divided into linked processes which could be running in series in certain areas and in parallel in other areas. These processes of the organization should be identified, named and their sequence put into a flowchart.

14) **Define processes and their interrelationships:** This is an absolutely new requirement and the basis of the new standard's philosophy. It requires the system and its people to switch over from the traditional FUNCTIONAL approach to the PROCESS approach. (Functional Approach has already, been explained earlier in chapter 5). Do not however act in haste. It is really not possible to merely fragment existing functions and then integrate them to get processes. If done in this way, it would result in dislocations and confusion leading to organizational failure.

You cannot tell people that overnight their roles have changed the next day onwards the same jobs that they have done for so long successfully have to be done differently as their earlier method, though result producing is not-good-enough and requires a change. People will not only, disbelieve you but laugh at your ideas. Attempt gradual re-orientation which requires an attitudinal change. Results will be slow, do not despair.

Plan thoroughly, before attempting any change. Explain this concept in full detail to people. Only then attempt to train them. When they understand they will be able to give-up their traditional narrow functional role and perform on a wider multi-functional level.

When the functional structure of the organization is dismantled, you would have the same people using different processes at different times, depending on requirements. Thus for instance, in the purchasing process they would not only be responsible for buying and making the product available but also for inspecting it, storing and handing over to the next user process. In-fact there would be situations where a person uses one process in the morning and a different one later in the day. In situations like these it would be difficult to draw an organization chart with clear-cut lines of control and hence the traditional organization chart around which your organizations have been built, will need to be re-looked at.

15) **Classify the processes:** All processes do not have equal importance. Some processes are more important than others due to the impact they have on the organization. These processes are normally the ones, which are essential to the organization's success and help the organization achieve its goals and objectives. They are normally called KEY or CORE processes. All other processes of the organization are called SUPPORTING or OTHER processes.

16) **Flatten the hierarchy:** The adoption of the process approach means having a flatter organization with lesser hierarchy, in place of the traditional pyramidal organization based on the functional approach. One of the key elements of process approach is this flattening of the hierarchy whereby managers instead of managing *people* begin to manage *processes*. The role of managers shifts from controlling people to contributing to the team effort. Thus rather than describing functional jobs, the approach requires describing people skills and how they can contribute to the team. The organization would have to then select people based on their skills and experience to use them wherever required and keep them in pockets or centers of skills, which remain available to all processes.

17) **Analyze key or core Processes:** It is necessary for an organization to analyze each of the 'Key or Core' macro processes vital to the organization's business

activity and then break-it into its respective micro processes. Each of these micro processes should then be put into a Flowchart.

18) **Draft the quality policy:** The quality policy is the top management statement that sets a direction for the organization. The QMS is designed and created to fulfill this. It may be drafted by anyone on behalf of the top management but should ultimately belong to the top management. It should therefore be endorsed by the Head of the organization under his own signature with date.

19) **Draft the quality objectives:** The quality objectives of the organization, in measurable terms and in-line with the primary goals, should be drafted by the person or team assigned with this task. There should also be some self-determined target dates by which time the organization would prefer to achieve these objectives. The objectives should be established not only for the entire organization as a whole but also for the various levels within, so that the levels also have more well-defined objectives, relevant to their area of work.

20) **Finalize the quality policy and the quality objectives:** The finalization of the quality policy, should be done by the top management since this is ultimately their policy. The draft quality objectives can then be discussed, debated and finalized in a meeting with the top management.

21) **Communicate the quality policy:** The most common methods of communicating the quality policy that are being practiced are as follows:

a) Printing it in the form of pocket cards, on organization brochures, on the first page of the organizations diary, on the reverse of identity cards, on the reverse of visiting cards, on pay slips, etc.,

b) Putting up big painted boards in the premises at prominent locations,

c) Displaying it in each room or area as posters or wall hangings,

d) Repeating it daily as an oath, at-least once, in a group or groups, and

e) Training people on the policy and its meaning and significance.

22) **Select suppliers and start monitoring them:** The existing suppliers assessment procedure has already been finalized. The organization should now begin to start monitoring them for assessing their performance. This would help identify and if necessary weed-out bad or indifferent suppliers.

23) **Prepare the quality plans:** The quality plans should be prepared so that every individual in the organization is clear about, the way quality would be achieved through the entire sequence of processes.

24) **Prepare the required QMS documents:** The required level 1, level 2, level 3 and level 4 documents ought to be prepared in consultation with the

concerned people of the organization. In preparing these documents it should be endeavored to try and make the least number of changes to the existing procedures and documents yet achieving complete compliance with the requirements of the standard.

25) **Implement the QMS:** After the QMS has been established and documented the benefits of the entire exercise would accrue only if the QMS is implemented methodically and practised in right spirit. This is a slow process and no instant results ought to be expected over-night. Constant and relentless effort alone can lead to success.

26) **Monitor progress:** The QMS installed and in use would gradually get settled and people would begin to understand its benefits. All this should be monitored, as also areas of deficiency needing corrections and improvements.

27) **Take corrective actions:** The feedback received from the monitoring followed by corrective actions would lead to improvements and strengthen the QMS ultimately. Finally everyone would get convinced and realise that the system is dynamic and so, changes, which lead to improvements, would be welcomed without reservations.

28) **Get pre-assessment done by an outsider:** This check will verify the following:

a) Adequacy of your QMS manual, and
b) Conformance of the QMS, implemented and in use, to the requirements.

Ideally this is best done by an outsider, may be even your consultant. This eliminates possibility of bias and provides opportunity to learn from experience.

29) **Take corrective actions:** The feedback from this pre-assessment should form the basis for further improvements to build confidence that the documentation is adequate and the QMS is in complete compliance.

30) **Apply for assessment:** You may then apply to any certifying organization of your choice for certification. They will assess the QMS. In-fact any organization seeking QMS certification is at liberty to apply for multiple-certification, if required on account of market compulsions.

31) **Undergo assessment:** The assessment is an arranged audit of your documentation and QMS by the certifying agency, who based on the outcome of their assessment will decide to award you with a certificate or else advise you to correct non-conformances and apply once again for assessment.

32) **Maintain the system:** The battle starts with certification. Maintaining the QMS without compromising and not allowing a downslide is the real battle. Its real reward besides the prestige and recognition is the strengthening, improvement and the growth of your organization.

33) **Practise continual improvement:** The QMS that has been designed, established and is being maintained is basically a framework on which the organization has to progress. This progress can only come from building-in continual improvement into the system. Certification is just the beginning and merely confirms that the organization has a system for the management of quality. The organization must take-off from here to reach greater heights.

ISO

eighteen

Auditing the Quality Management System

1. QUALITY AUDIT

A quality audit is a systematic, independent and documented process of examining any activity of an organization based on objective evidence, to determine,

(i) The extent to which quality activities and related results comply with the planned arrangements,

(ii) The extent to which these arrangements have been implemented effectively, and

(iii) Whether these arrangements are suitable to achieve the quality objectives.

2. ADEQUACY AUDIT VS. COMPLIANCE AUDIT

Adequacy audit is the process of comparing the 'QMS manual' against 'the requirements of ISO 9001:2000' to ensure that the manual has suitably and sufficiently addressed all the requirements of the standard and meets each of these requirements in full.

In carrying out this audit the standard is read clause by clause and it is ensured that the organization's manual contains all requirements of the clauses. This being a methodical comparison of the standard and the manual, it is best for the organization to number and sequence the QMS manual exactly as the standard, to ensure a one-to-one comparison between the standard and the manual. Thus co-relation becomes easy.

Remember that, unless the 'QMS Manual' passes an adequacy audit no certifying agency will proceed further.

Compliance audit on the other hand is the process of checking whether the organization has implemented what they haves stated and whether the people are doing what the documents had asked them to do.

3. TYPES OF AUDIT

a) **First party audit or self-audit or internal audit** - Carried out by people of the organization or on behalf of the organization itself to examine its own QMS.

b) **Second party audit or audit by customers or audit on or external audit** - carried out by the Customer on the organization or by the organization on the suppliers to examine the quality of the auditor's supplier.

c) **Third party audit or independent agency audit or external audit**-carried out by an external independent agency to assess compliance, usually for the purpose of certification.

We are more interested in setting the organization's own QMS in order, and so shall concentrate on the internal audit only.

4. INTERNAL AUDIT

Internal Audit acts as the organizations eyes and ears to gather feedback for correction and improvement. Normally an audit should have a positive approach with the objective of 'Finding Facts rather than Faults'. However in the case of internal audit by the organization where the primary goal is 'Correction and Improvement' the more the faults found the more the corrections and the greater the compliance. Hence, a marginal element of fault finding, would do more good than harm. These audits must be conducted regularly in accordance with the audit plan. Any deviations from the plan, if made as a special case consciously with proper justification and approvals, are also acceptable. Normally the audits must be carried out as per plan and schedules prepared each time for the audit.

4.1 Requirements for Internal Audit

a, Plan The audit plan is a formal document, which covers every area, process and department for the audit activity. It is normally prepared for a full year and specifies the following:

(i) The area, process or department to be audited

(ii) The frequency of the audit, preferably giving the month in which the area, process or department will be audited. As a good practice every area, process or department ought to be audited at-least once every year.

(iii) The qualification of the auditors. The standard requires they should be trained suitably.

(iv) The procedure to be followed. This could state that the audit be more stringent if more number of non-conformances are detected, with more time being given to the audit.

(v) The method of reporting the audit findings.

b. Timing The best time to audit is when people are at their busiest and tempted to take short cuts or make mistakes. However the convenience of the auditee is essential and their readiness and concurrence should be determined before proceeding on an audit.

If during an internal audit everything is found to be in order, well then it is a 'win - win situation' for the auditee as well as the organization.

c. Schedule The audit schedule is a document that gives details of the area, process or department to be audited during the scheduled audit. It also specifies the following:

(i) The dates of the audit,

(ii) The names of the auditor and the corresponding auditee area, process or department, and

(iii) The provision for acceptance of the scheduled audit by each auditor and auditee in token of accepting convenience and readiness for the audit on the scheduled date.

d. Internal Auditors Internal auditors are people from within the organization who have been trained to conduct audits. This training can be done by the organization itself if the expertise exists within and there can be more than one auditor per department. The most important precaution to be taken is to ensure that people do not audit their own work (because that would make them biased). They must be taught to treat an audit as a fact finding exercise and so should do a professional job.

e. Checklist Checklists are a methodical way of ensuring that all necessary areas are audited and right questions asked. A checklist is therefore a useful tool. However the auditors should adopt a flexible approach and use their own judgment to deviate, if necessary.

5. AUDITING YOUR OWN QMS

In order to assist the readers in this exercise the entire standard has been converted into a series of questions, which would help you determine and assess:

1) Conformance of the QMS, and
2) Objective evidence for proving conformance.

Just answering the "Audit questions for conformance" would help you determine the extent of implementation. After obtaining the answers in the form of 'YES or NO", all those requirements for which the answer is either, NO or even a partial YES, need to be strengthened and supported. Also the results of this audit over a period of time can be used to assess the maturity level of the organization. Therefore, do not discourage people from finding faults, in-fact encourage them to develop skill and be critical.

Answers to the "Audit questions for objective evidence" would determine, the organization's list of objective evidence for each of the requirement. This list once generated for all requirements would give you the complete and comprehensive list of, "Objective evidence needed by your QMS". You would have all four levels of documents figuring in this list of evidences.

TABLE 15

List of Audit Questions and Objective Evidences

Clause Number (of ISO 9001: 2000)	**Requirement**	**Audit Questions for determining and assessing**	
		Conformance	Objective Evidence (A few obvious documents that can be used as objective evidence have been listed against a few clauses, but the list specific to their needs must actually be prepared by the organization itself)
4	Quality Management System	[title only]	

4.1	General requirements	1. Is the QMS established, documented and implemented? 2. Is the QMS maintained as per the requirements of this standard? 3. Is the QMS being continually improved for its effectiveness? 4. Are the processes needed for the QMS along with their application in the organization identified? 5. Are the sequence and interaction of the identified processes determined? 6. Are the criteria and methods needed for ensuring effectiveness of the operation and control of the identified processes determined? 7. Is the availability of resources and information needed for supporting the operation and monitoring of these processes ensured? 8. Are these processes monitored, measured and analyzed? 9. Are the actions necessary to achieve planned results and continual improvement of these processes implemented? 10. Are these processes managed by the organization in line with the requirements of the standard? 11. Are any processes that effect product conformity with requirements out-sourced?	1. The QMS documentation 2. List of processes, with their sequence, interaction & application in the organization 3. List of outsourced processes 4. Criteria and methods for operation and control of processes 5. List of resources required and information necessary for the operation and monitoring of processes

		12. Are the out-sourced processes controlled? 13. Are the required controls on the out-sourced processes identified within the QMS?	
4.2	Documentation requirements	[title only]	
4.2.1	General	1. Are the quality policy and quality objectives statement documented? 2. Is the QMS manual documented? 3. Are the 6 mandatory procedures required by this standard established, documented, implemented and maintained? 4. Does the QMS documentation include the documents required for ensuring effective planning, operation and control of the processes? 5. Are the records required by this standard maintained?	1. Documented statements of the quality policy and quality objectives. 2. QMS manual document. 3. The 6 mandatory procedures in documented form. 4. Documents relating to planning, operation and control of the processes under the QMS. 5. Records.
4.2.2	Quality manual	1. Is the QMS manual established and is it being maintained? 2. Does the Manual include the following: a) The scope of the QMS? b) Details and justification of any exclusions? c) The documented procedures established for the QMS or are in reference to them?	1. The QMS Manual.

		d) A description of the interactions between the processes of the QMS?	
4.2.3	Control of documents	1. Are the documents required by the QMS controlled? 2. Are records also treated as documents (of a special type) within the QMS? 3. Is the procedure for defining the controls needed on documents established? 4. Does the procedure control approval for adequacy prior to issue? 5. Does the procedure control review, updating and re-approval? 6. Do the controls of the procedure ensure that changes and the current revision status of documents are identified? 7. Do the controls of the procedure ensure that the relevant versions of applicable documents are available at point of use? 8. Do the controls of the procedure ensure that documents remain legible and are readily identifiable? 9. Do the controls of the procedure ensure that documents of external origin are identified and their distribution controlled?	1. Document control related records. 2. Records control procedure related records. 3. Availibility of documented procedure(s) for document control. 4. Record for document approval prior to issue. 5. Record for review, updation and re-approval for changed documents. 6. The revision status marking on any document. 7. Issue to and availability of relevant documents at the place of use. 8. Identification numbering on every document. 9. List of external origin documents taken under control and availability of the relevant documents as controlled copies. 10. Lack of availability of current documents at place of use. 11. Obsolete documents file with all obsolete documents retained marked as 'Obsolete'.

		10. Do the controls of the procedure prevent unintended use of obsolete documents? 11. Do the controls of the procedure apply suitable identification to the obsolete documents if they are retained for any purpose?	
4.2.4	Control of records	1. Are records required by the QMS for effective operations established? 2. Are these records sufficient for providing evidence of effective operations of the QMS? 3. Are these records maintained to provide evidence of conformity to requirements? 4. Do these records provide evidence of actual effectiveness in the operation of the QMS? 5. Do the records remain legible? 6. Do the records remain readily identifiable? 7. Do the records remain easily retrievable? 8. Is the procedure established, documented, implemented and maintained to define the controls needed for the 'control of records'? 9. Does this procedure for control of records define the method for identification, storage, protection, retrieval, retention time and disposition of records?	1. QMS records. 2. Legibility of all records being maintained. 3. Numbering on the documents for identification. 4. Availability of the documented procedure(s) for control of records. 5. Determining whether the procedure(s) define the methods of identification, storage, protection, retrieval, retention time and disposition.

5	Management responsibility	[title only]	
5.1	Management commitment	1. Can the top management provide evidence of its commitment to the development and implementation of the QMS? 2. Can the top management provide evidence of its commitment to the continual improvement of the effectiveness of the QMS? 3. Has the top management established, implemented and maintained a method for communicating to the organization the importance of meeting the customer as well as the statutory and regulatory requirements? 4. Has the top management established their quality policy? 5. Has the top management ensured that the quality objectives have been established? 6. Does the top management conduct management reviews? 7. Does the top management ensure the availability of necessary resources?	1. Evidence of top management involvement and support to the QMS. 2. Evidence of top management support and encouragement to continual improvement. 3. Procedure for internal communication. 4. Availability of the quality policy. 5. Availibility of the quality objectives. 6. Management review meeting minutes. 7. List of needed resources and their availability 8. Follow-up document for determining changing resource requirements.

5.2	Customer focus	1. Can the organization provide evidence to demonstrate that it is customer focused? 2. Does the top management ensure that customer requirements are determined? 3. Does the top management ensure that the customer requirements, which have been determined, are met? 4. Does the top management aim at enhancing customer satisfaction?	1. Reference to customer focus in the quality policy and quality objectives. 2. The records of the determination of customer requirements. 3. The procedure for meeting customer requirements.
5.3	Quality policy	1. Has the top management ensured that the quality policy is appropriate to the purpose of the organization? 2. Does the quality policy include a commitment to comply with the requirements? 3. Does the quality policy include a commitment to continually improve the effectiveness of the QMS? 4. Does the quality policy provide a framework for establishing and reviewing quality objectives? 5. Is the quality policy communicated within the organization? 6. Is the quality policy understood by the people within the organization? 7. Is the quality policy reviewed for its continuing suitability? 8. Does the top management provide for maintaining the quality policy dynamic and changeable based on the feedback of the review?	

5.4	Planning	[title only]	
5.4.1	Quality objectives	1. Has the top management ensured that the quality objectives are established? 2. Do the quality objectives include those needed to meet the product requirements? 3. Are the quality objectives established at relevant functions and levels within the organization? 4. Are the established quality objectives measurable? 5. Are the established quality objectives consistent with the quality policy?	
5.4.2	Quality management system planning	1. Has the top management ensured that, planning of the QMS is carried out in order to meet the requirements given in clause 4.1? 2. Does the planning ensure that the requirements of the quality objectives are met? 3. Does the planning ensure that the integrity of the QMS is maintained even when changes to the QMS are planned and implemented?	
5.5	Responsibility, authority & communication	[title only]	
5.5.1	Responsibility and authority	1. Has the top management ensured that the responsibility and authority have been defined? 2. Are the responsibilities communicated within the organization?	

5.5.2	Management representative	1. Has the top management appointed a Management Representative (MR)? 2. Is the MR a member of the management of the organization? 3. Does the MR's responsibility and authority also include the following: a) Ensuring the processes needed for the QMS are established, implemented and maintained? b) Reporting to the top management on the performance of the QMS? c) Reporting to the top management on any need for improvement to the QMS? d) Ensuring the promotion of awareness of customer requirements throughout the organization? 4. Has anyone in the organization been made responsible for liaison with external parties on matters relating to the QMS?	
5.5.3	Internal communication	1. Has the top management ensured that appropriate communication processes have been established within the organization? 2. Is the top management ensuring that communication regarding the effectiveness of the QMS is taking place within the organization? 3. Is the top management ensuring that communication is taking place within the organization by using the processes established?	
5.6	Management review	[title only]	

5.6.1	General	1. Does the top management review the organization's QMS at planned intervals? 2. Does this review ensure the continuing suitability, adequacy and effectiveness of the QMS? 3. Does this review assess opportunities for improvement? 4. Does this review assess the need for change to the QMS? 5. Does this review assess the need for change to the quality policy and the quality objectives? 6. Are records of the management reviews maintained?	
5.6.2	Review inputs	1. Do the inputs to the management reviews include information on the following: a) Results of external or internal audits? b) Customer feedback? c) Process performance? d) Product conformity? e) Status of corrective actions? f) Status of preventive actions? g) Follow-up actions from previous audits? h) Changes that could affect the QMS? i) Recommendations for improvements?	
5.6.3	Review outputs	1. Do the outputs from the management reviews include decisions and actions on the following: a) Improvement of the effectiveness of the QMS and its processes? b) Improvement of product as per customer requirements? c) Resources needed?	
6	Resource management	[title only]	

6.1	Provision of resources	1. Has the organization determined the resources needed to implement and maintain the QMS? 2. Has the organization determined the resources needed to continually improve the effectiveness of the QMS? 3. Has the organization determined the resources needed to enhance customer satisfaction by meeting customer requirements? 4. Has the organization provided these resources?	
6.2	Human resources	[title only]	
6.2.1	General	1. Are those personnel who are performing work affecting product quality competent, based on their education, training, skill and experience?	
6.2.2	Competence, awareness and training	1. Has the organization determined the necessary competence for personnel performing work affecting product quality? 2. Has the organization provided necessary training or taken any other actions necessary to fulfill this need for competence? 3. Does the organization evaluate the effectiveness of the training or other actions to ensure their suitability and adequacy? 4. Does the organization ensure that its people are aware of the relevance and importance of their work? 5. Does the organization ensure that its people are aware on how they contribute to the achievement of the quality objectives? 6. Does the organization maintain appropriate records of education, training, skills and experience for personnel performing work affecting product quality?	

6.3	Infrastructure	1. Has the organization determined, provided and maintained the infrastructure needed to achieve product conformity to requirements? 2. In determining the infrastructure have the following been included: a) Building, workspace and associated utilities? b) Process Equipment (both hardware and software)? c) Supporting services (such as transport or communication)?	
6.4	Work environment	1. Has the organization determined, the work environment needed to achieve conformity of the product to requirements? 2. Does the organization provide the determined work environment? 3. Does the provided work environment, help in achieving product conformity to requirements?	
7	Product realization	[title only]	
7.1	Planning for product realization	1. Has the organization planned and developed the processes needed for product realization? 2. Is the planning of product realization consistent with the requirements of other processes of the QMS? 3. Through planning, is the organization determining the following: a) The quality objectives? b) The requirements for the product? c) The need to establish processes and documents? d) The need to provide resources specific to the product? e) The required verification, validation, monitoring, inspection and test activities specific to the product? f) The criteria for product acceptance?	

		g) The records needed to provide evidence that the product realization processes meet requirements? h) The records needed to provide evidence that the resulting product from the product realization processes meets requirements?	
7.2	Customer related processes	[title only]	
7.2.1	Determination of requirements related to the product	1. Has the organization determined the requirements specified by the customer? 2. Do the customer requirements determined by the organization also include the requirements for delivery and post delivery activities? 3. Has the organization determined the requirements not stated by the customer but necessary for specified or intended use, where ever known? 4. Has the organization determined the statutory and regulatory requirements related to the product? 5. Has the organization determined any other additional requirements felt necessary by the organization itself?	

7.2.2	Review of requirements related to the product	1. Does the organization review requirements related to the product? 2. Is this review of the requirements conducted prior to the organization committing to supply a product to a customer? 3. Does this review, conducted prior to committing to supply a product to a customer, cover submission of tenders, acceptance of contracts or orders, acceptance of changes to contracts or orders, etc? 4. Does this review ensure that product requirements are defined? 5. Does this review ensure that contracts or orders differing from those previously expressed and accepted are resolved? 6. Does this review ensure that only those orders are accepted for which the organization has the ability to meet the defined requirements? 7. Are the records of the results of review maintained? 8. Are the records of the actions arising out from the reviews maintained? 9. Does the organization define the requirements on its own where the customer does not provide documented statement of requirements? 10. Does the organization confirm these requirements from the customer prior to acceptance of the order? 11. Does the organization ensure that where the product requirements are changed the relevant documents are amended? 12. Does the organization ensure that where product requirements are changed the concerned personnel are made aware of the changed requirements?	

7.2.3	Customer communication	1. Has the organization determined the effective arrangements for communicating with the customer? 2. Has the organization effectively implemented these arrangements determined by it for communicating with the customer? 3. Does the communication with the customer occur in relation to: a) Product information? b) Enquiries, contracts or order handling, including amendments? c) Customer feedback, including customer complaints?	
7.3	Design and development	[title only]	
7.3.1	Design and development planning	1. Does the organization plan the design and development of the product? 2. Does the organization control the design and development of the product? 3. Does the organization determine the design and development stages during the planning, for the product? 4. Does the organization determine the review, verification and validation appropriate for each design and development stage during the planning, for the product? 5. Does the organization determine the responsibility and authority for design and development during the planning for the product? 6. Does the organization manage the interfaces between the different groups involved in design and development of the product? 7. Does the organization ensure through planning, that effective communication takes place during the design and development of the product?	

		8. Does the organization ensure that responsibility for the design and development of the product is clearly assigned? 9. Does the organization ensure that the planning output is appropriately updated as the design and development progresses?	
7.3.2	Design and development inputs	1. Does the organization determine the inputs relating to the product requirements? 2. Are the records relating to the determined input requirements maintained? 3. Are the functional and performance requirements of the product a part of the input requirements determined? 4. Are the applicable statutory and regulatory requirements of the product a part of the input requirements? 5. Is the information derived from previous similar designs where ever applicable used as a base to determine the input requirements of the product? 6. Are other requirements felt essential for the product design and development a part of the input requirements? 7. Are the determined inputs reviewed for adequacy? 8. Is it ensured that the requirements are complete, unambiguous and not in conflict with each other?	
7.3.3	Design and development outputs	1. Are the outputs of design and development provided in a form that enables verification against the design and development inputs? 2. Are the outputs of design and development approved prior to release? 3. Is it ensured that design and development outputs meet the input requirements of design development? 4. Is it ensured that design and development outputs provide appropriate information for purchasing, production and for servicing provision?	

		5. Is it ensured that design and development outputs contain or give reference to product acceptance criteria? 6. Is it ensured that the design and development outputs specify the characteristics of the product that are essential for its safe and proper use?	
7.3.4	Design and development review	1. Is a systematic review of design and development performed at suitable stages? 2. Is this review performed in accordance with planned arrangements? 3. Does the review at various stages evaluate the ability of the results of design and development to meet requirements? 4. Does the review at various stages identify any problems in the design and development that prevent it from meeting requirements? 5. Does the review at various stages also propose necessary corrective actions in the design and development? 6. Do the participants in such reviews include representatives of functions concerned with the design and development stages? 7. Are records of the results of design and development reviews maintained? 8. Are records of all necessary corrective actions on the design and development based on the reviews maintained?	
7.3.5	Design and development verification	1. Is the verification of the design and development planned? 2. Is the verification of the design and development performed as per the planned arrangements? 3. Does this planned verification of the design and development ensure that the design and development outputs meet the design and development input requirements?	

		4. Are records of the results of design and development verification maintained? 5. Are records of any necessary actions on the design and development based on the verification maintained?	
7.3.6	Design and development validation	1. Is the validation of the design and development planned? 2. Is the validation of the design and development performed as per the planned arrangements? 3. Does this planned validation of the design and development ensure that the resulting product is capable of meeting the requirements for the specified application or intended use. 4. If this validation is not done is because the specified application or intended use, are not known? 5. Is the validation of the design and development completed prior to delivery or implementation of the product release? 6. If this validation is not completed prior to delivery of service or release of the product, is it because, it is not practical to do so? 7. Are records of the results of design and development validation maintained? 8. Are records of all actions on the design and development based on the validation, maintained?	
7.3.7	Control of design and development changes	1. Are the design and development changes identified? 2. Are records of these identified design and development changes maintained? 3. Are these design and development changes reviewed, verified and validated as appropriate? 4. Are the design and development changes approved before implementation?	

		5. Does the review of the design and development changes include evaluation of the effect of the changes on the constituent parts?	
7.4	Purchasing	[title only]	
7.4.1	Purchasing process	1. Does the organization ensure that the purchased product conforms to the specified purchase requirements? 2. Is it ensured that the type and extent of controls applied to suppliers, is in proportion to the impact the product has on the final product? 3. Is it ensured that the type and extent of controls applied to the purchased product are in proportion to their effect on subsequent product realization or the final product? 4. Does the organization select and evaluate suppliers? 5. Is selection and evaluation of suppliers based on their ability to supply products in accordance with the organization's own requirements? 6. Are the criteria for selection, evaluation and re-evaluation established? 7. Are records of the results of evaluation of suppliers maintained? 8. Are records of any necessary action arising from the evaluation maintained?	
7.4.2	Purchasing information	1. Does the purchasing information describe the product to be purchased? 2. Does this purchase information include where appropriate: a) Requirements for approval of product, procedures, processes and equipment? b) Requirements for qualification of personnel? c) Quality management system requirements?	

		3. Does the organization ensure the adequacy of specified purchase requirements? 4. Is this adequacy of the requirements ensured prior to communication to the supplier?	
7.4.3	Verification of purchased product	1. Has the organization established the inspection or other activities necessary for ensuring that the purchased products meet specified purchase requirements? 2. Has the organization implemented the inspection or other activities established as necessary for ensuring that the purchased products meet specified purchase requirements? 3. Does the organization or its customers intend to perform any type of verification at the supplier's premises? 4. When any type of verification at the supplier's premises is intended does the organization state the intended verification arrangements in the purchase information? 5. When any type of verification at the supplier's premises is intended does the organization state in the purchase information the method of product release based on the verification?	
7.5	Production and service provision	[title only]	
7.5.1	Control of production and service provision	1. Does the organization plan its production and service provision? 2. Does the organization carry out its production and service provision as per plan? 3. Does the organization carry out its production and service provision under controlled conditions? 4. Do the controlled conditions include as applicable: a) The availability of information that describes the characteristics of the product? b) The availability of work instructions, as necessary?	

		c) The use of suitable equipment? d) The availability and use of monitoring and measuring devices? e) The implementation of monitoring and measurement? f) The implementation of release, delivery and post-delivery activities?	
7.5.2	Verification of production and service provision	1. Does the organization validate any process for production and servicing provision? 2. Are the processes, for production and servicing provision where the resulting output cannot be verified by subsequent monitoring or measurement, the ones that are validated? 3. Do these processes that are validated also include processes where deficiencies become apparent only after the product is in use or the service has been delivered? 4. Does the validation demonstrate the ability of these processes to achieve planned results? 5. Has the organization established arrangements for these processes? 6. Do these arrangements established include: a) Defined criteria for review and approval of the processes b) Approval of equipment and qualification of personnel c) Use of specific methods and procedures d) Requirements for records e) Revalidation	

7.5.3	Identification and traceability	1. Does the organization where ever appropriate identify 'the product' by suitable means? 2. Is this identification of the product available throughout the product realization process? 3. Does the organization identify 'the status of the product' within the product realization process? 4. Is this identification of the product status based on the monitoring and measurement requirements? 5. Does the organization control the unique identification of the product where traceability is the requirement? 6. Where traceability is a requirement, does the organization record the unique identification of the product? 7. In the organization's industry sectors, is configuration management a means by which identification and traceability are maintained? 8. Does the organization use configuration management as a means to maintain identification and traceability?	
7.5.4	Customer property	1. Does the organization exercise care with customer property while it is under the organization's control? 2. Does the organization exercise care with customer property while it is being used by the organization? 3. Does the organization identify, protect and safeguard customer property provided for use? 4. Does the organization identify, protect and safeguard customer property provided for incorporation into the product? 5. If any customer property is lost, damaged or otherwise found to be unsuitable for use, is this reported to the customer.	

		6. Are records maintained for customer property, especially for property lost, damaged or otherwise found to be unsuitable for use? 7. Is the intellectual property of the customer treated as Customer property? 8. Are all the above mentioned controls also exercised on intellectual property?	
7.5.5	Preservation of product	1. Does the organization preserve the conformity of product during internal processing? 2. Does the organization preserve the conformity of product during delivery to the intended destination? 3. Does this preservation include identification, handling, packaging, storage and protection? 4. Does the organization also apply preservation to the constituent parts of a product?	

7.6	Control of monitoring and measuring devices	1. Does the organization determine the monitoring and measurement to be undertaken? 2. Does the organization determine the monitoring and measuring devices needed? 3. Are these monitoring and measuring devices that have been found necessary capable of providing evidence of conformity of product to determined requirements? 4. Does the organization establish the processes needed to ensure that monitoring and measurement can be carried out? 5. Does the organization ensure that monitoring and measurement are actually carried out? 6. Does the organization ensure that monitoring and measurement is done in a manner that is consistent with the monitoring and measurement requirements? 7. To ensure valid results, are measuring equipment: a) Calibrated or verified at specified intervals, or prior to use, against measurement standards traceable to national or international level? b) Used only after recording the basis of calibration or verification in cases where no such standards exist? c) Adjusted or re-adjusted as necessary? d) Identified to enable the calibration status to be determined? e) Safeguarded from adjustments that would invalidate the measurement result? f) Protected from damage and deterioration during handling, maintenance and storage?	

7.6	Control of monitoring and measuring devices (continued ---)	8. Does the organization assess the validity of the results measured previously, when the equipment is found not conforming to requirements? 9. Does the organization record the validity of the results measured previously, based on assessment, when the equipment is found not conforming to requirements? 10. Does the organization take appropriate action on the equipment when it is found not conforming to requirements? 11. Does the organization take appropriate action on any product affected when the equipment is found not conforming to requirements? 12. Does the organization maintain records of the results of calibration of monitoring and measuring devices? 13. Does the organization maintain records of the results of verification of monitoring and measuring devices? 14. Is computer software used in the monitoring and measurement of specified requirements? 15. Is the ability of this computer software to satisfy the intended application confirmed when it is used in the monitoring and measurement of specified requirements? 16. Is this confirmation of the ability of the software undertaken prior to initial use? 17.Is this ability of the software reconfirmed as necessary? 18. Does the organization use ISO 10012-1 and ISO 10012-2 for guidance?	
8	Measurement, analysis and improvement	[title only]	

8.1	General	1. Does the organization plan the monitoring, measurement, analysis and improvement processes needed by the organization? 2. Does the organization implement the monitoring, measurement, analysis and improvement processes needed as per the plans? 3. Are these processes, which are used for the monitoring, measurement, analysis and improvement needed to demonstrate conformity of the product? 4. Are these processes, which are used for the monitoring, measurement, analysis and improvement needed to ensure conformity of the QMS? 5. Are these processes, which are used for the monitoring, measurement, analysis and improvement needed to continually improve the effectiveness of the QMS? 6. Does this monitoring, measurement, analysis and improvement include determination of methods that can be applied to these processes? 7. Do the processes of monitoring, measurement, analysis and improvement including the use of statistical techniques giving the extent of their use?	
8.2	Monitoring and measurement	[title only]	
8.2.1	Customer satisfaction	1. Does the organization assess and monitor customer satisfaction? 2. Does this customer satisfaction endeavor to assess whether the customers perceive, that the organization has succeeded in meeting their requirements? 3. Does the organization monitor information relating to customer perception as one of the measurements of the performance of the QMS?	

		4. Has the organization defined the methods that shall be applied for obtaining this information? 5. Has the organization determined the methods of using this obtained information regarding customer satisfaction?	
8.2.2	Internal audit	1. Does the organization plan their internal audits? 2. Does the organization conduct the internal audits at planned intervals? 3. Do these internal audits try to determine whether the QMS: a) Conforms to planned arrangements? b) Conforms to the requirements of this International Standard? c) Conforms to those QMS requirements that have been established by the organization? d) Has it been effectively implemented? e) Is it being effectively maintained? 4. Are the audit programs planned? 5. Is this planning done taking into consideration the status and importance of the processes and areas to be audited? 6. Are the results of previous audits also taken into account during the planning of the audit? 7. Are the audit criteria, scope, frequency and method of internal audit defined? 8. Does the selection of auditors and conduct of audits ensure objectivity and impartiality of the audit process? 9. Is it ensured that auditors do not audit their own work? 10. Does the organization have a documented procedure for internal audit?	

8.2.2	Internal audit (Continued ---)	13. Has the responsibility, for ensuring of actions without undue delay, to eliminate detected non-conformities and their causes, in the area being audited, been given to the management responsible for that area? 14. Are actions taken without undue delay to eliminate detected non-conformities and their causes? 15. Do the follow-up activities to the audit include the verification of the actions taken and the reporting of verification results? 16. Does the organization use ISO 10011-1, ISO 10011-2 and ISO 10011-3 for guidance?	
8.2.3	Monitoring and measurement of processes	1. Does the organization apply suitable methods for monitoring and, where applicable, measurement of the QMS processes? 2. Do these methods demonstrate the ability of the processes to achieve planned results? 3. Whenever planned results are not achieved, are corrections made and corrective action taken as appropriate to ensure conformity of the product?	

8.2.4	Monitoring and measurement of product	1. Does the organization monitor and measure the characteristics of the product? 2. Is this monitoring and measurement done to verify that product requirements have been met? 3. Is the monitoring and measurement carried out at appropriate stages of the product realization process? 4. Is the monitoring and measurement carried out in accordance with the planned arrangements? 5. Is the evidence of conformity with the acceptance criteria maintained in the form of records? 6. Do these records indicate the person(s) authorizing release of product? 7. Is it ensured that product release and service delivery do not proceed till the planned arrangements have been satisfactorily completed? 8. Is this rule of ensuring product release only after planned arrangements have been satisfactorily completed always followed, unless otherwise approved by an appropriate authority, and where applicable, by the customer?	

8.3	Control of non-conforming product	1. Does the organization ensure that products which do not conform to product requirements are identified? 2. Does the organization ensure that products which do not conform to product requirements are controlled to prevent their unintended use or delivery? 3. Does the organization have a documented procedure for control of non-conforming product? 4. Are the controls and related responsibilities and authorities for dealing with non-conforming product defined in the documented procedure for control of non-conforming product? 5. Does the organization deal with non-conforming product by one or more of the following ways : a) By taking action to eliminate the detected non-conformity? b) By authorizing its use, release or acceptance under concession by an appropriate authority and where applicable by the customer? c) By taking action to preclude its original intended use or application? 6. Are records maintained detailing the nature of non- conformities and any actions taken consequently, including concessions obtained? 7. When non-conforming product is corrected is it subject to re-verification to demonstrate conformity to the requirements? 8. When non-conforming product is detected after delivery or use has started does the organization take action appropriate to the effects or potential effects of the non- conformity?	

8.4	Analysis of data	1. Does the organization determine, collect and analyze appropriate data to demonstrate the suitability and effectiveness of the QMS? 2. Does the organization determine, collect and analyze appropriate data to evaluate where continual improvement of the effectiveness of the QMS can be made? 3. Is it ensured that the data analyzed includes data generated as a result of monitoring and measurement and from other relevant sources? 4. Is it ensured that the analysis of data provides information relating to: a) Customer satisfaction? b) Conformity to product requirements? c) Characteristics and trends of processes and products including opportunities for preventive action? d) Suppliers data?	
8.5	Improvement	[title only]	
8.5.1	Continual improvement	1. Does the organization continually improve the effectiveness of the QMS? 2. Does the organization use the quality policy, quality objectives, audit results, analysis of data, corrective and preventive actions and management review as a means for continual improvement?	

8.5.2	Corrective action	1. Does the organization take action to eliminate the cause of non-conformities in order to prevent recurrence? 2. Are the corrective actions appropriate to the effects of the non-conformities encountered? 3. Has the organization established a documented procedure to define requirements for: a) Reviewing non-conformities (including customer complaints)? b) Determining the causes of non-conformities? c) Evaluating the need for action to ensure that non-conformities do not recur? d) Determining and implementing action needed? e) Recording of the results of action taken? f) Reviewing corrective action taken?	
8.5.3	Preventive action	1. Does the organization determine action to eliminate the causes of potential non- conformities in order to prevent their occurrence? 2. Are the preventive actions taken by the organization appropriate to the effects of the potential problems? 3. Has the organization established a documented procedure to define the requirements for: a) Determining potential non-conformities and their causes? b) Evaluating the need for action to prevent occurrence of non-conformities? c) Determining and implementing action needed? d) Recording of results of action taken? e) Reviewing preventive action taken?	

6. SELF-ASSESSMENT OF THE CONFORMANCE OF THE ESTABLISHED QMS

The following can be used as a tool for formally carrying out a self-verification of the conformance of the implemented QMS in relation to the requirements of the standard. For each question under each clause indicate the level of conformance and assess percentage of compliance to determine the extent of conformance

TABLE 16

Format for Self-assessment

Conformance assessment question for requirement under each clause of ISO 9001:2000	Level of Conformance				Score
	Full	Part	Nil	Not Applicable	

Enter the various questions for the requirements of the standard clause-wise in the first column and then verify and judge the level of compliance of the requirement within your established and implemented QMS. For each such question, indicate the level of conformance by entering the marks for the respective level. Allot 10 marks for full compliance against the requirement. Similarly allot 5 marks for part compliance and 0 marks for nil compliance. In case the requirements are not applicable for your system and has been indicated in the exclusions, allot 10 marks. The total score at the end of the exercise when compared to the maximum marks obtainable will give an estimate of the level of conformance of the QMS.

If your score is:

1) **More than 85%**: Most of your QMS conforms to ISO 9001:2000. However, you need to strengthen your weak areas but can still go ahead for the assessment. Use of ISO 9004 will help you.

2) **Between 70 to 85%**: Many of the areas of your QMS, conform to ISO 9001:2000, but a significant part does not. Therefore, you need to strengthen your weak areas and can only then go ahead for the assessment. Use of ISO 9004:2000 will help you but you must also take more help of your consultant.

3) Between 55 to 70%: Most of your QMS does not conform to ISO 9001:2000 and a lot of work still needs to be done. You must seek the help of your consultant and work seriously towards compliance.

4) Less than 55%: Your QMS is practically non-existent. You need to put in whole- hearted effort, but your WILL being there, you cannot but succeed.

Section

V

Sample Documents

[I_S_O]

nineteen

QMS Manual of XYZ Corporation (As Per ISO 9001: 2000)

****

Plot No. 11, Street No. 08,

ABC Chambers, Hyderabad,

India

Ph. +91-40-110890

Fax. +91-40-290987

****

****

****

**

XYZ Co.	XYZ CORPORATION	Doc. No. XYZQMS – 4.2.3/P-01/I-XX/F-02
	QMS Manual	Rev. No. Nil
	Contents	Rev. Date. Nil

S.No	Document Number	Name of the Document	No. of Pages
1.	XYZQMS-4.2.3 /P-01/I-XX/F-01	Amendment Data Record	1
2.	**XYZQMS-1.**	**Profile of XYZ Corporation**	X
3.	**XYZQMS-2.**	**Mandatory Documents**	X
4.	XYZQMS-1.1	Quality Policy	X
5.	XYZQMS-1.2	Scope of the QMS and List of Exclusions	X
6.	XYZQMS-1.3	List of Outsourced Processes	X
7.	XYZQMS-1.4	Process Inter-relationship Diagram	X
8.	**XYZQMS-3.**	**Organizational Documents**	X
9.	XYZQMS-3.1	Control of the QMS Manual	1
10.	XYZQMS-3.2	Distribution List for QMS Documentation	X
11.	XYZQMS-3.3	Organization Chart	X
12.	XYZQMS-3.4	List classifying processes into Key & Supporting	X
13.	**XYZQMS-4.**	**Quality Management System**	1
14.	XYZQMS-4.1	General Requirements	2
-	-	Documentation Requirements	-
15.	XYZQMS-4.2.1	General	2
16.	XYZQMS-4.2.2	Manual	1
17.	XYZQMS-4.2.3	Control of Documents	2
18.	XYZQMS-4.2.4	Control of Records	1
		Readers to Kindly Note: All documents marked as "X" in "No. of Pages" column, have not been included in this sample manual and have to be prepared by organizations on their own, for their particular activity, based on their organizational policies and top management decisions.	

Issue No. 1	Issue Date: 29.09.2001	Page No. 1 of 3
Reviewed By:		Approved By:

XYZ Co.	XYZ CORPORATION	Doc. No. XYZQMS – 4.2.3/P-01/I-XX/F-02
	QMS Manual	Rev. No. Nil
	Contents	Rev. Date. Nil

S.No.	Document Number	Name of the Document	No. of Pages
19.	**XYZQMS-5.**	**Management Responsibility**	1
20.	XYZQMS-5.1	Management Commitment	1
21.	XYZQMS-5.2	Customer Focus	1
22.	XYZQMS-5.3	Quality Policy	1
-	-	Planning	-
23.	XYZQMS-5.4.1	Quality Objectives	1
24.	XYZQMS-5.4.2	QMS Planning	1
-	-	Responsibility, Authority &	-
		Communication	-
25.	XYZQMS-5.5.1	Responsibility & Authority	1
26.	XYZQMS-5.5.2	Management Representative	1
27.	XYZQMS-5.5.3	Internal Communication	1
-	-	Management Review	-
28.	XYZQMS-5.6.1	General	1
29.	XYZQMS-5.6.2	Review Inputs	1
30.	XYZQMS-5.6.3	Review Outputs	1
31.	**XYZQMS-6.**	**Management Responsibility**	1
32.	XYZQMS-6.1	Provision of Resources	1
-	-	Human Resources	-
33.	XYZQMS-6.2.1	General	1
34.	XYZQMS-6.2.2	Competence, Awareness & Training	1
35.	XYZQMS-6.3	Infrastructure	1
36.	XYZQMS-6.4	Work Environment	1
37.	**XYZQMS-7.**	**Product Realization**	1
38.	XYZQMS-7.1	Planning of Product Realization	1
-	-	Customer Related Processes	-
39.	XYZQMS-7.2.1	Determination of Requirements	1
-	-	related to the Product	-
40.	XYZQMS-7.2.2	Review of Requirements related to the Product	1
41.	XYZQMS-7.2.3	Customer Communication	1

Issue No. 1	Issue Date: 29.09.2001	Page No. 2 of 3
Reviewed By:		Approved By:

XYZ Co.	XYZ CORPORATION	Doc. No. XYZQMS – 4.2.3/P-01/I-XX/F-02
	QMS Manual	Rev. No. Nil
	Contents	Rev. Date. Nil

S.No.	Document Number	Name of the Document	No. of Pages
-	-	Design & Development	-
42.	XYZQMS-7.3.1	Design & Development Planning	1
43.	XYZQMS-7.3.2	Design & Development Inputs	1
44.	XYZQMS-7.3.3	Design & Development Outputs	1
45.	XYZQMS-7.3.4	Design & Development Review	1
46.	XYZQMS-7.3.5	Design & Development Verification	1
47.	XYZQMS-7.3.6	Design & Development Validation	1
48.	XYZQMS-7.3.7	Control of Design & Development	1
-	-	Changes Purchasing	-
49.	XYZQMS-7.4.1	Purchasing Process	1
50.	XYZQMS-7.4.2	Purchasing Information	1
51.	XYZQMS-7.4.3	Verification of Purchased Product	1
-	-	Production & Service Provision	-
52.	XYZQMS-7.5.1	Control of Production & Service Provision	1
53.	XYZQMS-7.5.2	Validation of Processes for Production & Service Provision	1
54.	XYZQMS-7.5.3	Identification & Traceability	1
55.	XYZQMS-7.5.4	Customer Property	1
56.	XYZQMS-7.5.5	Preservation of Product	1
57.	XYZQMS-7.6	Control of Monitoring & Measuring Devices	2
58.	**XYZQMS-8.**	**Measurement, Analysis & Improvement**	1
59.	XYZQMS-8.1	General	2
-	-	Monitoring & Measurement	-
60.	XYZQMS-8.2.1	Customer Satisfaction	1
61.	XYZQMS-8.2.2	Internal Audits	1
62.	XYZQMS-8.2.3	Monitoring & Measurement of Processes	1
63.	XYZQMS-8.2.4	Monitoring & Measurement of Product	1
64.	XYZQMS-8.3	Control of Non-conforming Product	1
65.	XYZQMS-8.4	Analysis of Data	1
-	-	Improvement	-
66.	XYZQMS-8.5.1	Continual Improvement	1
67.	XYZQMS-8.5.2	Corrective Action	1
68.	XYZQMS-8.5.3	Preventive Action	1

Issue No. 1	Issue Date: 29.09.2001	Page No. 3 of 3
Reviewed By:		Approved By:

<table>
<tr><td rowspan="3">XYZ Co.</td><td>XYZ CORPORATION</td><td>Doc. No. XYZQMS – 4.2.3/P-01/I-XX/F-01</td></tr>
<tr><td>QMS Manual</td><td>Rev. No. Nil</td></tr>
<tr><td>Amendment Data Record</td><td>Rev. Date. Nil</td></tr>
</table>

S.No.	Doc. No.	Doc. Name	Page No. Of Doc. Changed	Issue No / Issue Date	Rev. No. / Rev. Date	Nature of change / Amendment

Issue No. 1	Issue Date: 29.09.2001	Page No. 1 of 1
Reviewed By:		Approved By:

<table>
<tr><td rowspan="3">XYZ Co.</td><td>XYZ CORPORATION</td><td>Doc. No. XYZQMS – 3.1</td></tr>
<tr><td>Organizational Documents</td><td>Rev. No. Nil</td></tr>
<tr><td>Control of the QMS Manual</td><td>Rev. Date. Nil</td></tr>
</table>

This QMS manual has been prepared with the intention of documenting the Quality Management System at XYZ Corporation, for establishing, implementing and continually improving it, in line with the requirements of ISO 9001:2000.

The contents of this QMS Manual and all other related documents are the sole property of XYZ corporation and shall not be copied or reproduced, in part or whole by anyone whosoever, without the written permission of the Corporation.

XYZ Corporation may however make as many copies of this manual as required for its own use. These copies shall be used for distribution within the Corporation. Copies of the manual given to those individuals listed in the distribution list shall be controlled and updated. Uncontrolled copies if and when issued may or may not be updated.

All control copies shall be identified by rubber stamping the 'Control Copy No.___' in red color on each page, followed by the control copy number written by hand, again using a red pen.

<table>
<tr><td>Issue No. 1</td><td>Issue Date: 29.09.2001</td><td>Page No. 1 of 1</td></tr>
<tr><td colspan="2">Reviewed By:</td><td>Approved By:</td></tr>
</table>

XYZ Co.	XYZ CORPORATION	Doc. No. XYZQMS - 4.
	4. Quality Management System	Rev. No. Nil
	Section Identification Page	Rev. Date. Nil

Quality

Management

System

Issue No. 1	Issue Date: 29.09.2001	Page No. 1 of 1
Reviewed By:		Approved By:

<table>
<tr><td rowspan="3">XYZ Co.</td><td>XYZ CORPORATION</td><td>Doc. No. XYZQMS - 4.1</td></tr>
<tr><td>4. Quality Management System</td><td>Rev. No. Nil</td></tr>
<tr><td>4.1 General Requirements</td><td>Rev. Date. Nil</td></tr>
</table>

The Quality Management System (QMS) of XYZ Corporation is established, documented, implemented and maintained in line with the requirements of ISO 9001:2000. Continual Improvement of the effectiveness of this QMS in as many processes and areas as possible, consistent with the requirements of this international standard, is constantly endeavoured and practised. The entire QMS has been developed and implemented based on the **"Process Approach".**

At XYZ Corporation the various processes need to comply with the QMS requirement of the ISO Standard and hence the management has taken the following actions:

The processes needed for the effective functioning of the QMS have been identified and the applicability of these processes to all areas and functions, have been defined, specific to XYZ Corporation's requirements. Further,

(i) The sequence of the different processes at XYZ Corporation, is clearly defined. Besides this, the interaction of these processes with each other are additionally determined and specified,

(ii) The criteria and methods needed to ensure the effectiveness of actual operation and the controls thereof for the smooth running of the processes are determined,

(iii) The availability of the necessary resources and information required to support the operation and the monitoring of these processes are ensured.

(iv) The processes are regularly monitored, systematically measured and thoroughly analyzed, and

(v) In order to achieve the results as planned, proper actions are implemented. These actions also serve the objective of continual improvement.

Issue No. 1	Issue Date: 29.09.2001	Page No. 1 of 2
Reviewed By:		Approved By:

<table>
<tr><td rowspan="3">XYZ
Co.</td><td>XYZ CORPORATION</td><td>Doc. No.
XYZQMS - 4.1</td></tr>
<tr><td>4. Quality Management System</td><td>Rev. No. Nil</td></tr>
<tr><td>4.1 General Requirements</td><td>Rev. Date. Nil</td></tr>
</table>

At XYZ Corporation all the processes are managed totally inline with the "**Process Approach**" detailed in ISO 9001:2000 and the processes have been classified into "**Key Processes**" and "**Supporting Processes**". The procedure for QMS by process approach, gives details of the processes, their inter-relationship, inter-linkages, inputs, outputs and other relevant details.

Presently the only process outsourced is "**Computer and Information Service**". If however in future any of the other processes are to be outsourced, they shall also be suitably assessed and necessary controls exercised on them.

Ref:

Issue No. 1	Issue Date: 29.09.2001	Page No. 2 of 2
Reviewed By:		Approved By:

<table>
<tr><td rowspan="3">XYZ Co.</td><td>XYZ CORPORATION</td><td>Doc. No.
XYZQMS - 4.2.1</td></tr>
<tr><td>4. Quality Management System</td><td>Rev. No. Nil</td></tr>
<tr><td>4.2 Documentation Requirements</td><td>Rev. Date. Nil</td></tr>
</table>

4.2.1 General

XYZ Corporation has documented its entire QMS requirements to facilitate effective implementation, maintenance and continual improvement of the system. The documents, structured to meet the requirements of ISO 9001:2000, are capable of dynamic changes and consist of following:

a) Documented statements of the quality policy and the quality objectives form a part of this manual. XYZ Corporation's quality policy is used to convey and affirm to every member of the organization, the top management's commitment to quality with continual improvements through anticipatory methods. The quality policy is explained to all employees of the organization through training sessions and a copy of the policy in 'English and Vernacular' is provided to each employee. This quality policy is prominently displayed at various locations within the organization's premises.

b) XYZ Corporation has structured its QMS such that it aims at ensuring conformance of the products with specified requirements and helps XYZ Corporation achieve its stated quality policy and quality objectives. This structure has been created such that the whole set of documents are divided into four levels as under:

Level-1
This level of document consists of the quality manual, which defines the scope of XYZ Corporation's activities to which the QMS, as per ISO 9001:2000 applies. It describes how the QMS, that has been installed and maintained, addresses each clause of the standard to fulfill all requirements. Reference to the relevant documents of other levels to link them with the quality manual are also provided.

Level-2
The documents at this level consist of the QMS procedures, required by both the system as well as the process, under ISO 9001:2000.These are also in line with XYZ Corporation's stated quality policy and quality objectives. The procedures describe the purpose of the processes, how they should operate and the controls to be exercised for their smooth operation and consistency. Further, they provide references to the instructions of work, calibration, maintenance, inspection and relevant documents of other levels.

<table>
<tr><td>Issue No. 1</td><td>Issue Date: 29.09.2001</td><td>Page No. 1 of 2</td></tr>
<tr><td colspan="2">Reviewed By:</td><td>Approved By:</td></tr>
</table>

<table>
<tr><td rowspan="3">XYZ Co.</td><td>XYZ CORPORATION</td><td>Doc. No. XYZQMS - 4.2.1</td></tr>
<tr><td>4. Quality Management System</td><td>Rev. No. Nil</td></tr>
<tr><td>4.2 Documentation Requirements</td><td>Rev. Date. Nil</td></tr>
</table>

Level-3

This level consists of documents required for effective operation and control of the various processes in use. The primary operational document consist of the quality plan in the form of a flow chart. This chart details the process flow and specifies each stage by its instruction name and document number. Instructions are provided for all activities such as inspection, work, calibration, safety and maintenance. They describe how the activity is performed with due stress on safety and other precautions. They also specify the functions responsible for the particular activity and give reference of records to be maintained at that particular stage.

Level-4

Documents of this level, consist of forms, formats, records, product specifications, reference exhibits, certificates and other reports to demonstrate conformity to requirements.

Ref:

Issue No. 1	Issue Date: 29.09.2001	Page No. 2 of 2
Reviewed By:	Approved By:	

<table>
<tr><td rowspan="3">XYZ Co.</td><td>XYZ CORPORATION</td><td>Doc. No. XYZQMS - 4.2.2</td></tr>
<tr><td>4. Quality Management System</td><td>Rev. No. Nil</td></tr>
<tr><td>4.2 Documentation Requirements</td><td>Rev. Date. Nil</td></tr>
</table>

4.2.2 Quality Manual

The quality manual requirements have been documented and maintained with the intention of establishing a progressive and dynamic QMS at XYZ Corporation, as per the international standard ISO 9001: 2000.

The contents of this manual and the related documents are the exclusive property of XYZ Corporation and shall not be reproduced, in part or in whole by any one, whosoever.

a) The **Scope** of the QMS established, documented and maintained is as under:

"Design, manufacture and supply of XYZ Corporation's products"

At XYZ Corporation, "positive recall" is not a part of the QMS established, implemented and maintained, since for the products manufactured, "Positive recall is not essential and can be avoided". This is therefore an **Exclusion** from the QMS.

b) In order to operate the implemented QMS at XYZ Corporation effectively, **Procedures** necessary are established and documented as level-2 documents. These QMS Procedures are consistent with ISO 9001:2000 requirements and XYZ Corporation's quality policy and quality objectives.

c) A detailed description of the **interaction** between various processes of the QMS are prepared to exhibit the role of each process in the entire setup. This is annexed to the QMS Manual in the form of analysis, flowcharts, diagrams and tables for process approach.

Ref:

Issue No. 1	Issue Date: 29.09.2001	Page No. 1 of 1
Reviewed By:		Approved By:

XYZ Co.	XYZ CORPORATION	Doc. No. XYZQMS - 4.2.3
	4. Quality Management System	Rev. No. Nil
	4.2 Documentation Requirements	Rev. Date. Nil

4.2.3 Control of Documents

XYZ Corporation has established and maintained documented procedures to control all the documents pertaining to QMS. The procedures define the controls needed to ensure satisfactory operation.

a. Issue and Approval
The Procedure for document control identifies the methodology for issue of all the controlled documents to various locations/users depending upon their applicability to them. Documents are issued as per the approved distribution list. The procedure also specifies the authority, which shall approve documents, prior to issue.

b. Review, Update and Re-approval
The Procedure for document control specifies the authority which reviews the documents, and only after this review are they approved. When change or revision in documents become necessary due to improvements in system or practice, they are amended and updated. This update version is then reviewed afresh by the same authority, which had reviewed it earlier. These changed documents are then re-approved by the designated re-approving authority.

c. Changes and Revision Status Identification
All documents pertaining to the QMS at XYZ Corporation, are identified by a unique numbering system, which is detailed in the procedure for document control. It is ensured that all the changes to documents are prepared, reviewed, updated and then put forth for approval to the same authority which had conducted the original review and approval. The changes in the revised document are made as per procedure for document and data changes and recorded in the amendment data record.

d. Control
All documents under QMS are controlled as per the procedure for document control and issued in the form of 'Controlled Copies'. All the controlled copies are identified by the 'Control Copy No.' stamped in red color ink and the copy number which is handwritten in red ink. Uncontrolled Copies of documents whenever necessary may be issued and these need not be controlled.

Issue No. 1	Issue Date: 29.09.2001	Page No. 1 of 2
Reviewed By:		Approved By:

<table>
<tr><td rowspan="3">XYZ
Co.</td><td>XYZ CORPORATION</td><td>Doc. No. XYZQMS - 4.2.3</td></tr>
<tr><td>Quality Management System</td><td>Rev. No. Nil</td></tr>
<tr><td>Documentation Requirements</td><td>Rev. Date. Nil</td></tr>
</table>

Availability of only the latest document, at the place of use, is ensured by replacing the current copy of the applicable document with its revised version, as soon as it is approved. To identify the current issue status of the documents in use, a master list of documents is maintained by the management representative which indicates the current issue status and the date of issue.

e. Codification

The Procedure for document control ensures that the relevant documents are easily identifiable. All the Level 1, Level 2 & Level 3 documents under the QMS are computer printouts, so as to ensure that they are clear and legible. All Level 4 documents are either printed or computer printouts where the data is hand-written or computer generated or typed in the form of records to make it readable.

f. External Origin

The procedure for document control ensures that all those external origin documents, which are needed by XYZ Corporation during the course of its operations are also controlled and available for use.

g. Obsolete

The procedure for document control ensures that only the latest issues of the relevant documents are available at all places of use and the obsolete documents are withdrawn and destroyed to avoid unintended use. The management representative however, retains one of the obsolete copies duly marked as 'OBSOLETE COPY' or 'SUPERCEDED', for future reference.

Ref:

Issue No. 1	Issue Date: 29.09.2001	Page No. 2 of 2
Reviewed By:	Approved By:	

<table>
<tr><td rowspan="3">XYZ Co.</td><td>XYZ CORPORATION</td><td>Doc. No. XYZQMS - 4.2.4</td></tr>
<tr><td>4. Quality Management System</td><td>Rev. No. Nil</td></tr>
<tr><td>4.2 Documentation Requirements</td><td>Rev. Date. Nil</td></tr>
</table>

4.2.4 Control of Records

XYZ Corporation has established a documented procedure for the control of records in order to collect, maintain and control data generated within the organization. The records generated are used as a means to provide evidence of conformity of the product to requirements, and display effective operation of the processes of the QMS. All records are maintained legible, readily identifiable and easily retrievable. The procedure for control of records specifies the methodology for identification, storage, protection, retrieval, retention period and disposition of the records.

Records being the means to demonstrate effective operation, are made available to the statutory and regulatory bodies, certifying bodies and the customer whenever required.

Ref:

<table>
<tr><td>Issue No. 1</td><td>Issue Date: 29.09.2001</td><td>Page No. 1 of 1</td></tr>
<tr><td colspan="2">Reviewed By:</td><td>Approved By:</td></tr>
</table>

<table>
<tr><td rowspan="3">XYZ
Co.</td><td>XYZ CORPORATION</td><td>Doc. No. XYZQMS - 5.</td></tr>
<tr><td>5. Management Responsibility</td><td>Rev. No. Nil</td></tr>
<tr><td>Section Identification Page</td><td>Rev. Date. Nil</td></tr>
</table>

Management

Responsibility

<table>
<tr><td>Issue No. 1</td><td>Issue Date: 29.09.2001</td><td>Page No. 1 of 1</td></tr>
<tr><td colspan="2">Reviewed By:</td><td>Approved By:</td></tr>
</table>

XYZ Co.	XYZ CORPORATION	Doc. No. XYZQMS - 5.1
	5. Management Responsibility	Rev. No. Nil
	5.1 Management Commitment	Rev. Date. Nil

At XYZ Corporation, the top management is totally committed to quality, in all areas of work, irrespective of their apparent unimportance. The QMS is established, documented, implemented, maintained and constantly reviewed with the object of providing evidence of the commitment that the management has towards its implementation and development. The regular review that is undertaken, is to ensure continual improvement in the effectiveness of the QMS.

a. Compliance to Requirements: The top management has made it amply clear to all people of the organization that meeting the customer requirement is of the greatest importance. Further, under no circumstances any deviations from statutory or regulatory requirements should be made and none of them contravened.

b. Quality Policy: At XYZ Corporation, the top management has clearly laid down and made known its quality policy, in order to give direction to the employees for achieving the quality objectives of the organization. The quality policy is used as a means to ensure that every member of the organization understands the company's quest for quality and harmonizes his working with it. For achieving this, the policy is explained to all employees of the organization through training sessions and a copy of the "Quality policy in English and in Vernacular" is distributed to each employee. The quality policy is also prominently displayed at various locations within the organization.

c. Quality Objectives: XYZ Corporation has established and documented its quality objectives and made them known, within the organization, to ensure that all members are aware of the goals they have to reach, by making a continual effort towards improvement, through preventive and corrective measures.

d. Management Review: The top management remains directly involved with the management reviews carried out regularly on the QMS, giving special emphasis on using them as a tool for assessment and improvement .

e. Resources: At XYZ Corporation the top management is well-aware of its direct responsibility towards providing and ensuring the availability of all resources necessary for the success of the QMS, and constantly ensures its availability.

Ref :

Issue No. 1	Issue Date: 29.09.2001	Page No. 1 of 1
Reviewed By:	Approved By:	

<table>
<tr><td rowspan="4">XYZ
Co.</td><td rowspan="2">XYZ CORPORATION</td><td>Doc. No.
XYZQMS - 5.2</td></tr>
<tr><td></td></tr>
<tr><td>5. Management Responsibility</td><td>Rev. No. Nil</td></tr>
<tr><td>5.2 Customer Focus</td><td>Rev. Date. Nil</td></tr>
</table>

At XYZ Corporation, the top management ensures that, the entire organization in every area of its operation, has a clear focus towards meeting and exceeding the customer requirements. With this objective the first step is towards determining these requirements, both stated and implied, from the customers. The effort then is towards not only satisfying the customers, by fulfilling their requirements, but also towards enhancing the level of their satisfaction.

Ref:

<table>
<tr><td>Issue No. 1</td><td>Issue Date: 29.09.2001</td><td>Page No. 1 of 1</td></tr>
<tr><td colspan="2">Reviewed By:</td><td>Approved By:</td></tr>
</table>

<table>
<tr><td rowspan="4">XYZ
Co.</td><td rowspan="2">XYZ CORPORATION</td><td>Doc. No. XYZQMS - 5.3</td></tr>
<tr><td></td></tr>
<tr><td>5. Management Responsibility</td><td>Rev. No. Nil</td></tr>
<tr><td>5.3 Quality Policy</td><td>Rev. Date. Nil</td></tr>
</table>

The top Management of XYZ Corporation, in defining and stating their quality policy ensure that the policy is in line with the stated quality objectives. They have ensured that:

a. The quality policy stated is appropriate to the activity carried out at XYZ Corporation, which is manufacture and supply of a product that is extremely safe and of the highest quality.

b. Compliance to laid down requirements and continual improvement is included in the quality policy, with the object of improving the effectiveness of the QMS.

c. The stated quality objectives being the goals that XYZ Corporation wishes to achieve, provides a frame-work for not only establishing but also regularly reviewing the achievements in relation to the objectives.

d. Communication of the quality policy within the organization is done by making known the policy and its meaning and relevance with reference to every employee's function. The policy is therefore explained in detail analytically so that it is clearly understood. Further to enable the employees remember the policy, pocket-sized cards with the policy printed in, "English and in Vernacular" are given to all employees.

e. The quality policy itself is also maintained in a dynamic way, by reviewing it for its continuing suitability, during each management review meeting.

Ref :

<table>
<tr><td>Issue No. 1</td><td>Issue Date: 29.09.2001</td><td>Page No. 1 of 1</td></tr>
<tr><td colspan="2">Reviewed By:</td><td>Approved By:</td></tr>
</table>

<table>
<tr><td rowspan="3">XYZ Co.</td><td>XYZ CORPORATION</td><td>Doc. No. XYZQMS - 5.4.1</td></tr>
<tr><td>5. Management Responsibility</td><td>Rev. No. Nil</td></tr>
<tr><td>5.4 Planning</td><td>Rev. Date. Nil</td></tr>
</table>

5.4.1 Quality Objectives

At XYZ Corporation the top management has ensured that the quality objectives have been established at relevant functions and levels within the organization. These objectives ensure that requirements of the product are not only identified and met, but also constantly reviewed and improved.

The management of XYZ Corporation realizes that to make the objectives achievable and to enable verification of the continual improvements necessary to achieve them, the objectives ought to be measurable. They have therefore stated the objectives consistent with the quality policy, in measurable terms to make this verification possible. By making them measurable, they ensure that the objectives once achieved, can again be set at higher measurable levels.

Ref :

<table>
<tr><td>Issue No. 1</td><td>Issue Date: 29.09.2001</td><td>Page No. 1 of 1</td></tr>
<tr><td colspan="2">Reviewed By:</td><td>Approved By:</td></tr>
</table>

<table>
<tr><td rowspan="3">XYZ Co.</td><td>XYZ CORPORATION</td><td>Doc.No. XYZQMS - 5.4.2</td></tr>
<tr><td>5. Management Responsibility</td><td>Rev. No. Nil</td></tr>
<tr><td>5.4 Planning</td><td>Rev. Date. Nil</td></tr>
</table>

5.4.2 Quality Management System Planning

a. The planning at XYZ Corporation is done not only to maintain the QMS implemented, but also monitor, measure, analyze and improve on a continual basis. Through the process of planning 'Achieving the Quality Objectives' is targeted.

b. The integrity and soundness of the QMS is maintained by ensuring that all changes, whenever effected, are carried out in a planned manner. Thus planning ensures, that the implementation of the changes bring about improvement, since, the process of planning anticipates, identifies and addresses all problems likely to be encountered due to the change.

Ref :

Issue No. 1	Issue Date: 29.09.2001	Page No. 1 of 1
Reviewed By:		Approved By:

<table>
<tr><td rowspan="3">XYZ Co.</td><td>XYZ CORPORATION</td><td>Doc. No. XYZQMS - 5.5.1</td></tr>
<tr><td>5. Management Responsibility</td><td>Rev. No. Nil</td></tr>
<tr><td>5.5 Responsibility, Authority and Communication</td><td>Rev. Date. Nil</td></tr>
</table>

5.5.1 Responsibility and Authority

XYZ Corporation has structured its activities to ensure that its products meet customer requirements consistently. The responsibility, authority and interrelation of the personnel who carry out, manage and verify processes are defined individually, in annexures 1 to __. Further for each quality system procedure, the primary responsibility for implementing is specified and listed in the annexure. This annexure is enclosed along with the set of QMS procedures given to each control copy holder for easy reference. The organization chart of XYZ Corporation, indicating the structure of the organization and interrelation amongst its personnel, is also enclosed with this manual. The responsibility and authority given in the annexures1 to __, also identifies and indicates the personnel who have to:

a. Initiate action to prevent the occurrence of non-conformities relating to the product and processes of the QMS.

b. Identify and record problems relating to the product and processes of the QMS.

c. Initiate, recommend or provide solutions through designated channels.

d. Verify the implementation of solutions.

e. Control further processing, delivery or installation of non-conforming products until the deficiency or unsatisfactory condition has been corrected.

At XYZ Corporation, every individual is encouraged to identify non-conformities in product and processes of the QMS to enable further improvements, which are then dealt by personnel of specified responsibility and authority.

Ref :

Issue No. 1	Issue Date: 29.09.2001	Page No. 1 of 1
Reviewed By:		Approved By:

<table>
<tr><td rowspan="3">XYZ Co.</td><td>XYZ CORPORATION</td><td>Doc. No. XYZQMS - 5.5.2</td></tr>
<tr><td>5. Management Responsibility</td><td>Rev. No. Nil</td></tr>
<tr><td>5.5 Responsibility, Authority and Communication</td><td>Rev. Date. Nil</td></tr>
</table>

5.5.2 Management Representative

The management of XYZ Corporation, appointed Mr. A.B.C. (part of the management) as the 'Management Representative' (MR) whose responsibilities and authorities are given in Annexure ___. The 'MR', as a part of his responsibility:

a. Ensures that all processes needed for the QMS, as per the requirements of ISO 9001:2000 are established, implemented and maintained,

b. Reports to the top management on the performance and health of QMS to enable review, which shall be the basis for further improvement,

c. Ensures that the customer requirements are known throughout the organization, and

d. Ensures liaison is maintained with external agencies on all matters relating to the QMS.

Ref :

Issue No. 1	Issue Date: 29.09.2001	Page No. 1 of 1
Reviewed By:		Approved By:

<table>
<tr><td rowspan="3">XYZ Co.</td><td>XYZ CORPORATION</td><td>Doc. No. XYZQMS – 5.5.3</td></tr>
<tr><td>5. Management Responsibility</td><td>Rev. No. Nil</td></tr>
<tr><td>5.5 Responsibility, Authority and Communication</td><td>Rev. Date. Nil</td></tr>
</table>

5.5.3 Internal Communication

The management of XYZ Corporation has defined and implemented effective and efficient processes, for communicating the quality policy, quality objectives, customer requirements and targets for achievement of the QMS, to all its concerned employees. These communication processes that are established, ensure effective implementation and performance improvement of the QMS, to facilitate in achieving the quality objectives. The 'Procedure for Internal Communication', actively encourages feed-back and communication to give a clear picture of the status of QMS to the top management and thus involves people to bring about planned improvements.

Ref :

Issue No. 1	Issue Date: 29.09.2001	Page No. 1 of 1
Reviewed By:		Approved By:

XYZ Co.	XYZ CORPORATION	Doc.No. XYZQMS – 5.6.1
	5. Management Responsibility	Rev. No. Nil
	5.6 Management Review	Rev. Date. Nil

5.6.1 General

The management of XYZ Corporation shall conduct periodic reviews at least once in a quarter, during the implementation of the QMS and thereafter also during the course of its use. These reviews shall ensure monitoring of the QMS implementation. They shall also verify the continuing suitability, adequacy and effectiveness of the QMS, inline with the quality policy for achieving the quality objectives, in addition to the other requirements of ISO 9001:2000 standard. The reviews shall also assess the need for changes if any, required in the QMS including the quality policy and the quality objectives so that they also remain dynamic and changeable as per the current needs and future requirements. Such changes can not only bring about improvements in the existing processes but also create new system requirements. The minutes of these management review meetings, shall be recorded.

Ref :

Issue No. 1	Issue Date: 29.09.2001	Page No. 1 of 1
Reviewed By:		Approved By:

<table>
<tr><td rowspan="3">XYZ Co.</td><td>XYZ CORPORATION</td><td>Doc.No. XYZQMS – 5.6.2</td></tr>
<tr><td>5. Management Responsibility</td><td>Rev. No. Nil</td></tr>
<tr><td>5.6 Management Review</td><td>Rev. Date. Nil</td></tr>
</table>

5.6.2 Review Input

The management review shall cover the following:

a. The feedback and reports received from the internal and external audits.

b. The customer complaints and feedback, which shall be used as a tool for effecting improvements through corrective and preventive actions.

c. The performance of the various processes, and the reports for product testing indicating non-conformances, which shall be taken as feedback for effecting controls and improvements.

d. The status and performance of the various corrective and preventive actions already implemented.

e. Follow-up actions taken based on decisions of the previous management review meeting, indicating effective and sufficient implementation.

f. Changes, that could even effect the QMS are to be brought about, since they are found suitable and necessary.

g. All the recommendations for improvements discussed in-depth.

Ref :

<table>
<tr><td>Issue No. 1</td><td>Issue Date: 29.09.2001</td><td>Page No. 1 of 1</td></tr>
<tr><td colspan="2">Reviewed By:</td><td>Approved By:</td></tr>
</table>

<table>
<tr><td rowspan="3">XYZ
Co.</td><td>XYZ CORPORATION</td><td>Doc.No. XYZQMS – 5.6.3</td></tr>
<tr><td>5. Management Responsibility</td><td>Rev. No. Nil</td></tr>
<tr><td>5.6 Management Review</td><td>Rev. Date. Nil</td></tr>
</table>

5.6.3 Review Output

The management of XYZ Corporation during the management review meetings shall take decisions on actions to be taken, based on the discussions it had on the inputs to the review.

a. The most important decision shall be, with regard to the improvements required for enhancing the effectiveness of the QMS and all processes under its control.

b. Special emphasis shall be given to customer requirements, which bring about product related improvements, resulting in fulfillment of the customer expectations and meeting their needs.

c. The management being fully aware of the need to ensure availability of necessary resources, has decided to verify and document any specific requirements arising out of the discussions, which pertain to resources.

Ref :

Issue No. 1	Issue Date: 29.09.2001	Page No. 1 of 1
Reviewed By:	Approved By:	

<table>
<tr><td rowspan="3">XYZ Co.</td><td>XYZ CORPORATION</td><td>Doc. No. XYZQMS – 6.</td></tr>
<tr><td>6. Resource Management</td><td>Rev. No. Nil</td></tr>
<tr><td>Section Identification Page</td><td>Rev. Date. Nil</td></tr>
</table>

Resource

Management

Issue No. 1	Issue Date: 29.09.2001	Page No. 1 of 1
Reviewed By:		Approved By:

<table>
<tr><td rowspan="3">XYZ Co.</td><td>XYZ CORPORATION</td><td>Doc. No. XYZQMS – 6.1</td></tr>
<tr><td>6. Resource Management</td><td>Rev. No. Nil</td></tr>
<tr><td>6.1 Provision of Resources</td><td>Rev. Date. Nil</td></tr>
</table>

At XYZ Corporation, the management is fully conscious of the need and importance, of timely planning and provision of all resources in adequate quantity and of appropriate quality. They have therefore, determined the requirements, and made provisions for making them available at the appropriate locations in time, to ensure vibrancy of the QMS, as it is well understood that the QMS has to be continually improved to remain effective, efficient and viable.

The resources also include qualified, trained, experienced and skilled personnel for managing and performing work and verification activities. These resources have been identified and made available to ensure the following:

a. The effective implementation and maintenance of the QMS depends upon the availability of resources and hence their availability in adequate quality and quantity is ensured. Moreover, this QMS needs to be continually improved, to be effective, and this improvement is only possible with the availability of proper resources in time, whenever and wherever needed.

b. The customer requirements, form the basis of the various QMS processes, and hence with the object of enhancing customer satisfaction, availability of quality resources shall be ensured.

Ref:

Issue No. 1	Issue Date: 29.09.2001	Page No. 1 of 1
Reviewed By:		Approved By:

<table>
<tr><td rowspan="3">XYZ Co.</td><td>XYZ CORPORATION</td><td>Doc.No. XYZQMS – 6.2.1</td></tr>
<tr><td>6. Resource Management</td><td>Rev. No. Nil</td></tr>
<tr><td>6.2 Human Resources</td><td>Rev. Date. Nil</td></tr>
</table>

6.2.1 General

XYZ Corporation is fully aware of the importance of the human resources available within the organization and values them. People therefore are treated as an extremely valuable resource of the organization. At XYZ Corporation, it is recognized and accepted that product quality depends upon the work output of the personnel at various stages.

At XYZ Corporation, personnel performing work, directly affecting product quality are verified and screened for their competence to undertake the assigned work. This assessment of the competence of the employees, is carried out based on the individuals' background with regard to education, training, skill and work experience.

Ref :

Issue No. 1	Issue Date: 29.09.2001	Page No. 1 of 1
Reviewed By:		Approved By:

<table>
<tr><td rowspan="3">XYZ Co.</td><td>XYZ CORPORATION</td><td>Doc.No. XYZQMS – 6.2.2</td></tr>
<tr><td>6. Resource Management</td><td>Rev. No. Nil</td></tr>
<tr><td>6.2 Human Resources</td><td>Rev. Date. Nil</td></tr>
</table>

6.2.2 Competence, Awareness and Training

XYZ Corporation has established and maintained documented procedures for identifying the competence of personnel, for bringing about awareness and providing training to all its people. The organization has therefore identified means to determine the following with regard to the people, to ensure that each person is given a job that suits him the most.

a. The competence necessary for performing work, effecting product quality at various stages has been determined and is ensured while allocating the work.

b. All personnel are provided with the necessary training in order to ensure that the product meets specified requirements and the processes of QMS are handled and controlled efficiently. Training needs for individuals are also identified and suitable training programs are conducted periodically. Personnel performing special kinds of jobs, are given these assignments, on the basis of their education, previous training and experience. Such personnel are also given additional training whenever necessary and then considered qualified for these special jobs.

c. The effectiveness of the training imparted is reviewed and evaluated to verify the need for re-training.

d. The personnel carrying out the various allotted activities, are duly informed and made aware of the relevance and importance of their activity with regard to the product quality. They are also made aware, on how their job contributes towards the achievement of the quality objectives of the organization. Such training is organised and imparted periodically.

e. Appropriate records are maintained for all personnel with regard to their education, training, skill and experience. Such records are also updated periodically.

Ref :

Issue No. 1	Issue Date: 29.09.2001	Page No. 1 of 1
Reviewed By:		Approved By:

<table>
<tr><td rowspan="3">XYZ
Co.</td><td rowspan="2">XYZ CORPORATION</td><td>Doc. No. XYZQMS – 6.3</td></tr>
<tr><td></td></tr>
<tr><td>6. Resource Management</td><td>Rev. No. Nil</td></tr>
<tr><td></td><td>6.3 Infrastructure</td><td>Rev. Date. Nil</td></tr>
</table>

The infrastructure needed to achieve the product requirements has been identified and created at XYZ Corporation. This infrastructure determined and provided is not only maintained but also verified for possible improvement. It includes the following:

a. The land, building, work space and all associated utilities which form the basis of infrastructure are created and provided.

b. The process of design, manufacture and supply consists of various processes which require process-equipment (both hardware and software). These equipments including those suitable for the monitoring and measuring needs, are made available.

c. The support services (such as transport, means of communication, etc.) which form an essential part of the basic infrastructure are also provided for ensuring the satisfactory performance of QMS.

Ref :

Issue No. 1	Issue Date: 29.09.2001	Page No. 1 of 1
Reviewed By:		Approved By:

XYZ Co.	XYZ CORPORATION	Doc. No. XYZQMS – 6.4
	6. Resource Management	Rev. No. Nil
	6.4 Work Environment	Rev. Date. Nil

At XYZ Corporation it is recognized that work area and the environment form an essential part of the basic resources to be provided. These are determined and made available to achieve the product requirements without compromising either on the quality or on the needed work environment.

Ref :

Issue No. 1	Issue Date: 29.09.2001	Page No. 1 of 1
Reviewed By:		Approved By:

<table>
<tr><td rowspan="3">XYZ
Co.</td><td>XYZ CORPORATION</td><td>Doc. No. XYZQMS – 7.</td></tr>
<tr><td>7. Product Realization</td><td>Rev. No. Nil</td></tr>
<tr><td>Section Identification Page</td><td>Rev. Date. Nil</td></tr>
</table>

Product

Realization

Issue No. 1	Issue Date: 29.09.2001	Page No. 1 of 1
Reviewed By:		Approved By:

<table>
<tr><td rowspan="3">XYZ Co.</td><td>XYZ CORPORATION</td><td>Doc. No. XYZQMS – 7.1</td></tr>
<tr><td>7. Product Realization</td><td>Rev. No. Nil</td></tr>
<tr><td>7.1 Planning of Product Realization</td><td>Rev. Date. Nil</td></tr>
</table>

Realization of the product requires planning and development of the processes necessary to carry out the various operations. As such, alignment of the process of planning for product realization along with the other processes of QMS is done for satisfactory performance.

During the process of planning for the realization of the product, the following are borne in mind to determine the appropriate requirements :

a. XYZ Corporation's quality objectives and requirements of the product with regard to quality and customer needs.

b. The various processes used, the documents generated and the resources utilized are established and taken into account.

c. The product acceptance criteria which are determined, are then verified, validated, monitored, inspected and tested to ensure conformity.

d. All records needed to provide evidence, that the realization process and the resulting product meet specified requirements, are maintained.

As a result of this planning process, it shall be ensured that suitable documents are generated for the organization's satisfactory performance. These documents shall be in the form of quality plans detailing the processes and resources necessary for the QMS.

Ref :

Issue No. 1	Issue Date: 29.09.2001	Page No. 1 of 1
Reviewed By:		Approved By:

<table>
<tr><td rowspan="3">XYZ Co.</td><td>XYZ CORPORATION</td><td>Doc.No. XYZQMS – 7.2.1</td></tr>
<tr><td>7. Product Realization</td><td>Rev. No. Nil</td></tr>
<tr><td>7.2 Customer Related Processes</td><td>Rev. Date. Nil</td></tr>
</table>

7.2.1 Determination of requirements related to the Product

The products manufactured at XYZ Corporation, form the very basis for the existence of the organization. This is therefore an extremely important entity on which the entire business and reputation of XYZ Corporation rests. XYZ Corporation has therefore given due importance for determining the customer's requirements in the following manner:

a. The various requirements specified by the customer, including requirements for delivery and post-delivery activities are taken note of and are duly addressed.

b. The customer at times does not state certain requirements which are necessary for the specified or intended use. Such requirements are also duly taken care of.

c. The products manufactured and supplied by XYZ Corporation need extreme care with regard to compliance to all statutory and regulatory requirements. All these requirements are duly addressed and followed.

d. XYZ Corporation has determined certain additional requirements not covered above which are also complied with, in order to maintain product quality.

Ref :

<table>
<tr><td>Issue No. 1</td><td>Issue Date: 29.09.2001</td><td>Page No. 1 of 1</td></tr>
<tr><td colspan="2">Reviewed By:</td><td>Approved By:</td></tr>
</table>

XYZ Co.	XYZ CORPORATION	Doc.No. XYZQMS – 7.2.2
	7. Product Realization	Rev. No. Nil
	7.2 Customer Related Processes	Rev. Date. Nil

7.2.2 Review of Requirements Related to the Product

At XYZ Corporation, the various requirements relating to the products manufactured, are regularly reviewed to ensure that the requirements accepted previously are being followed and met with. This review of requirements is conducted prior to acceptance of any order and before making any commitment for supply to the customer. These requirements could originate from tenders, contracts or direct orders, or 'change-orders' received. During the process of review it is ensured that the following are taken care of:

a. The procedure for review explicitly defines the methodology to ensure that the customer's requirements are clearly understood and documented . All product-related requirements are defined unambiguously to ensure clarity. The unstated but implied requirements of the customer, regulatory requirements and other requirements determined and felt necessary by XYZ Corporation are also reviewed for determining conformity.

b. The differences if any, from the previously stated requirements of the customers, are clarified and resolved. The procedure also describes the methodology of processing any amendment either from the customer's end or from XYZ Corporation.

c. For all acceptances given to the customers relating to tenders, purchase orders or amendments, it is ensured that XYZ Corporation has the capability to meet the defined requirements.

Records of all reviews and action arising from them, are maintained for reference.

Ref :

Issue No. 1	Issue Date: 29.09.2001	Page No. 1 of 1
Reviewed By:		Approved By:

<table>
<tr><td rowspan="3">XYZ
Co.</td><td>XYZ CORPORATION</td><td>Doc.No. XYZQMS – 7.2.3</td></tr>
<tr><td>7. Product Realization</td><td>Rev. No. Nil</td></tr>
<tr><td>7.2 Customer Related Processes</td><td>Rev. Date. Nil</td></tr>
</table>

7.2.3 Customer Communication

XYZ Corporation has established and maintained channels of communication with the customers, to ensure effective implementation of the QMS. These channels have been determined, defined and established for the following :

a. To determine and clarify all information with regard to product requirements since the product is the basic entity required by the customer.

b . To communicate with regard to, the enquiries received, contracts and orders accepted including amendments, etc.

c. To act on every feedback and complaint, received from customers by assigning them the highest priority and importance. In fact at XYZ Corporation all feedback are treated with the same diligence given to complaints and the same amount of efforts are put for correction and improvement based on this feedback. This method of handling feedback, results in building an extra level of confidence in the customers.

Ref :

Issue No. 1	Issue Date: 29.09.2001	Page No. 1 of 1
Reviewed By:	Approved By:	

<table>
<tr><td rowspan="3">XYZ Co.</td><td>XYZ CORPORATION</td><td>Doc.No. XYZQMS – 7.3.1</td></tr>
<tr><td>7. Product Realization</td><td>Rev. No. Nil</td></tr>
<tr><td>7.3 Design and Development</td><td>Rev. Date. Nil</td></tr>
</table>

7.3.1 Design and Development Planning

At XYZ Corporation, the management, based on the QMS established, implemented and maintained, carryout design and development of all products with predetermined plans and systematic controls.

During this planning, the organization shall determine and establish the following to facilitate the process of design and development of the product:

a. The different stages of design and development to complete the exercise satisfactorily.

b. Appropriate methods of review, verification and validation used at every stage of design and development undertaken at XYZ Corporation.

c. Determine who is responsible for the various activities of design and development and what is their authority.

It shall judiciously manage and smoothly mesh the interfaces of various groups involved in this important process. This careful handling of the groups shall be done to ensure that the communication is not only clear and unambiguous but also effective with regard to information exchange. This shall also ensure a clear assignment of responsibility amongst the people.

It shall be ensured that the planning output is updated appropriately as the design and development of the product progresses.

Ref :

Issue No. 1	Issue Date: 29.09.2001	Page No. 1 of 1
Reviewed By:		Approved By:

XYZ Co.	XYZ CORPORATION	Doc.No. XYZQMS – 7.3.2
	7. Product Realization	Rev. No. Nil
	7.3 Design and Development	Rev. Date. Nil

7.3.2 Design and Development Inputs

At XYZ Corporation, the inputs relating to the product shall be determined before any design and development activity commences. Moreover all records of these inputs shall be essentially maintained and preserved.

Inputs being the very basis of design and development, shall ensure that the following are ascertained in advance.

a. The functional and performance requirements of the product being designed,

b. All applicable statutory and regulatory requirements which pertain to the product, right from its inputs, through its processes, to its delivery and use, with special reference to health and safety

c. Where applicable and possible, any information derived from previous similar designs done in-house or by competitors, and

d. All other requirements, which are found to be essential for the particular product's design and development

These inputs determined prior to use shall be reviewed to ensure that they are adequate for the purpose of design and development. To ensure that these projected input requirements of design, are not rendered useless and surplus later, they shall be complete, unambiguous and not in conflict with each other.

Ref :

Issue No. 1	Issue Date: 29.09.2001	Page No. 1 of 1
Reviewed By:		Approved By:

<table>
<tr><td rowspan="3">XYZ Co.</td><td>XYZ CORPORATION</td><td>Doc.No. XYZQMS – 7.3.3</td></tr>
<tr><td>7. Product Realization</td><td>Rev. No. Nil</td></tr>
<tr><td>7.3 Design and Development</td><td>Rev. Date. Nil</td></tr>
</table>

7.3.3 Design and Development Outputs

The outputs of the design and development at XYZ Corporation, shall be determined in a form (such as drawings, specifications, prototypes, etc) so that they can be correlated to the inputs and verified. Upon completion of the determination of outputs for each design and development, they shall be released only after approval by the designated approving authority.

These outputs of the design and development shall essentially fulfill the following requirements:

a. Meet all the input requirements of design already determined.

b. Provide appropriate information based on which the processes of purchasing, production and service provision can function satisfactorily.

c. Give reference to the acceptance criteria for the products and information on the reasons for rework and rejection.

d. Specify all the characteristics of the product that are essential for its safe and proper use.

Ref :

Issue No. 1	Issue Date: 29.09.2001	Page No. 1 of 1
Reviewed By:	Approved By:	

<table>
<tr><td rowspan="3">XYZ Co.</td><td>XYZ CORPORATION</td><td>Doc.No. XYZQMS – 7.3.4</td></tr>
<tr><td>7. Product Realization</td><td>Rev. No. Nil</td></tr>
<tr><td>7.3 Design and Development</td><td>Rev. Date. Nil</td></tr>
</table>

7.3.4 Design and Development Review

At XYZ Corporation it is ensured that during the planning itself, suitable stages for systematic reviews of design and development are identified, formally documented and carried out. The Corporation considers it obligatory that these reviews shall be undertaken with a view to target the following objectives:

a. To evaluate the ability of the results of design and development to meet requirements,

b. To identify any problems that appear or likely to occur, and

c. To propose necessary actions to these anticipated problems.

Participants in such design and development reviews, shall include suitable representatives of all functions concerned, with the particular design and development stage(s) being reviewed. It shall be ensured that records of the results of every review carried out and any action that has become necessary on account of the review are maintained.

Ref :

Issue No. 1	Issue Date: 29.09.2001	Page No. 1 of 1
Reviewed By:		Approved By:

<table>
<tr><td rowspan="3">XYZ Co.</td><td>XYZ CORPORATION</td><td>Doc.No. XYZQMS – 7.3.5</td></tr>
<tr><td>7. Product Realization</td><td>Rev. No. Nil</td></tr>
<tr><td>7.3 Design and Development</td><td>Rev. Date. Nil</td></tr>
</table>

7.3.5 Design and Development Verification

At XYZ Corporation the design and development planning ensures that verification of design and development is a part of the design process itself. This verification shall ensure that at each stage of design and development, the design outputs meet the design and development input requirements.

It shall be ensured that records of the results of each verification and any action that becomes necessary on account of the verification shall be maintained.

Ref :

Issue No. 1	Issue Date: 29.09.2001	Page No. 1 of 1
Reviewed By:		Approved By:

<table>
<tr><td rowspan="3">XYZ
Co.</td><td>XYZ CORPORATION</td><td>Doc.No. XYZQMS – 7.3.6</td></tr>
<tr><td>7. Product Realization</td><td>Rev. No. Nil</td></tr>
<tr><td>7.3 Design and Development</td><td>Rev. Date. Nil</td></tr>
</table>

7.3.6 Design and Development Validation

The validation of design and development carried out at XYZ Corporation is in line with the initial plans made for these validation processes. During this validation it is ensured that the product being produced as a result of the design and development is capable of meeting all the known requirements for the specific application or use for which it is intended.

Unless it is impractical or impossible to conduct this validation, it shall always be carried out prior to delivery (for goods) or implementation (for service) of the product.

It shall be ensured that records of the results of every validation carried out and any action that becomes necessary on account of this validation are maintained.

Ref :

Issue No. 1	Issue Date: 29.09.2001	Page No. 1 of 1
Reviewed By:		Approved By:

XYZ Co.	XYZ CORPORATION	Doc.No. XYZQMS – 7.3.7
	7. Product Realization	Rev. No. Nil
	7.3 Design and Development	Rev. Date. Nil

7.3.7 **Control of Design and Development Changes**

At XYZ Corporation, it is ensured that all changes and modifications to design and development are duly identified, documented, reviewed, verified, validated appropriately and approved before their incorporation or implementation.

Should a review of these design and development changes be carried out, it shall verify the effect of the change on the following also:

a. The constituent parts of the product, and

b. The product already delivered.

It shall be ensured that records of the results of the review of every design and development change made, and any action that becomes necessary on account of this review are maintained.

Ref :

Issue No. 1	Issue Date: 29.09.2001	Page No. 1 of 1
Reviewed By:		Approved By:

<table>
<tr><td rowspan="3">XYZ Co.</td><td>XYZ CORPORATION</td><td>Doc.No. XYZQMS – 7.4.1</td></tr>
<tr><td>7. Product Realization</td><td>Rev. No. Nil</td></tr>
<tr><td>7.4 Purchasing</td><td>Rev. Date. Nil</td></tr>
</table>

7.4.1 Purchasing Process

To ensure consistency and reliability of incoming products, XYZ Corporation has established and maintained documented procedures, which ensure that the purchased products conform to specified requirements.

The type and extent of control on the purchased product is defined, based on the effect of the purchase on the final product. Thus, the purchases are categorized into critical and other items. The category of critical items includes those purchased items, which are directly used as input in the product or contribute to product quality and effect the subsequent product realization.

The documented procedures for supplier evaluation ensure that the suppliers are evaluated and selected, on the basis of their ability to meet the demands of the anticipated product requirements. The procedure also defines the extent of control which shall be exercised on the suppliers.

A list of approved suppliers is maintained. Further the procedure also elucidates the methodology of monitoring and re-evaluating the approved suppliers on an yearly basis, which would enable deleting the names of suppliers (from the approved supplier list) who do not perform to acceptable norms.

The process of selecting, evaluating, monitoring and re-evaluating the suppliers shall apply only to critical item suppliers. Records of all such supplier evaluations are maintained.

Ref :

<table>
<tr><td>Issue No. 1</td><td>Issue Date: 29.09.2001</td><td>Page No. 1 of 1</td></tr>
<tr><td colspan="2">Reviewed By:</td><td>Approved By:</td></tr>
</table>

XYZ Co.	XYZ CORPORATION	Doc.No. XYZQMS – 7.4.2
	7. Product Realization	Rev. No. Nil
	7.4 Purchasing	Rev. Date. Nil

7.4.2 Purchasing Information

The procedure for purchasing at XYZ Corporation stipulates and thereby ensures that complete and unambiguous purchasing data shall be provided to all suppliers. The purchase requirements provided to the supplier shall be verified within XYZ Corporation for adequacy prior to communication to the supplier. The purchase information shall describe the product to be purchased and the supplier has to comply with the following:

a. The requirements of the product shall be detailed in the 'Purchase Order' generated,. clearly specifying and describing the required specifications. Other relevant technical information, including method of inspection shall also be given in addition to the commercial details. This information shall always be provided irrespective of whether this purchasing is for product, procedures, processes or equipment, since all of them require such detailed specifications.

b. In case personnel skills, capabilities and expertise in various specialized areas are sought to be purchased, the purchase documents shall clearly specify the requirements for qualifying the concerned personnel.

c. The QMS requirements shall be made known to the supplier to ensure compliance.

Ref :

Issue No. 1	Issue Date: 29.09.2001	Page No. 1 of 1
Reviewed By:		Approved By:

<table>
<tr><td rowspan="3">XYZ Co.</td><td>XYZ CORPORATION</td><td>Doc.No. XYZQMS – 7.4.3</td></tr>
<tr><td>7. Product Realization</td><td>Rev. No. Nil</td></tr>
<tr><td>7.4 Purchasing</td><td>Rev. Date. Nil</td></tr>
</table>

7.4.3 Verification of Purchased Product

The verification of purchased product is covered in the procedure for verification of incoming products. This procedure established and implemented, states and thereby ensures that the purchased products meet specified requirements.

No procedure for verification of purchased products at supplier's premises exists, since the entire verification of the purchased products shall be done by XYZ Corporation within its own premises.

Where it is specified in the contract that the customer would like to verify any aspect at XYZ Corporation's suppliers premises, the same shall be taken note of in the procedure for review of product requirements. It shall be intimated to the suppliers well in advance, to keep them aware and then, the customer shall be afforded the right for verification. Such verifications if carried out shall not be used as evidence to reduce any control measures, and XYZ Corporation shall continue to exercise effective controls on its suppliers' product.

Ref :

<table>
<tr><td>Issue No. 1</td><td>Issue Date: 29.09.2001</td><td>Page No. 1 of 1</td></tr>
<tr><td colspan="2">Reviewed By:</td><td>Approved By:</td></tr>
</table>

XYZ Co.	XYZ CORPORATION	Doc.No. XYZQMS – 7.5.1
	7. Product Realization	Rev. No. Nil
	7.5 Production and Service Provision	Rev. Date. Nil

7.5.1 Control of Production and Service Provision

To enable timely delivery of quality products, XYZ Corporation decides on a "Production Plan" every month. The quality plan for each product, indicates the various production processes, inspection and tests to be carried out. In view of the past performance and experience, all processes and equipment in operation are considered, as suitable and approved. To enable process control, XYZ Corporation has documented procedures, which define the manner in which the operations of production are carried out and the controls exercised on them, through all stages affecting quality. This documented procedure states that the controlled conditions for operating these processes shall include:

a. The information that describes the characteristics of the products, is made available in the form of specifications, drawings and reference samples.

b. The work instructions at various stages of production along with reference standards and workmanship criteria, illustration of defects and defective samples wherever practical are provided, in order that they act as a guide for work instructions to achieve satisfactory product characteristics.

c. The equipment necessary for carrying out the operations at the various stages of work have been listed in the work instructions provided.

d. The work instructions highlight the methodology and parameters to be monitored and controlled to give satisfactory product characteristics. These instructions specify the monitoring and measuring devices to be used, which are made available to the various stages of production.

e. The monitoring and measurement devices are themselves controlled as per procedure for their control and only calibrated devices are issued for use.

f. The release of products by ensuring complete compliance to the requirements of the specification and availability of statutory compliance certificate is ensured prior to despatch. Once such products are delivered to the customer, any feedback or complaint whenever received on delivered products requiring postdelivery activities, is given the highest priority to ensure customer satisfaction.

Ref :

Issue No. 1	Issue Date: 29.09.2001	Page No. 1 of 1
Reviewed By:		Approved By:

XYZ Co.	XYZ CORPORATION	Doc.No. XYZQMS – 7.5.2
	7. Product Realization	Rev. No. Nil
	7.5 Production and Service Provision	Rev. Date. Nil

7.5.2 Validation of Processes for Production and Service Provision

At XYZ Corporation, any of the processes of production and service where the resulting output cannot be verified by subsequent monitoring or measurement are validated. The corporation has decided that all such processes shall be designated 'Special Processes' since the deficiency in them becomes apparent only after the product is in use or has been delivered.

In the manufacturing process such special processes are always identified and work instructions are provided accordingly. XYZ corporation's policy ensures that the records for validation, of these special processes, to achieve planned results shall be maintained for future reference.

XYZ Corporation has established arrangements for the 'Special Processes' with regard to the following:

a. The process parameters shall be reviewed and approved by the technical head of the process, based on in-house trials. Only after the approval is accorded, the control parameters shall be frozen.

b. To ensure maintenance of the process capability, all equipment used for these special processes and the personnel performing them shall be controlled. The equipment shall also be maintained in good working condition and the personnel given regular training.

c. The methods and procedures for carrying out these operations shall be detailed in the relevant work instructions .

d. All records for the review and approval for qualifying and validating the special process parameters shall be maintained properly.

e. Revalidation of the parameters, if felt necessary shall be done based on trials and in-house reapproval of parameters, followed by review and approval, by the same authority which had accorded the initial approval.

Ref :

Issue No. 1	Issue Date: 29.09.2001	Page No. 1 of 1
Reviewed By:		Approved By:

XYZ Co.	XYZ CORPORATION	Doc.No. XYZQMS – 7.5.3
	7. Product Realization	Rev. No. Nil
	7.5 Production and Service Provision	Rev. Date. Nil

7.5.3 **Identification and Traceability**

Regulatory and customer requirements necessitate that during the process of product realization, the input product realization and later its traceability, should be ensured as this corporation follows the undermentioned system.

Identification
XYZ Corporation shall establish and maintain documented procedures to identify incoming, in-process, and final products during the entire process of product realization.

XYZ Corporation has also identified means for product status identification, in the process of monitoring and measuring its conformity and effecting corrective actions as and when required.

The methodology used for product identification includes location, orientation, sizes, color codes, markings, tags, etc.

Traceability
The procedure for product identification and traceability also elucidates the methodology of ensuring traceability for every product produced, throughout the manufacturing process. This is ensured through color code, customer's name, product size, serial number, batch number, markings, stampings, records, etc.

Ref :

Issue No. 1	Issue Date: 29.09.2001	Page No. 1 of 1
Reviewed By:		Approved By:

<table>
<tr><td rowspan="3">XYZ Co.</td><td>XYZ CORPORATION</td><td>Doc.No. XYZQMS – 7.5.4</td></tr>
<tr><td>7. Product Realization</td><td>Rev. No. Nil</td></tr>
<tr><td>7.5 Production and Service Provision</td><td>Rev. Date. Nil</td></tr>
</table>

7.5.4 Customer Property

At XYZ Corporation, all care is exercised with regard to customer property while it is in XYZ Corporation's control. The products received from the customers are both for conversion as well as incorporation.

To enable control of this customer property, XYZ Corporation has established, maintained and documented procedures to identify, verify, protects, tore, maintain and safeguard the customer property.

The procedure elucidates the methodology of identification, verification, use, storage, safeguarding and maintenance of the product.

Any complaints regarding unsuitability of the product during use, loss or damage are also recorded and intimated to the customer, as per laid down procedures.

Ref :

<table>
<tr><td>Issue No. 1</td><td>Issue Date: 29.09.2001</td><td>Page No. 1 of 1</td></tr>
<tr><td colspan="2">Reviewed By:</td><td>Approved By:</td></tr>
</table>

<table>
<tr><td rowspan="3">XYZ Co.</td><td>XYZ CORPORATION</td><td>Doc.No. XYZQMS – 7.5.5</td></tr>
<tr><td>7. Product Realization</td><td>Rev. No. Nil</td></tr>
<tr><td>7.5 Production and Service Provision</td><td>Rev. Date. Nil</td></tr>
</table>

7.5.5 Preservation of Product

In order to ensure that the product reaches the customer in good condition, XYZ Corporation has established and maintained documented procedures to identify, handle, package, store, preserve and protect the product.

Identification
The product is identified as indicated in the procedure for product identification and traceability.

Handling
Materials on receipt, and while in-process are handled with suitable care to avoid damage. The methodologies used are manual handling, conveyors, forklifts, cranes, trolleys, trucks, etc. The procedure for handling indicates the method and equipment to be used for handling the product at the various stages.

Packaging
The specific packaging methodology is detailed in the procedure to protect it during storage, handling and transportation. The package also provides the customer with necessary information, which is printed on it. The packaging is also used as a powerful tool for marketing the product through its aesthetic appeal.

Storage and Protection
All materials are stored at designated locations to avoid damage and deterioration of the product prior to use. The procedure for storage states the methodology of receipts and issues, of various products from designated locations. Periodic checks are undertaken to assess deterioration of stored material as per procedure for stores. Pending delivery, finished products are stored as per procedure for storage of the finished products.

Preservation
The product is preserved from the detrimental effects of the environment as per the procedure for preservation of the product.

Ref:

<table>
<tr><td>Issue No. 1</td><td>Issue Date: 29.09.2001</td><td>Page No. 1 of 1</td></tr>
<tr><td colspan="2">Reviewed By:</td><td>Approved By:</td></tr>
</table>

XYZ Co.	XYZ CORPORATION	Doc. No. XYZQMS – 7.6
	7. Product Realization	Rev. No. Nil
	7.6 Control of Monitoring and Measuring Devices	Rev. Date. Nil

At XYZ Corporation, the monitoring and measurements to be undertaken are determined based on the technical requirements at the stages where this monitoring and measurement have to be done. The various monitoring and measuring devices needed to provide evidence of conformity of the product, to the determined requirements have been identified, listed and provided at the place of use. The list of the measuring equipment, detailing their specifications are maintained as technical data.

XYZ Corporation has established processes in order to ensure that monitoring and measurements can be carried out. Further, it is ensured that the measurements are carried out in such a way that they are consistent with the monitoring and measuring requirements. All measurements are treated as valid, only if the following actions on the monitoring and measuring equipment have been ensured :

a. The equipment shall be calibrated or verified at specified intervals or prior to use. The verification or calibration is done against standards traceable to any national or international standards. For measurements where no such standards exist, the calibration is still done and the method and basis for this verification or calibration is recorded. The instructions for calibration indicate the environmental conditions required for calibration, when done in-house.

b. Equipments, whenever found to be out of calibration are rectified by adjustments or readjustments wherever necessary, prior to their use.

c. The calibration status of all monitoring and measuring equipment is indicated on the equipment itself with calibration stickers and are supported by the calibration records available. All such equipment that effect product quality are uniquely identified giving calibration status and stated interval of recalibration. The calibration is carried out both, in-house and through external agencies. When done in-house the process of calibration is clearly defined.

Issue No. 1	Issue Date: 29.09.2001	Page No. 1 of 2
Reviewed By:		Approved By:

<table>
<tr><td rowspan="3">XYZ Co.</td><td>XYZ CORPORATION</td><td>Doc. No. XYZQMS – 7.6</td></tr>
<tr><td>7. Product Realization</td><td>Rev. No. Nil</td></tr>
<tr><td>7.6 Control of Monitoring and Measuring Devices</td><td>Rev. Date. Nil</td></tr>
</table>

d. Care is also taken to ensure that the calibration of the equipment remains valid during use. It is ensured that the setting and adjustments do not get disturbed, invalidating the measurements made. This safeguard of the instrument ensures its accuracy, and its fitness for use continues throughout the period, till the next calibration is due, or done.

e. Protection of these equipments to avoid damage and deterioration during handling, maintenance and storage is ensured since confidence and validity of measurements depend upon the proper upkeep of these equipments.

At XYZ Corporation, when the equipment, in use are found out-of-calibration, they are not only rectified or scrapped, but also the previous measurements carried out in the process are reassessed and the results are documented as observed. Further, for those products on which measurements had been done with the defective equipment, appropriate action as given in the procedure is taken. All measuring equipments are selected and used with known measurement accuracy consistent with the requirements of the measurement to be made.

The software used at XYZ Corporation, for monitoring and measurement is assessed for suitability, prior to use, for the intended application. The ability of this software to satisfy the intended application is also periodically reconfirmed. Thus the desired confidence level in the process of monitoring and measurement is ensured.

Ref :

Issue No. 1	Issue Date: 29.09.2001	Page No. 2 of 2
Reviewed By:		Approved By:

<table>
<tr><td rowspan="3">XYZ
Co.</td><td>XYZ CORPORATION</td><td>Doc. No. XYZQMS – 8</td></tr>
<tr><td>8. Measurement, Analysis and Improvement</td><td>Rev. No. Nil</td></tr>
<tr><td>Section Identification Page</td><td>Rev. Date. Nil</td></tr>
</table>

Measurement,

Analysis

and

Improvement

Issue No. 1	Issue Date: 29.09.2001	Page No. 1 of 1
Reviewed By:		Approved By:

<table>
<tr><td rowspan="3">XYZ Co.</td><td>XYZ CORPORATION</td><td>Doc. No. XYZQMS – 8.1</td></tr>
<tr><td>8. Measurement, Analysis and Improvement</td><td>Rev. No. Nil</td></tr>
<tr><td>8.1 General</td><td>Rev. Date. Nil</td></tr>
</table>

XYZ Corporation has established and maintained documented procedures to plan and implement the measurement, analysis and improvement processes within the QMS as per the requirements of the standard to ensure that the product meets the specified requirements. This process of planning and implementation is carried out on a regular basis to ensure the following:

a. Conformity of the product to specified requirements

Incoming Product
The procedure for inspection and testing of the incoming product (receiving inspection), details the methodology and sampling to be carried out on the incoming products and the extent of control to be exercised, which depends on the control exercised at the supplier's end. At XYZ Corporation no product is released for use unless, receiving-inspection has been done. Hence, no system of positive recall exists. However, the procedure clearly mentions that in the event of such situations arising in future positive recall shall essentially be practised.

In - process Product
The procedure for inspection and testing of inprocess product at XYZ Corporation, gives in detail the inspection and testing to be conducted at the relevant stages of inspection, as per the quality plan. In-process products are released to the next stage only after necessary inspection and tests are completed, and hence no system for positive recall exists.

Finished Product
The procedure for inspection and testing of the finished product, at XYZ Corporation ensures that all tests as per the quality plan are completed and evidenced accordingly in the inspection and test records. No product is despatched until all inspection and test activities are completed and the related data and documentation are available and authorized.

b. Conformity of the QMS
XYZ Corporation, plans and implements procedures, to ensure conformity of QMS to stated requirements, in line with its quality policy and quality objectives.

<table>
<tr><td>Issue No. 1</td><td>Issue Date: 29.09.2001</td><td>Page No. 1 of 2</td></tr>
<tr><td colspan="2">Reviewed By:</td><td>Approved By:</td></tr>
</table>

<table>
<tr><td rowspan="3">XYZ Co.</td><td>XYZ CORPORATION</td><td>Doc. No. XYZQMS – 8.1</td></tr>
<tr><td>8. Measurement, Analysis and Improvement</td><td>Rev. No. Nil</td></tr>
<tr><td>8.1 General</td><td>Rev. Date. Nil</td></tr>
</table>

c. Continual improvement of the QMS

The plans and procedures implemented at XYZ Corporation, facilitate continual improvement of the effectiveness of the QMS, to ensure dynamism and achievement of the quality objectives, which require not only to improve in steps but also to upgrade the quality objectives themselves.

This planning and implementation shall include methods for measuring, analyzing and improving the products, processes and system for which XYZ Corporation has identified the use of appropriate statistical techniques. The procedure for statistical techniques, which is applied to as many areas of work as possible, specifies the extent of their use.

Ref :

Issue No. 1	Issue Date: 29.09.2001	Page No. 2 of 2
Reviewed By:		Approved By:

<table>
<tr><td rowspan="3">XYZ
Co.</td><td>XYZ CORPORATION</td><td>Doc.No. XYZQMS – 8.2.1</td></tr>
<tr><td>8. Measurement, Analysis and Improvement</td><td>Rev. No. Nil</td></tr>
<tr><td>8.2 Monitoring and Measurement</td><td>Rev. Date. Nil</td></tr>
</table>

8.2.1 Customer Satisfaction

XYZ Corporation has documented and implemented procedures for determining the customer satisfaction. The performance of the QMS can be effectively judged based on the feedback as per this procedure. Information from the customers relating to their perception, of XYZ Corporation having met their requirements, is requested, received, analyzed, assessed and thereafter conclusions are drawn for improvement. This information generated is used as a tool for continual improvement and upgradation of the product, process and system.

Ref :

<table>
<tr><td>Issue No. 1</td><td>Issue Date: 29.09.2001</td><td>Page No. 1 of 1</td></tr>
<tr><td colspan="2">Reviewed By:</td><td>Approved By:</td></tr>
</table>

<table>
<tr><td rowspan="3">XYZ
Co.</td><td>XYZ CORPORATION</td><td>Doc.No. XYZQMS – 8.2.2</td></tr>
<tr><td>8. Measurement, Analysis and Improvement</td><td>Rev. No. Nil</td></tr>
<tr><td>8.2 Monitoring and Measurement</td><td>Rev. Date. Nil</td></tr>
</table>

8.2.2 Internal Audit

To determine and monitor the effectiveness of the QMS, XYZ Corporation has established, implemented and maintained documented procedures for planning and carrying out the internal audits. These audits are aimed at verifying, if the quality activities are functioning as per planned arrangements and the requirements of the standard and QMS are being adhered to meticulously. Internal audits are carried out at least once every six months, as per the audit plan.

a. The audit activity is carried out as per planned arrangements, by ensuring that it is in line with XYZ Corporation's 'Quality Objectives' and requirements of the product. The schedules for the internal audits are prepared in advance to ensure that all processes get covered under the QMS and all findings of the audits are properly recorded.

b. The audits are aimed at verifying the effective implementation and maintenance of the QMS, and all the results of the audits are recorded and communicated to the concerned personnel having direct responsibility for the process audited, who then take necessary corrective actions for the deviations or shortcomings to avoid recurrence, thereby assisting in continual improvement.

At the planned intervals given in the 'Audit Plan' the internal audits are taken up as per a planned schedule, giving due regard to the status and importance of the activity. Due consideration is also given to the results of the previous audit findings. All audits that are scheduled, specify the criteria, scope and method to be adopted during the audit. It is ensured that all internal audits are carried out with objectivity and impartiality to the auditee, by trained and responsible personnel selected for the activity. Auditor selection is done in such away that they do not audit their own work. The responsibility and requirements for planning and conducting the audits as also reporting results and recording them have been defined at XYZ Corporation in the procedure for internal audits. The persons responsible for the area audited under the procedure, ensures that corrective actions are taken without undue delay to eliminate the detected non-conformity and their cause. A follow-up verification of the corrective action and its effectiveness pertaining to the deviation observed is carried out to ensure the satisfactory implementation.

Ref :

Issue No. 1	Issue Date: 29.09.2001	Page No. 1 of 1
Reviewed By:		Approved By:

<table>
<tr><td rowspan="3">XYZ
Co.</td><td>XYZ CORPORATION</td><td>Doc.No. XYZQMS – 8.2.3</td></tr>
<tr><td>8. Measurement, Analysis and Improvement</td><td>Rev. No. Nil</td></tr>
<tr><td>8.2 Monitoring and Measurement</td><td>Rev. Date. Nil</td></tr>
</table>

8.2.3 Monitoring and Measurement of Processes

XYZ Corporation has developed suitable methods for monitoring and measurement of the QMS. To demonstrate the ability of this monitoring and measurement process and to achieve planned results, XYZ Corporation has documented procedures which define the manner in which the operation of production is to be carried out through all stages affecting quality. Conformity of the product being the prime objective, whenever it is found that the planned results have not been achieved, correction and corrective action as appropriate shall be taken, as per the procedure.

Ref :

Issue No. 1	Issue Date: 29.09.2001	Page No. 1 of 1
Reviewed By:		Approved By:

XYZ Co.	XYZ CORPORATION	Doc.No. XYZQMS – 8.2.4
	8. Measurement, Analysis and Improvement	Rev. No. Nil
	8.2 Monitoring and Measurement	Rev. Date. Nil

8.2.4 Monitoring and Measurement of Product

XYZ Corporation monitors and measures all the necessary characteristics of its products to ensure that product requirements are met. Achievement of these product requirements is ensured by carrying out measurement and monitoring at various appropriate stages of the product realization process, in accordance with the 'Quality Plan'.

Conformity of the product to the acceptance criteria is evidenced through records where the authority / personnel authorized to release the product is clearly identified.

At XYZ Corporation, it is ensured that the incoming product, in-process and also the finished product are not released until all the planned requirements are met satisfactorily.

Ref :

Issue No. 1	Issue Date: 29.09.2001	Page No. 1 of 1
Reviewed By:		Approved By:

<table>
<tr><td rowspan="4">XYZ Co.</td><td>XYZ CORPORATION</td><td>Doc. No. XYZQMS – 8.3</td></tr>
<tr><td rowspan="2">8. Measurement, Analysis and Improvement</td><td></td></tr>
<tr><td>Rev. No. Nil</td></tr>
<tr><td>8.3 Control of Non-Conforming Product</td><td>Rev. Date. Nil</td></tr>
</table>

To ensure that non-conforming products identified at various stages are controlled, and not passed on to the next stage, or used unintentionally, XYZ Corporation has established and maintained documented procedures to control the non-conforming products. This procedure for non-conforming products also highlights the responsibility and authority for dealing with the non-conforming product, through the review and disposition, which could result in rework, acceptance by degrading for alternate use or rejection.

Whenever non-conformity in the product is observed the procedure provides for dealing with it by one or more of the following ways :

a. Reworking the product to eliminate the detected non- conformities in future.

b. Authorizing its use, release or acceptance for alternative purposes by authorized personnel or customer where applicable.

c. Rejecting it outright.

The procedure provides for the identification, documentation, segregation, evaluation, notification and disposition of the non-conforming products. Records for all such actions indicating reason for non- conformity shall be maintained. Any reworked product shall be reinspected in accordance with the procedure for inspection and testing, to demonstrate conformity to the requirements upon reverification.

Any non-conformity in the product, detected after delivery or use of the product has commenced, is viewed as a complaint. Such non-conformities are used as feedback for either correcting the system, wherever necessary, or preventing such non-conformities.

Ref :

Issue No. 1	Issue Date: 29.09.2001	Page No. 1 of 1
Reviewed By:		Approved By:

<table>
<tr><td rowspan="3">XYZ Co.</td><td>XYZ CORPORATION</td><td>Doc. No. XYZQMS – 8.4</td></tr>
<tr><td>8. Measurement, Analysis and Improvement</td><td>Rev. No. Nil</td></tr>
<tr><td>8.4 Analysis of Data</td><td>Rev. Date. Nil</td></tr>
</table>

At XYZ Corporation, the data generated as a result of monitoring and measurement, from all sources, is collected and analyzed to demonstrate suitability and effectiveness of the QMS. Evaluation of this data is used to show continual improvement of the QMS.

The Procedure for analysis of data, facilitates proper analysis of the relevant data pertaining to the following specific areas of the QMS:

a. Customer satisfaction

b. Product conformity to requirements

c. Scope for correction and prevention based on characteristics and trends of product and process observed leading to continual improvement

d. Suppliers assessment

Ref :

Issue No. 1	Issue Date: 29.09.2001	Page No. 1 of 1
Reviewed By:		Approved By:

<table>
<tr><td rowspan="3">XYZ Co.</td><td>XYZ CORPORATION</td><td>Doc.No. XYZQMS – 8.5.1</td></tr>
<tr><td>8. Measurement, Analysis and Improvement</td><td>Rev. No. Nil</td></tr>
<tr><td>8.5 Improvement</td><td>Rev. Date. Nil</td></tr>
</table>

8.5.1 Continual Improvement

At XYZ Corporation, the effectiveness of the QMS is continually improved by systematically using the quality policy, quality objectives, audit results, analysis of data, corrective and preventive actions, and management reviews.

The improvement so achieved is entered in records along with the details of the activity responsible for raising the level of performance of the QMS.

Ref :

Issue No. 1	Issue Date: 29.09.2001	Page No. 1 of 1
Reviewed By:		Approved By:

XYZ Co.	XYZ CORPORATION	Doc.No.XYZQMS-8.5.2
	8. Measurement, Analysis and Improvement	Rev. No. Nil
	8.5 Improvement	Rev. Date. Nil

8.5.2 Corrective Action

XYZ Corporation has established, implemented and maintained documented procedures to affect corrective actions. The purpose of this procedure is to ensure the following:

a) Dynamism in the QMS with continual improvement

b) Elimination of the root causes of non-conformities

c) Prevention of the recurrence of problems

This documented procedure has been established and maintained to define the requirements for the following :

a) The method of reviewing the non-conformities observed or reported and also customer complaints or feedback received.

b) The method of determining the cause of non-conformity and the controls needed to prevent it.

c) The method of evaluating the need for actions to avoid recurrence of non-conformities.

The method for determining and implementing actions needed for eliminating erved non-conformities.

records to be maintained for actions taken.

ethod of reviewing corrective actions based on feedback received.

	Issue Date: 29.09.2001	Page No. 1 of 1
		Approved By:

<table>
<tr><td rowspan="3">XYZ Co.</td><td>XYZ CORPORATION</td><td>Doc.No. XYZQMS - 8.5.3</td></tr>
<tr><td>8. Measurement, Analysis and Improvement</td><td>Rev. No. Nil</td></tr>
<tr><td>8.5 Improvement</td><td>Rev. Date. Nil</td></tr>
</table>

8.5.3 Preventive Action

The procedure for preventive action at XYZ Corporation highlights the methodology of determining and using appropriate sources of information to eliminate potential non-conformities . The procedure helps in the following ways:

a. Determining the non-conformities and their probable root causes

b. Evaluating the need for actions to prevent occurrence of non-conformities

c. Determining and initiating actions needed

d. Recording results of actions taken

e. Verifying the effectiveness of actions by review of preventive actions taken

Ref:

Issue No. 1	Issue Date: 29.09.2001	Page No. 1 of 1
Reviewed By:		Approved By:

ISO

twenty

"SIX" MANDATORY PROCEDURES OF XYZ CORPORATION (AS PER ISO 9001:2000)

****

Plot No. 11, Street No. 08,

ABC Chambers, Hyderabad,

India

Ph. +91-40-110890

Fax. +91-40-290987

****

****

****

**

XYZ Co.	XYZ CORPORATION	Doc. No. XYZQMS – 4.2.3/P-01/I-XX/F-02	
	Mandatory Procedures of the QMS	Rev. No. Nil	
	Contents	Rev. Date. Nil	

Sl.No.	Document Number	Name of the Document	No. of Pages
1.	XYZQMS-4.2.3/P-01	Procedure for Control of Documents	4
2.	XYZQMS-4.2.4/P-01	Procedure for Control of Records	1
3.	XYZQMS-8.2.2/P-01	Procedure for Internal Audit	2
4.	XYZQMS-8.3/P-01	Procedure for Control of Non-Conforming Product	2
5.	XYZQMS-8.5.2/P-01	Procedure for Corrective Actions	1
6.	XYZQMS-8.5.3/P-01	Procedure for Preventive Actions	2

Issue No. 1	Issue Date: 29.09.2001	Page No. 1 of 1
Reviewed By:	Approved By:	

<table>
<tr><td rowspan="3">XYZ Co.</td><td>XYZ CORPORATION</td><td>Doc. No. XYZQMS – 4.2.3/P-01/I-XX/F-01</td></tr>
<tr><td>Mandatory Procedures of the QMS</td><td>Rev. No. Nil</td></tr>
<tr><td>Amendment Data Record</td><td>Rev. Date. Nil</td></tr>
</table>

Sl. No.	Doc. No.	Doc. Name	Page No. of Doc. Changed	Issue No / Issue Date	Rev. No. / Rev. Date	Nature of change / Amend-ment

Issue No. 1	Issue Date: 29.09.2001	Page No. 1 of 1
Reviewed By:	Approved By:	

XYZ Co.	XYZ CORPORATION	Doc. No. XYZQMS – 4.2.3/P- 01
	4. Quality Management System	Rev. No. Nil
	Procedure for Control of documents	Rev. Date. Nil

Purpose : To ensure that all QMS documents are controlled by

a) Issuing them when authorised and ensuring their adequacy before approval,
b) Reviewing, updating when necessary and reapproving them
c) Changing in an authorized manner
d) Making available at the correct place of use
e) Ensuring their Legibility, identification, indexing & codification
f) Listing and preserving documents of external origin
g) Preventing unintended use of obsolete documents

Responsibility : MR

Scope : All processes.

Procedure : All levels of documents under the 'QMS' shall be controlled to ensure satisfactory performance and operation. All level 4 documents generated during the course of the operation of the QMS shall be written legibly and shall be properly filed. All these Files shall be numbered. All files of documents maintained for the satisfactory functioning of the QMS in the ISO Cell shall be listed as "Files Available in ISO Cell" which can be referred for locating the document based on the serial number allotted to the relevant file.

a) **Issue and Approval :** The MR shall ensure that only approved documents are issued to the user as "Control Copies" as per the 'Distribution List'. This formal issue to the specified individuals or location shall be done to ensure availability of relevant documents at the respective places of use. All issues shall be recorded in the document issue record and acknowledgement taken. The 'QMS' manual shall be issued in full to all personnel listed in the distribution list, but the procedures and instructions shall be issued, based on whether the particular procedures or instructions are applicable to the concerned personnel's area of work. All approved formats shall be available for use but shall not be issued.

The manual, procedures, work instructions, inspection instructions, maintenance instructions, calibration instructions, specifications and lists issued in separate files shall have "Contents pages" at the beginning, listing all the documents of the type available and shall also indicate which of documents have been issued to the control copy holder and hence available in the control copy file issued.

Issue No. 1	Issue Date: 29.09.2001	Page No. 1 of 4
Reviewed By:	Approved By:	

XYZ Co.	**XYZ CORPORATION**	Doc. No. XYZQMS – 4.2.3/P- 01
	4. Quality Management System	Rev. No. Nil
	Procedure for Control of Documents	Rev. Date. Nil

b) Review, Update & Reapproval: The first three levels of documents shall bear signatures for 'Reviewed by' and 'Approved by' on all control copies but in the fourth level documents, only master copies shall be signed for 'Reviewed by' and 'Approved by'. After any updation, the documents shall once again be reviewed and reapproved by the same authority, which had reviewed and approved the earlier document. All four levels of 'QMS' documents shall be reviewed and approved by the following authorities at XYZ Corporation:

Level	Reviewed by	Approved by
1	Management Representative	Executive Director
2	Management Representative	Executive Director
3	Management Representative	Executive Director
4	Management Representative	Executive Director

c) Changes and revision status identification : Change in any level of document can be initiated by any person at XYZ Corporation, by requesting the change through the document change form, indicating the change suggested and its justification. This document change form shall be forwarded to the MR through the concerned area head or process owner. The MR will discuss the change suggested and if found appropriate, shall modify the document incorporating the change. After this the changed document shall be reapproved by the same authority, which had reviewed and approved the earlier documents. The changes could be initiated based on difficulties encountered, possibility of better or improved practices, internal audits, external audits, etc.

Note: During the process of document change or new document creation, draft documents are to be prepared by the ISO Cell. They shall therefore be permitted to simultaneously maintain such, 'Drafts undergoing change or being created' along with the earlier control copies, since the modified document and the earlier document are compared and only then finalized for approval. Hence, for some-time they would have both the documents together. The modified document would be as an uncontrolled copy until it is approved.

d) Revision status: Only those pages, which are amended or revised, shall be replaced and corresponding obsolete pages withdrawn. The nature of change shall be recorded in the amendment data record. The modified document shall be issued and recorded in the document issue record.

Issue No. 1	Issue Date: 29.09.2001	Page No. 2 of 4
Reviewed By:		Approved By:

<table>
<tr><td rowspan="3">XYZ
Co.</td><td>XYZ CORPORATION</td><td>Doc. No.
XYZQMS – 4.2.3/P- 01</td></tr>
<tr><td>4. Quality Management System</td><td>Rev. No. Nil</td></tr>
<tr><td>Procedure for
Control of Documents</td><td>Rev. Date. Nil</td></tr>
</table>

After changes have been made, the document change form, obsolete document and if the changes have been initiated by an observation / Non Conformance Report NCR then this also, shall be marked with a common number at the top right corner to inter-relate the documents.

e) **Codification** : The quality system documents shall be numbered as indicated below.

Level	Document	Numbering
1	Manual	XYZQMS-X.XX
2	Procedures	XYZQMS-X.XX/P-XX
3	Instructions for Work/Inspection / Maintenance/Calibration/ Specifications	XYZQMS-X.XX/P-XX/I-XX
4	Formatted Records/ Log Sheets/ Proformae/ Files/ Registers.	XYZQMS-X.XX/P-XX/I-XX/F-XX

XYZQMS	*XYZ Corporation's Quality Management System*
P	*Procedures*
I	*Instructions*
F	*Formatted Records, Log-Sheets, Proformae, Files, Registers*
X	*Numerical Digit*

In case any manual, document or procedure directly refers either to an instruction or a record, then while numbering the document, the missing level shall not be skipped in the number given. Within the number allotted to the document the procedure or instruction location shall be retained as merely P-XX or I-XX indicating that the level of document does not exist for the particular case.

Example: The format of 'Amendment Data Record' is a level 4 document, which has no instruction and directly figures under the procedure as XYZQMS-4.2.3/P-01. Since there is no level 3 instruction under the level 2 procedure and the procedure directly refers to the level 4 document 'Amendment Data Record', this level 4 document shall be numbered as XYZQMS-4.2.3/P-01/I-XX/F-01 and not as XYZQMS-4.2.3/P-01/F-01.

Issue No. 1	Issue Date: 29.09.2001	Page No. 3 of 4
Reviewed By:		Approved By:

<table>
<tr><td rowspan="3">XYZ
Co.</td><td>XYZ CORPORATION</td><td>Doc. No.
XYZQMS – 4.2.3/P- 01</td></tr>
<tr><td>4. Quality Management System</td><td>Rev. No. Nil</td></tr>
<tr><td>Procedure for
Control of Documents</td><td>Rev. Date. Nil</td></tr>
</table>

The level 1,2,3 documents of the quality system shall be in the formats enclosed. The first issue of all documents shall be 01 and the page revision number shall be 0. Any page amended shall be indicated by upgrading the page revision status to, 1, 2, 3,...etc. After 15 revisions, the particular page of the document shall be re-issued and the issue number incremented by 1 and the page revision status shall become "0" for this revised issue.

f) Documents of external origin: The documents of external origin taken under control shall be entered in the list of external origin documents, which include 'National & International Standards', 'Customer Drawings' and 'Operation & Maintenance Manuals of Equipment' (retained for reference only).

The national & international standards shall be verified for amendments or revision at-least once every year for ensuring availability of latest amendments and revisions.

g) Obsolete: Whenever revised documents are formally issued to users, the corresponding obsolete documents shall be withdrawn and destroyed by the ISO Cell. The formal handing over of the current issue shall be recorded in the same format as for document issue. One copy of all withdrawn documents shall be retained for knowledge purpose. For this purpose the 'Master Copy' of the documents that became obsolete shall be extracted from the master file and after striking off with pen across the master copy stamp, and stamping them 'Obsolete Copy', shall be shifted to the obsolete documents file.

Ref :

<table>
<tr><td>Issue No. 1</td><td>Issue Date: 29.09.2001</td><td>Page No. 4 of 4</td></tr>
<tr><td colspan="2">Reviewed By:</td><td>Approved By:</td></tr>
</table>

<table>
<tr><td rowspan="4">XYZ
Co.</td><td>XYZ CORPORATION</td><td>Doc. No.
XYZQMS – 4.2.4/P- 01</td></tr>
<tr><td>4. Quality Management System</td><td>Rev. No. Nil</td></tr>
<tr><td>Procedure for
Control of Records</td><td>Rev. Date. Nil</td></tr>
</table>

Purpose : To ensure that all records are identified, collected, indexed, accessed, filed, stored, maintained, retained and disposed to demonstrate the conformance to specified requirements.

Responsibility : Processes Owners.

Scope : All processes.

Procedure : Records at XYZ Corporation shall be filled with the required data, collected at the place of use. All data entered, shall be 'as generated and as observed' to ensure it is factual. These records shall be maintained by the respective stage / location of use, stated in the master list of documents. When bound registers are used and a register gets filled, it shall be stored in the records room and a fresh register taken. In case loose sheets are used, they shall be properly filed in the relevant file. All records shall be countersigned by the personnel authorized to do so, in the relevant manual document / procedure / work instruction. Whenever data is entered into records the persons filling the data shall ensure that the entries are neat, legible and readable. In case corrections are to be made due to an incorrect entry, it is to be ensured that, it is unambiguous and does not lead to doubts or confusion.

The records generated during the course of implementation of QMS shall be referred in the relevant higher-level document. All such records / files shall be identified by a unique codification system as per 'Procedure for Control of Documents.' The records after filling in the data, shall be indexed chronologically and stored in the form of files / registers. Whenever required the records shall be retrieved and made available.

At the end of every financial year, all latest running records shall be closed and fresh records started. All obsolete records shall be sequentially numbered and stored / retained in the records room. The master list of documents shall state the retention period of every record. On completion of the retention period, the particular record shall be destroyed.

The formats of all controlled records shall have their specimen controlled copies available in the ISO Cell, as approved Level 4 documents.

Ref:

Issue No. 1	Issue Date : 29.09.2001	Page No. 1 of 1
Reviewed By:		Approved By:

<table>
<tr><td rowspan="3">XYZ Co.</td><td>XYZ CORPORATION</td><td>Doc. No.
XYZQMS – 8.2.2/P- 01</td></tr>
<tr><td>8. Measurement, Analysis & Improvement</td><td>Rev. No. Nil</td></tr>
<tr><td>Procedure for Internal Audit</td><td>Rev. Date. Nil</td></tr>
</table>

Purpose : To determine and monitor the effectiveness of the QMS implemented within the organization by ensuring that internal audits are planned and carried out.

Responsibility: Management Representative

Scope : All processes.

Procedure : The internal quality audit shall be carriedout by one or more trained members from within the organization and by outside experts, as a second party audit for feedback and advice.

The internal quality audits shall be planned in advance for a full calendar year to ensure that each department is audited at least once every six months. In case the need is felt and it is required to carry out additional audits, there shall be no bar on it. Care shall be taken in the appointing auditor(s) to ensure that one does not have to audit ones own work.

A tentative schedule shall be prepared by the MR and forwarded to all auditees at least a week in advance to ensure the convenience and availability of their key personnel. During the audit, it allotted shall be ensured that all areas as per the plan are audited.

The auditor(s) shall audit the department as per the schedule. The entire audit shall be done with a positive approach and positive reporting shall be adopted, through the use of "Internal Audit Reports" giving actual findings. Any deficiencies observed shall also be reported therein. If these deficiencies are non-conformities, they shall be reported in the format 'Internal Audit NC Report' and if they are mere observations they shall be reported in 'Internal Audit Observation Report'. If as a result of audit, non-conformities are not found for the particular audited department, the same shall be reported in the format 'Internal Audit Report for No NC Found'.

At the end of the audit, the auditors shall appraise the auditee about their findings. The auditors shall ensure that all facts are agreed upon and signature of the auditee is obtained. These reports shall be submitted to the MR for information and necessary action.

Issue No. 1	Issue Date: 29.09.2001	Page No. 1 of 2
Reviewed By:		Approved By:

<table>
<tr><td rowspan="3">XYZ
Co.</td><td>XYZ CORPORATION</td><td>Doc. No.
XYZQMS – 8.2.2/P- 01</td></tr>
<tr><td>8. Measurement, Analysis &
Improvement</td><td>Rev. No. Nil</td></tr>
<tr><td>Procedure for
Internal Audit</td><td>Rev. Date. Nil</td></tr>
</table>

The deficiencies brought out by the audit team in the form of NC & observations shall be corrected effectively, within an agreed time frame. This shall be verified and reported through a follow-up audit or visit to ensure necessary corrective actions have been taken.

The auditee department heads, shall ensure they maintain a file containing all their previous NCR's and observations and show them to the auditors as and when required.

The '**Internal Quality Audit Reports**' and report for second party audit shall be maintained and the findings of the audit shall be presented by the MR for review during the management review meetings.

Ref :

Issue No. 1	Issue Date: 29.09.2001	Page No. 2 of 2
Reviewed By:		Approved By:

<table>
<tr><td rowspan="3">XYZ Co.</td><td>XYZ CORPORATION</td><td>Doc. No.
XYZQMS – 8.3/P- 01</td></tr>
<tr><td>8. Measurement, Analysis & Improvement</td><td>Rev. No. Nil</td></tr>
<tr><td>Procedure for Control of Non-Conforming Products (NCP)</td><td>Rev. Date. Nil</td></tr>
</table>

Purpose : To ensure that the non-conforming products are neither sent to the next stage nor put to use even unintentionally, and are reviewed and disposed suitably.
Responsibility : Process Owners

Scope : All processes.

Procedure : All Products whether incoming, in-process or finished shall be inspected as per the relevant inspection instructions, to verify and ensure their conformity prior to use.

Incoming Products: All incoming products found non-conforming shall be identified, rejected and returned to the supplier except for those items which when found non-conforming can be downgraded and used for alternative applications, where the downgraded material is acceptable. The decision to degrade and accept for alternative use shall be the authority of the Works Manager.

In-process Products: The various possible in-process non-conformities in the product, at different stages of production shall be provided in the form of a list within the respective inspection instructions. Non-conformity whenever identified shall be marked on the non-conforming product as per instructions for test status marking and the NCP shifted to the area designated for such NCP. All reworkable NCP shall be reworked as per the Instructions for rework.

Finished Products: In case of non-conformity observed in finished products in relation to the specified standards, appropriate action to review shall be taken by the Head Q.C./ Works Manager/ General Manager to rework / reject. All NCs in the product detected and reported after delivery has been effected or if its use has commenced shall be treated as complaints and dealt with as per the procedure for handling complaints.

In case of non-conformities identified other than the possible NCs listed in the various inspection instructions provided, the Head Q.C. along with the Head of the relevant section shall review the non-conformity and take a decision. All non-conforming products that can neither be reworked nor downgraded and used for alternative use shall be disposed off as per the instructions for disposal of NCP.

<table>
<tr><td>Issue No. 1</td><td>Issue Date: 29.09.2001</td><td>Page No. 1 of 2</td></tr>
<tr><td colspan="2">Reviewed By:</td><td>Approved By:</td></tr>
</table>

<table>
<tr><td rowspan="3">XYZ
Co.</td><td>XYZ CORPORATION</td><td>Doc. No.
XYZQMS – 8.3/P- 01</td></tr>
<tr><td>8. Measurement, Analysis &
Improvement</td><td>Rev. No. Nil</td></tr>
<tr><td>Procedure for Control of
Non-Conforming Products (NCP)</td><td>Rev. Date. Nil</td></tr>
</table>

All non-conformities shall be reported as feedback for corrective and preventive actions, if the percentage of non-conforming product increases beyond the limits specified in the table of acceptable limits of NCP. Such NCs shall be taken up for discussion during the management review meetings.

For materials that undergo rework and reinspection, the same record as for the original inspection shall be used to record their inspection status.

Ref:

Issue No. 1	Issue Date: 29.09.2001	Page No. 2 of 2
Reviewed By:	Approved By:	

<table>
<tr><td rowspan="4">XYZ Co.</td><td>XYZ CORPORATION</td><td>Doc. No. XYZQMS – 8.5.2/P-01</td></tr>
<tr><td rowspan="2">8. Measurement, Analysis & Improvement</td><td></td></tr>
<tr><td>Rev. No. Nil</td></tr>
<tr><td>Procedure for Corrective Actions</td><td>Rev. Date. Nil</td></tr>
</table>

Purpose : a) To ensure dynamism in the QMS with continual improvement
b) To eliminate the root cause of identified NCs, and
c) To avoid recurrence of problems

Responsibility : Process Owners

Scope : All processes.

Procedures : The Executive Director and the Head Q.C. shall coordinate the corrective actions to be undertaken by investigating the causes of non-conformities in the product, process and the system to avoid recurrence. The extent of stress and control that shall be put on the corrective actions shall depend upon the impact of the NC on the product, process or system and its consequent influence on other areas.

Product related NCs identified during inspection, if observed to be higher than the acceptable limits of NC specifies, shall be taken up for corrective action immediately. For all such corrective actions, records shall be maintained using the proforma for corrective action. The corrective action identified shall be assessed for suitability prior to implementation and shall also be verified subsequently for effectiveness. The document changes arising out of the corrective action shall be taken up, as per the Procedure for Control of Documents.

Information and feedback from the various processes and work operations, internal quality audit reports, customer complaints and feedback shall be reviewed and NCs shall be reported to the concerned personnel so as to investigate the cause and suggest corrective action.

The corrective action for quality system related NCs shall be dealt as per the Procedure for Internal Audit.

Ref :

<table>
<tr><td>Issue No. 1</td><td colspan="2">Issue Date: 29.09.2001</td><td>Page No. 1 of 1</td></tr>
<tr><td colspan="2">Reviewed By:</td><td colspan="2">Approved By:</td></tr>
</table>

<table>
<tr><td rowspan="3">XYZ Co.</td><td>XYZ CORPORATION</td><td>Doc. No.
XYZQMS –8.5.3/P-01</td></tr>
<tr><td>8. Measurement, Analysis & Improvement</td><td>Rev. No. Nil</td></tr>
<tr><td>Procedure for Preventive Actions</td><td>Rev. Date. Nil</td></tr>
</table>

Purpose : a) To anticipate and identify likely problems in the QMS
b) To eliminate the root cause of the potential problems
c) To avoid occurrence of these problems
d) To ensure effectiveness in this process of prevention

Responsibility: Process Owners

Scope : All processes

Procedures : The Executive Director and the Head Q.C. shall coordinate the preventive action to be undertaken by assessing the impact of the potential non-conformities in the product, process and the system on other related areas to avoid any new problems from arising.

All information/feedback from various sources such as processes, work operations, internal quality audit reports, customer feedback, etc., shall be reviewed and the potential non-conformities shall be reported to concerned personnel to investigate the cause and suggest preventive action. The preventive action suggested shall be discussed with other functionaries regarding its effect in their areas.

All potential non-conformities with respect to product, process and system after they have been identified shall be reported to the Executive Director and the related Head. They shall also be recorded in 'preventive actions taken proforma'. These shall then be discussed and the possible preventive action identified. From the identified solution the optimum preventive action shall be implemented temporarily for study. The implemented action if found effective and useful shall be incorporated into the procedures appropriately for permanent implementation, through the procedure for document and data changes. In case the implemented action is found to be lacking in any way, an alternative action shall be identified and implemented.

Product / process related preventive actions, are based on the impact of corrective actions on other related areas, where, prevention helps avoid likely problems. All such actions taken based on the likelihood of problems arising and the consequent prevention measures are recorded in the 'preventive action taken proforma'. The preventive actions once determined shall be discussed prior to implementation and later verified for effectiveness. All document changes arising out of the preventive action shall be taken up as per the procedure for document and data changes.

<table>
<tr><td>Issue No. 1</td><td>Issue Date: 29.09.2001</td><td>Page No. 1 of 2</td></tr>
<tr><td colspan="2">Reviewed By:</td><td>Approved By:</td></tr>
</table>

XYZ Co.	**XYZ CORPORATION**	Doc. No. XYZQMS – 8.5.3/P-01
	5. Management Responsibility	Rev. No. Nil
	Procedure for Preventive Actions	Rev. Date. Nil

The preventive actions for quality system related potential non-conformities shall be dealt as per the procedure for internal audits.

Ref :

Issue No. 1	Issue Date: 29.09.2001	Page No. 2 of 2
Reviewed By:		Approved By:

[I S O] *twenty-one*

Optional Procedures of XYZ Corporation for a Few New Requirements (As per ISO 9001:2000)

****

Plot No. 11, Street No. 08,

ABC Chambers, Hyderabad,

India

Ph. +91-40-110890

Fax. +91-40-290987

****

****

****

**

XYZ Co.	XYZ CORPORATION	Doc. No. XYZQMS – 4.2.3/P-01/I-XX/F-02
	Optional Procedures of the QMS	Rev. No. Nil
	Contents	Rev. Date. Nil

Sl.No.	Document Number	Name of the Document	No. of Pages
1.	XYZQMS-4.1/P-01	Procedure for Identifying Processes, their Sequence and Interaction	2
2.	XYZQMS-4.1/P-02	Procedure for classifying processes into Key and Supporting Processes	2
3.	XYZQMS-4.1/P-03	Procedure for Process Approach	2
4.	XYZQMS-4.1/P-04	Procedure for Outsourcing Processes	3
5.	XYZQMS-5.1/P-01	Procedure for demonstrating Top Management commitment	1
6.	XYZQMS-5.2/P-01	Procedure for Customer Focus	1
7.	XYZQMS-5.5.3/P-01	Procedure for Internal Communication	2
8.	XYZQMS-6.2.2/P-01	Procedure for Identifying Work Affecting Product Quality	1
9.	XYZQMS-6.2.2/P-02	Procedure for Ensuring Competence of People	2
10.	XYZQMS-7.2.3/P-01	Procedure for Customer Communication	1
11.	XYZQMS-8.2/P-01	Procedure for Customer Satisfaction	3
12.	XYZQMS-8.5.1/P-01	Procedure for Continual Improvement	3

Issue No. 1	Issue Date: 29.09.2001	Page No. 1 of 1
Reviewed By:	Approved By:	

<table>
<tr><td rowspan="3">XYZ Co.</td><td colspan="3">XYZ CORPORATION</td><td colspan="3">Doc. No. XYZQMS – 4.2.3/P-01/I-XX/F-01</td></tr>
<tr><td colspan="3">Optional Procedures of the QMS</td><td colspan="3">Rev. No. Nil</td></tr>
<tr><td colspan="3">Amendment Data Record</td><td colspan="3">Rev. Date. Nil</td></tr>
<tr><td>Sl.No.</td><td>Doc. No.</td><td>Doc. Name</td><td>Page No. Of Doc. Changed</td><td>Issue No / Issue Date</td><td>Rev. No. / Rev. Date</td><td>Nature of change / Amend-ment</td></tr>
<tr><td></td><td></td><td></td><td></td><td></td><td></td><td></td></tr>
<tr><td colspan="3">Issue No. 1</td><td colspan="2">Issue Date: 29.09.2001</td><td colspan="2">Page No. 1 of 1</td></tr>
<tr><td colspan="4">Reviewed By:</td><td colspan="3">Approved By:</td></tr>
</table>

<table>
<tr><td rowspan="3">XYZ Co.</td><td>XYZ CORPORATION</td><td>Doc. No. XYZQMS – 4.1/P- 01</td></tr>
<tr><td>4.1 QMS General Requirements</td><td>Rev. No. Nil</td></tr>
<tr><td>Procedure for Identifying Processes needed, their Sequence and Interaction</td><td>Rev. Date. Nil</td></tr>
</table>

Purpose: To identify the 'Processes Needed for the QMS' through flow charting of existing processes under the QMS and aligning them with the requirements of the standard to arrive at 'their application'.

Responsibility: Process Owners

Scope : All Processes

Procedure: The following shall be the steps used to identify the 'Processes Needed under the QMS and their application, sequence and interaction' through flow charting:

(i) The existing value-adding processes, which convert inputs to outputs, shall be listed. Such processes could be planning, design and development, purchasing, product realization, marketing, servicing, etc.

(ii) A flow chart of these processes, in the sequence of their occurrence and use, shall then be prepared.

(iii) The supporting processes are then added to the flow chart e.g. Finance, Legal, Human resource, Infrastructure, Management, Information technology, etc.

(iv) Lines with arrows shall be drawn between the processes depicting flow of material (continuous line), information (broken line) or both (double line).

(v) Wherever there are decision-making processes, feedback loops shall be shown for:

a) Correction of the defectives
b) Corrective action for the defects
c) Preventive actions for associated areas.

(vi) These shall then be defined through a table, listing the identified processes, their inputs, outputs, required resources, the value-additions activity and thereby their application within the QMS.

(vii) The flow chart and table shall now be compared with the requirements of the standard and the following actions taken:

a) Each 'requirement of the standard' shall be assigned to the appropriate process based on the 'process requirements', and
b) Any new processes or activities that need to be fitted into the flowchart to take care of any leftover requirement of the standard, that does not have an appropriate corresponding process, shall be identified.

<table>
<tr><td>Issue No. 1</td><td>Issue Date: 29.09.2001</td><td>Page No. 1 of 2</td></tr>
<tr><td colspan="2">Reviewed By:</td><td>Approved By:</td></tr>
</table>

<table>
<tr><td rowspan="3">XYZ Co.</td><td>XYZ CORPORATION</td><td>Doc. No.
XYZQMS – 4.1/P- 01</td></tr>
<tr><td>4.1 QMS General Requirements</td><td>Rev. No. Nil</td></tr>
<tr><td>Procedure for Identifying Processes needed
their Sequence and Interaction</td><td>Rev. Date. Nil</td></tr>
</table>

(viii) A modified flow chart and table incorporating the necessary changes shall be prepared as the final flow process chart of XYZ Corporation.

(ix) Boundaries of the processes around those activities, that each process covers, shall be drawn to arrive at, and thereby define the 'Process Boundaries'.

(x) Each of these identified processes shall be given an appropriate name.

(xi) The identified processes and their defined boundaries shall be used for the development of their procedures and also for allocation of responsibility and authority for each one of them.

Ref :

Issue No. 1	Issue Date: 29.09.2001	Page No. 2 of 2
Reviewed By:		Approved By:

XYZ Co.	XYZ CORPORATION	Doc. No. XYZQMS – 4.1/P- 02
	4.1 QMS General Requirements	Rev. No. Nil
	Procedure for Classifying Processes into Key and Supporting Processes	Rev. Date. Nil

Purpose : To evaluate all processes of the organization for determining their importance in relation to the quality objectives, to identify "Key or Core Processes" and "Supporting or Other Processes".

Responsibility : Process Owners

Scope : All processes

Procedures : The following sequence of steps would help in zeroing onto these key or core processes:

(i) This task shall be assigned only to senior people, who with an overall view of the organization can identify core processes of critical importance to the operational existence of the corporation.
(ii) All the objectives of the organization shall be listed and processes associated with each of them shall be determined.
(iii) The processes shall then be linked to the appropriate objectives.
(iv) A matrix linking each objective with its associated macro as well as micro-processes shall be developed as shown below:

Shared & Linked Macro Processes With their Microprocesses	**Objectives to be achieved**			**Total Impact Based on Total Marks**
Macroprocess 1	**Objective 1**	**Objective 2**	**Objective 3**	
Microprocess 1				
Microprocess 2				
Macroprocess 2				
Microprocess 2				
Microprocess 2				
Microprocess 3				

Issue No. 1	Issue Date: 29.09.2001	Page No. 1 of 2
Reviewed By:	Approved By:	

<table>
<tr><td rowspan="3">XYZ Co.</td><td>XYZ CORPORATION</td><td>Doc. No.
XYZQMS – 4.1/P- 02</td></tr>
<tr><td>4.1 QMS General Requirements</td><td>Rev. No. Nils</td></tr>
<tr><td>Procedure for classifying processes into Key and Supporting Processes</td><td>Rev. Date. Nil</td></tr>
</table>

(v) The impact of each microprocess on each of the objectives shall then be established.

(vi) The type of impact shall be indicated by allotting 10 marks for a large impact, 5 marks for an average impact and 0 marks for small or no impact.

(vii) The marks of each microprocess for all the objectives put together shall be added to arrive at the total impact on the objectives of the organization and thereby identify the important microprocesses.

(viii) The marks for all the microprocesses under each macroprocess, shall be added to arrive at the total impact of the macroprocess. This would help in identifying the core or key processes out of all the listed processes.

The identifying characteristics of key or core processes shall be:

- They have an extremely large impact on the organization.
- They are crucial to the organization's success.
- Their proper performance gives the organization a competitive advantage.
- They affect the customers.
- They are multi-functional.
- They tend to be mostly large and complex.
- They would be the processes pertaining to the areas of specialization of the organization.

The 'Key or Core Processes' shall normally be those multi-departmental macroprocesses, which directly relate to 'the customers' or 'design and development' or 'product realization' or 'provision of resources'. All other processes shall be defined as 'Supporting or Other Processes'. After identifying these 'Key or Core' macroprocesses that are vital to XYZ Corporation's business activity, each of them shall then be brokenup into its respective micro processes.

Ref :

<table>
<tr><td>Issue No. 1</td><td>Issue Date: 29.09.2001</td><td>Page No. 2 of 2</td></tr>
<tr><td colspan="2">Reviewed By:</td><td>Approved By:</td></tr>
</table>

<table>
<tr><td rowspan="3">XYZ Co.</td><td>XYZ CORPORATION</td><td>Doc. No.
XYZQMS – 4.1/P- 03</td></tr>
<tr><td>4.1 QMS General Requirements</td><td>Rev. No. Nil</td></tr>
<tr><td>Procedure for
Process Approach</td><td>Rev. Date. Nil</td></tr>
</table>

Purpose : To apply and manage, the identified interacting system of processes of XYZ Corporation, within the organization, for its effective functioning and improvement.

Responsibility : Process Owners

Scope : All processes

Procedures : XYZ Corporation shall treat the entire organization as a network of interlinked processes that can be identified, documented, controlled and improved.

These processes being cross-functional, their impact on the associated functions as well as the other interacting processes, shall be assessed to ensure effective functioning and ascertain the scope for improvement. Each process shall also be defined giving its purpose, resource requirements, quality requirements, cycle time, measurement and monitoring, controls, variability, and constraints.

The application of the system of identified process of XYZ Corporation to the QMS shall be based on the following:

(i) Processes shall be organized around the *Outcomes* of the processes rather than the activities or *Outputs*, since outputs are the result of satisfactory operation of processes while outcomes are the result of satisfactory outputs. (*Outputs* measure the 'ability of the processes to deliver product conforming to specifications' while *Outcomes* measure the 'ability of the delivered product to satisfy customers').

(ii) All activities shall be linked in the natural order of their occurrence in the process chain to ensure a smooth flow.

(iii) Activities that can be performed in parallel, shall be performed in such a manner, so as to bring down cycle time.

(iv) As far as possible specialized competencies shall be centralized to create "Centers of Excellence".

<table>
<tr><td>Issue No. 1</td><td>Issue Date : 29.09.2001</td><td>Page No. 1 of 2</td></tr>
<tr><td colspan="2">Reviewed By:</td><td>Approved By:</td></tr>
</table>

XYZ Co.	XYZ CORPORATION	Doc. No. XYZQMS – 4.1/P- 03
	4.1 QMS General Requirements	Rev. No. Nil
	Procedure for Process Approach	Rev. Date. Nil

(v) All checks, controls and processing of information for taking decisions shall be placed in the process chain where their presence results in correction as well as immediate feedback for corrective action.

(vi) Information shall be collected once at the point of origination or where encountered first and then shall be used subsequently as it is, to avoid duplication and needless reconciliation.

(vii) Ownership of the processes shall be practised, so that during value-addition to the inputs, each owner ensures only conforming output are given to the internal customer. By practising this principle of ownership, satisfactory input to the next process, and the next and so on, shall be ensured, leading to satisfied customers. The process owners themselves shall define their specific task and controls needed, to achieve the required output 'Right First Time Every Time'. To achieve continual improvement they shall also identify, control, monitor and analyze problems within their process and at the interfaces.

(viii) Each Key process within the entire chain of interlinked processes of the QMS, at XYZ Corporation, shall be described adequately and its controls defined so that it can function correctly in harmony with other processes. The system of processes thus identified shall be utilized to achieve control over process-variability to eliminate non-conforming outputs. The acceptable limits of process-variability shall also be defined, and reasons for deviations beyond acceptable value leading to non-conformity shall be analyzed, for bringing about continual improvement.

The starting point for the application of the 'Processes Approach' to the QMS shall be based on the identified existing processes identified on account of historical reasons of satisfactory performance in the past. These processes shall form the initial base of the process chain as they already provide the 'Existing Quality Level'.

The Process Matrix shall then be aligned with the requirements of the standard by the addition of any process not already included in the chain but required by the standard.

Ref :

Issue No. 1	Issue Date: 29.09.2001	Page No. 2 of 2
Reviewed By:	Approved By:	

<table>
<tr><td rowspan="3">XYZ Co.</td><td>XYZ CORPORATION</td><td>Doc. No.
XYZQMS – 4.1/P- 04</td></tr>
<tr><td>4.1 QMS General Requirements</td><td>Rev. No. Nil</td></tr>
<tr><td>Procedure for
Outsourcing Processes</td><td>Rev. Date. Nil</td></tr>
</table>

Purpose : To transfer the selected processes and delegate responsibility for their routine operations to third party suppliers.

Responsibility: Top Management.

Scope : All processes

Procedure: The top management at XYZ Corporation, has decided to outsource the process of "**Computer and Information Service**" since this process takes up a lot of long-term investment and effort in its operation and maintenance and yet has a high and rapid rate of obsolescence. Moreover this is not a key process of XYZ Corporation.

The above however does not put a bar on outsourcing even key processes any time in the future, as long as the outsourced process complies with all requirements, and the outsourcing is approved by the 'Board of Directors' of the corporation through a resolution. Those processes which the Top management considers as the core competencies of XYZ Corporation, need to be guarded from competitors and hence shall not be outsourced.

The decision regarding outsourcing of processes shall be totally governed by the following:

(i) If it would help gain some sustainable competitive advantage in the market
(ii) If it would help in some reduction in cost even after accounting for the transaction cost and keeping own facilities idle
(iii) If this decision would help the organization maintain better controls and greater flexibility
(iv) If it would help the organization bring down processing and changeover cycle time
(v) If this decision would facilitate in flattening the organizational structure

It has been decided to outsource process from only those suppliers who comply with the following criterion:

(i) They are experts in certain technologies and they are prepared to provide them to users
(ii) Their Key Process, in view of their line of activity, is the outsourced process,

Issue No. 1	Issue Date: 29.09.2001	Page No. 1 of 3
Reviewed By:	Approved By:	

<table>
<tr><td rowspan="3">XYZ Co.</td><td>XYZ CORPORATION</td><td>Doc. No. XYZQMS – 4.1/P- 04</td></tr>
<tr><td>4.1 QMS General Requirements</td><td>Rev. No. Nil</td></tr>
<tr><td>Procedure for Outsourcing Processes</td><td>Rev. Date. Nil</td></tr>
</table>

(iii) They are prepared to and easily can take care of the slack and peak periods,
(iv) Their processes are efficient
(v) They have the capability to respond quickly to the organization's needs and changes
(vi) They have a wide base of available skills in the field of activity
(vii) They are able to draw on other experiences to propose and implement better or newer idea
(viii) They are able to provide a good control on the process
(ix) They are able to show accountability for the performance of the outsourced process
(x) They are prepared for a long-term partnership to mutual advantage
(xi) They are prepared to provide the latest cutting-edge technology at competitive price
(xii) Their Price is competitive (not necessarily the lowest) even after including the transaction costs
(xiii) They have a lean organization
(xiv) They are trustworthy and reliable
(xv) They have adequate capacity to spare and utilize in a better way
(xvi) They have some geographic location advantages giving differential costs for power, labor, taxes, material handling, etc
(xvii) They have a higher productivity in their organization than it is otherwise possible for XYZ Corporation to have

After deciding upon the supplier from whom a process shall be outsourced, a formal agreement shall be drawn-out and communicated to the process supplier. This agreement shall not only contain details of the process but also all requirements and expectations of XYZ Corporation in full detail to avoid misinterpretation and ambiguity leading to errors. XYZ Corporation shall also specify the required controls, methods of measurement, acceptable levels of performance, continual improvement requirements, etc. Records of all these shall be maintained. The outsourced process shall be monitored and controlled as per 'Procedure for control of outsourced processes'.

The above however does not in anyway mean, that since the organization is out-sourcing a process, all issues related to the process and its technology no longer concern XYZ Corporation. Rather, the 'Purchasing' process of XYZ Corporation would monitor and control the performance of this outsourced process for ensuring better performance. There shall, infact, be a conscious shift from operational to tactical and then to strategic management of the process.

Issue No. 1	Issue Date: 29.09.2001	Page No. 2 of 3
Reviewed By:	Approved By:	

<table>
<tr><td rowspan="3">XYZ Co.</td><td>XYZ CORPORATION</td><td>Doc. No. XYZQMS – 4.1/P-04</td></tr>
<tr><td>4.1 QMS General Requirements</td><td>Rev. No. Nil</td></tr>
<tr><td>Procedure for Outsourcing Processes</td><td>Rev. Date. Nil</td></tr>
</table>

The suppliers of every outsourced process shall be given the status of a 'Key Relationship Supplier' to differentiate them from the other suppliers in recognition of their ability and contribution to meeting and exceeding, XYZ Corporation's high growth need, coupled with the flexibility needed to make rapid changes.

Ref :

Issue No. 1	Issue Date: 29.09.2001	Page No. 3 of 3
Reviewed By:	Approved By:	

<table>
<tr><td rowspan="4">XYZ
Co.</td><td>XYZ CORPORATION</td><td>Doc. No.
XYZQMS – 5.1/P-01</td></tr>
<tr><td></td><td></td></tr>
<tr><td>5. Management Responsibility</td><td>Rev. No. Nil</td></tr>
<tr><td>Procedure for demonstrating
Top Management commitment</td><td>Rev. Date. Nil</td></tr>
</table>

Purpose : To provide evidence of commitment to development, implementation and continual improvement of effectiveness of QMS

Responsibility: Top Management

Scope : All processes

Procedure: The top management at XYZ Corporation shall treat their commitment to the QMS as an obligation, which can easily be verified. It shall therefore be stated, documented and communicated within the organization as under:

a) The document where this commitment shall be stated is the quality policy of the Corporation duly signed by the top management

b) The evidence for demonstrating commitment to the QMS shall be the following:
   (i) Establishment, documentation, maintenance and continual improvement of the entire QMS
   (ii) Endorsement of the established quality objectives shall provide evidence of top management commitment
   (iii) Ensuring whatever is committed or stated is done faithfully
   (iv) Encouraging feed-back from all interested parties
   (v) Ensuring sub-standard products are never dispatched, rather they are suitably attended
   (vi) Supporting corrective actions, preventive actions and improvement efforts
   (vii) Provision, allocation and replenishment of resources

c) The communication of their commitment shall be done as per "Procedure for communicating top management commitment within the organization"

Ref :

Issue No. 1	Issue Date: 29.09.2001	Page No. 1 of 1
Reviewed By:		Approved By:

<table>
<tr><td rowspan="3">XYZ
Co.</td><td>XYZ CORPORATION</td><td>Doc. No.
XYZQMS – 5.2/P-01</td></tr>
<tr><td>5. Management Responsibility</td><td>Rev. No. Nil</td></tr>
<tr><td>Procedure for
Customer Focus</td><td>Rev. Date. Nil</td></tr>
</table>

Purpose : To ensure customer requirements are determined and met to enhance customer satisfaction.

Responsibility : Top Management

Scope : All processes

Procedures : At XYZ Corporation, the entire focus of the organization shall remain towards ensuring customer satisfaction, by determining and assessing customer requirements and maintaining a congenial and harmonious customer relationship. The actual end user of the output product of the organization shall be identified. The *customer requirements* and other related information shall be determined, and then utilized for providing and improving products delivered. Flexibility for adjusting to future requirements and expectations shall be suitably addressed and provided for. The collection of data for assessing customer satisfaction shall be treated as a critical activity. This data shall be collected from any or all of the following available sources:

Internal	Third Party	Customers
Complaints Warranty claims Field service reports Refund Lost customer report Delivery receipts	Independent surveys Industry Analysts	Interviews Focus groups Surveys Comment cards

Customer interaction response mechanism shall be maintained at its fastest for maximum effectiveness. Access to customers shall be sought to facilitate collection of information and making them providing data. All issues leading to customer dissatisfaction shall be amicably and suitably resolved. Customer satisfaction data and feedback shall be pursued and actively followed-up. No efforts shall be spared to evaluate and improve *Customer-Relationship Management.* Compared to the practices adopted by competitors the organization shall setup methods to *determine customer satisfaction* level with the purpose of ensuring that the same customers keep coming back. This shall once again be treated as a critical process. The *customer satisfaction/dissatisfaction results* compared to competitors shall be determined. The assessment shall determine the current level of satisfaction and also the relative level of satisfaction compared to competitors.

Ref :

Issue No. 1	Issue Date: 29.09.2001	Page No. 1 of 1
Reviewed By:	Approved By:	

<table>
<tr><td rowspan="4">XYZ Co.</td><td rowspan="2">XYZ CORPORATION</td><td>Doc. No.
XYZQMS – 5.5.3/P-01</td></tr>
<tr><td></td></tr>
<tr><td>5. Management Responsibility</td><td>Rev. No. Nil</td></tr>
<tr><td>Procedure for
Internal Communication</td><td>Rev. Date. Nil</td></tr>
</table>

Purpose : To establish and implement an effective and efficient means for communicating the quality policy, requirements, objectives and accomplishments within the organization.

Responsibility : M.R

Scope : All processes

Procedures : Every individual at XYZ Corporation, shall be encouraged to communicate within the organization with effectiveness. In order to avoid making errors leading to mistakes they shall be suitably trained to ensure the following during their internal communication:

Clarity of expression
Preciseness of the subject
Focus on the objective
Ease of understanding
Atmosphere of friendliness and trust
Proper understanding by the receiver of the communication

At the Corporation, the quality policy and quality objectives shall be communicated to all levels through training sessions. Further, the quality policy and quality objectives shall be displayed at prominent places within the premises. Each individual shall also be given a laminated printed copy of the quality policy in English and vernacular. Daily repetition of the quality policy at work areas in groups shall also be practised. During the training sessions, the relevance of the quality policy and objectives to each individual's work function shall be communicated / elaborated.

The requirements of the customer with regard to product, process and system shall be made known to all levels. Further, the personnel within XYZ Corporation shall be informed of the need, to not only ensure compliance and conformity to stated needs but also to rise to the occasion and ensure customer satisfaction through fulfilling implied needs in the form of expectations, such as professionalism, promptness, reasonableness, adaptability, accuracy of information, transparency and ownership of problems.

Issue No. 1	Issue Date: 29.09.2001	Page No. 1 of 2
Reviewed By:	Approved By:	

<table>
<tr><td rowspan="4">XYZ
Co.</td><td rowspan="2">XYZ CORPORATION</td><td>Doc. No.
XYZQMS – 5.5.3/P-01</td></tr>
<tr><td></td></tr>
<tr><td>5. Management Responsibility</td><td>Rev. No. Nil</td></tr>
<tr><td>Procedure for
Internal Communication</td><td>Rev. Date. Nil</td></tr>
</table>

XYZ Corporation's accomplishments which affect the image shall be communicated within the organization to boost the morale and motivate people for better performance. Suitable means shall be adopted to reward individuals responsible for such accomplishments.

In order to obtain suggestions and feedback from employees on the product, process and system, suggestion boxes shall be placed at convenient locations, whereby even individuals not desiring to disclose their identity with regard to any suggestion, can also drop unsigned papers with their suggestions.

Team briefings, training sessions and meetings shall be regularly organized as per QMS and records of the same maintained in 'Meetings Attendance Register'. The notice boards provided on the shop floor, rest rooms, security gates, reception lobby, etc. shall be used for communicating general communications affecting all individuals.

Ref:

Issue No. 1	Issue Date: 29.09.2001	Page No. 2 of 2
Reviewed By:		Approved By:

<table>
<tr><td rowspan="3">XYZ
Co.</td><td>XYZ CORPORATION</td><td>Doc. No.
XYZQMS – 6.2.2/P-01</td></tr>
<tr><td>6. Resource Management</td><td>Rev. No. Nil</td></tr>
<tr><td>Procedure for
Work Affecting Product Quality</td><td>Rev. Date. Nil</td></tr>
</table>

Purpose : To identify those work areas of the organization whose activities affect product quality.

Responsibility : Process Owners

Scope : All processes

Procedure: At XYZ Corporation work shall be divided into the following types:
a) Those which are a part of the key processes
b) Those which are a part of the supporting processes
c) Those which are a part of other processes of the organization

The corporation recognizes the contribution of every individual process to the 'organizational quality commitment and effort'. However, in keeping with the requirements of the standard, the corporation has specified that those activities or work that form a part of either its key processes or its supporting processes shall be defined as "work affecting product quality".

Besides the above, health and safety although a part of the other processes shall be treated as "work affecting product quality" since this is one area, which directly affects the quality of people's outputs.

Ref :

Issue No. 1	Issue Date: 29.09.2001	Page No. 1 of 1
Reviewed By:	Approved By:	

<table>
<tr><td rowspan="3">XYZ Co.</td><td>XYZ CORPORATION</td><td>Doc. No.
XYZQMS – 6.2.2/P-02</td></tr>
<tr><td>6. Resource Management</td><td>Rev. No. Nil</td></tr>
<tr><td>Procedure for
Ensuring Competence of People</td><td>Rev. Date. Nil</td></tr>
</table>

Purpose : To ensure people possess the required knowledge, understanding and practical ability to consistently perform the assigned job and sustain it to the expected level, when compared against current and future requirements of the organization.

Responsibility : Top Management

Scope : All processes

Procedures : Objective assessment of people's 'capabilities to contribute in relation to the requirements of the job assigned' shall be carried out, to determine 'competence of people' at XYZ Corporation. It shall also be remembered that whenever the same type of job is being performed, but at different levels, the need for the measure of competence shall be different, depending upon the level.

As the first step, the following or more factors, that can be used as a basis for determining competence shall be defined. Next, the number of levels of competence required within the organization, shall be specified in the form of GRADES between a minimum of 3 and maximum of 7 levels based on the following requirements:

- Mental capability
- Knowledge and skill
- Scope of responsibility
- Physical capability
- Nature and type of work
- Complexity of work

Finally the required competence, which is a combination of the knowledge, understanding and practical ability to perform their jobs shall be determined. This shall be done by developing a matrix of the factors in relation to the different levels of competence required. Marks shall be assigned to each factor depending on its importance to the level. While allotting these marks, different levels would be given different weightage for different factors and they need not be linear.

A suitable matrix proforma for determining the competence of people is given separately on the next page.

Ref:

Issue No. 1	Issue Date: 29.09.2001	Page No. 1 of 2
Reviewed By:	Approved By:	

XYZ Co.	XYZ CORPORATION	Doc. No. XYZQMS – 6.2.2/P-02
	6. Resource Management	Rev. No. Nil
	Procedure for Ensuring Competence of People	Rev. Date. Nil

COMPETENCE DETERMINATION FORM

Employee Name: **Employee No:**
Designation: **Process:**
Grade: **Date:**

Sl. No.	Related Factors Competence	Weightage marks for each Level of Competence					
		1	2	3	4	5	6
1.	Qualification and experience						
2.	Areas of expertise						
3.	Professional or technical knowledge						
4.	Commercial or business knowledge						
5.	Knowledge of internal processes, procedures and products						
6.	Decision-making and initiative						
7.	Management, planning and organizing capability						
8.	Written and verbal communication						
9.	Inter-personal relationship and teamwork						
10.	Mathematical ability						
11.	Logic and reasoning						
12.	Problem solving						
13.	Creativity and innovation						
14.	Information technology skills						
15.	Physical and manual skills						
16.	Leadership						
17.	Resources to be controlled						
18.	Any special appreciation / awards						

NAME OF ASSESSOR: SIGN:

Issue No. 1	Issue Date: 29.09.2001	Page No. 2 of 2
Reviewed By:	Approved By:	

<table>
<tr><td rowspan="3">XYZ Co.</td><td>XYZ CORPORATION</td><td>Doc. No. XYZQMS – 7.2.3/P-01</td></tr>
<tr><td>7. Product Realization</td><td>Rev. No. Nil</td></tr>
<tr><td>Procedure for Customer Communication</td><td>Rev. Date. Nil</td></tr>
</table>

Purpose : To determine and implement suitable and effective arrangements for maintaining communication with customers for receiving and transmitting necessary information.

Responsibility : Process Owners

Scope : All processes

Procedures : Channels of communication shall be established and maintained with XYZ Corporation's customers for obtaining information with regard to the product being supplied. The following procedure should be followed:

Before accepting any order from the customer, the entire information with regard to 'Product Requirements' shall be obtained from the customers through the 'enquiry form'. Any other queries arising shall be clarified, assessed and then accepted. Orders finally accepted shall also be communicated to the customer. All changes communicated by the customers shall be taken note of and incorporated as required. The changed requirements acceptance shall also be communicated to the customers.

Any enquiries received from the Customers / Potential Customers, shall be studied, clarified and assessed before acceptance through communication.

All communications received from customers and other sources in the nature of feedback as also, customer complaints shall be immediately acknowledged. They shall then be handled at top priority as per the procedure for 'Customer Complaints'. During the entire process, feedback and complaints shall be treated as identical, so that, every individual feedback acts as a means for improvement, leading to enhancement of performances.

Ref :

Issue No. 1	Issue Date: 29.09.2001	Page No. 1 of 1
Reviewed By:	Approved By:	

<table>
<tr><td rowspan="3">XYZ
Co.</td><td>XYZ CORPORATION</td><td>Doc. No.
XYZQMS – 8.2/P-01</td></tr>
<tr><td>8. Measurement, Analysis and Improvement</td><td>Rev. No. Nil</td></tr>
<tr><td>Procedure for Customer Satisfaction</td><td>Rev. Date. Nil</td></tr>
</table>

Purpose :To lay down guidelines for obtaining, evaluating and using information relating to customers' perception of the organization. Having met their requirements to measure and monitor the performance of the QMS earlier, sustain and improve upon it..

Responsibility: Top Management

Scope :All processes

Procedures : XYZ Corporation has adopted a positive approach towards determining and improving the customer satisfaction by taking the following specific actions to improve customer perception of our quality, in relation to the quality of our main competitors.

(i) Establishing a system for determining the requirements important to the customer such as cost, safety, reliability, etc. and then finding ways and means to achieve them.

(ii) Listening to the customer and taking appropriate actions.

(iii) Never making unrealistic promises.

(iv) Ensuring promises are kept.

(v) Determining customers perception of our quality, in comparison to our main competitors and acting on the feedback.

(vi) Customer satisfaction is rated in the form of easy to understand pictorial representation such as graphs or histograms.

Feedback from the customers shall be sought in writing through the 'Customer Feedback Form' on a three-monthly basis. The form shall be mailed to the customer by the marketing head and follow-up done to ensure that the data is returned completed in all respects. This form shall be sent to all customers.

All verbal feedback, written feedback and formal complaints received shall be processed as per procedure for customer complaints and actions taken expeditiously. Feedback arising out of these complaints shall be used to measure customer satisfaction, through 'Number of Complaint trend graph' updated on a monthly basis.

Customer requirements shall be disseminated and strictly enforced company-wide to eliminate or minimize costly errors.

Issue No. 1	Issue Date: 29.09.2001	Page No. 1 of 3
Reviewed By:	Approved By:	

XYZ Co.	XYZ CORPORATION	Doc. No. XYZQMS – 8.2/P-01
	8. Measurement, Analysis and Improvement	Rev. No. Nil
	Procedure for Customer Satisfaction	Rev. Date. Nil

The contact points with the customers shall be trained to ensure professionalism, competence and genuine concern for the customer, while dealing with them.

Evaluation of Customer Satisfaction to arrive at 'Customer Satisfaction / Dissatisfaction Index' is done based on the following:

(i) Are the requirements of customer verified and updated?
(ii) Are the requirements communicated within the organization?
(iii) Is the plot of customer satisfaction rating, maintained regularly?
(iv) Is continual improvement promoted, based on customer feedback?
(v) What is customer perception of our performance in relation to our main competitors?
(vi) Are all external customers contacted regularly for obtaining feed-back?
(vii) Is there an easy means for registering customer complaints?
(viii) Are complaints dealt with quickly and effectively ?
(ix) Is the customer educated in relevant areas ?
(x) Are the information and manuals reviewed for clarity, simplicity and latest information ?
(xi) Is there a change in the relative importance of requirements communicated earlier?
(xii) Do the products satisfy stated needs, implied needs and meet desired expectations?

The 'Customer Satisfaction Form' for rating the customer satisfaction level shall state:

The **overall satisfaction with performance of our product/service in relation to your expectations**, on a 5 Point Scale, where the range is from extremely dissatisfied to extremely satisfied and the discrete values are translated into descriptions such as

1) Extremely dissatisfied
2) Dissatisfied
3) Neither satisfied 'nor' satisfied
4) Satisfied
5) Extremely satisfied.

Issue No. 1	Issue Date: 29.09.2001	Page No. 2 of 3
Reviewed By:		Approved By:

<table>
<tr><td rowspan="3">XYZ Co.</td><td>XYZ CORPORATION</td><td>Doc. No.
XYZQMS – 8.2/P-01</td></tr>
<tr><td>8. Measurement, Analysis and Improvement</td><td>Rev. No. Nil</td></tr>
<tr><td>Procedure for Customer Satisfaction</td><td>Rev. Date. Nil</td></tr>
</table>

Further our performance is rated in relation to our main competitor on a scale of 5 by indicating satisfaction with our product when compared to our closest competitor as follows:

1) Much less satisfied than competitor
2) Less satisfied than competitor
3) Equally satisfied
4) More satisfied than competitor
5) Much more satisfied than competitor

List of attributes to be used for assessing customer satisfaction.

(i) Product conformance to specification.
(ii) Promptness of delivery.
(iii) Completeness of documentation.
(iv) Effectiveness in problem resolution.
(v) Responsiveness to queries.
(vi) Accuracy of information.
(vii) Price.
(viii) Adaptability to changing requirements and future needs..
(ix) Correction / Improvement based on feedback.

Ref:

Issue No. 1	Issue Date: 29.09.2001	Page No. 3 of 3
Reviewed By:		Approved By:

<table>
<tr><td rowspan="3">XYZ Co.</td><td>XYZ CORPORATION</td><td>Doc. No. XYZQMS – 8.5.1/P-01</td></tr>
<tr><td>8. Measurement, Analysis and Improvement</td><td>Rev. No. Nil</td></tr>
<tr><td>Procedure for Continual Improvement</td><td>Rev. Date. Nil</td></tr>
</table>

Purpose : To plan and manage continual improvements of the effectiveness and efficiency of the product, process and system in order to enhance XYZ Corporation's overall performance and benefit all interested parties.

Responsibility : Process Owners

Scope :All processes

Procedures :Planning for continual improvement shall be done by the top management and wholehearted support in its implementation shall be provided for achieving performance enhancement. All individuals shall be encouraged to spare no efforts towards continual improvement in their work or activity. The following shall form the basis of improvements:

a) The applicability of the quality objectives in relation to each 'Process or Function'

b) Competitors performance

c) Best practices

d) Suggestions from personnel who are encouraged to seek opportunities for improvement

These improvements shall advocate a systematic approach to problem solving, with a focus on accomplishments and results, leading to benefits in any of the following:

a) Improvement in the effectiveness by meeting requirements
b) Improvement in efficiency by proper utilization of resources
c) Compliance to statutory and regulatory requirements
d) Improvement in potential by-weak areas
e) Opportunities for all round betterment
f) Need for control on planned and un-planned changes
g) Measurement of planned benefits
h) Tackling cross-functional boundary and interface problems

<table>
<tr><td>Issue No. 1</td><td>Issue Date: 29.09.2001</td><td>Page No. 1 of 3</td></tr>
<tr><td colspan="2">Reviewed By:</td><td>Approved By:</td></tr>
</table>

<table>
<tr><td rowspan="3">XYZ Co.</td><td>XYZ CORPORATION</td><td>Doc. No. XYZQMS – 8.5.1/P-01</td></tr>
<tr><td>8. Measurement, Analysis and Improvement</td><td>Rev. No. Nil</td></tr>
<tr><td>Procedure for Continual Improvement</td><td>Rev. Date. Nil</td></tr>
</table>

Continual improvement being a planned activity, desired objectives shall be set, actions planned, implemented, monitored, corrected, improved, studied and then goals reset. This shall be done to keep up with the competitors who are also constantly improving, since competitive requirements are constantly getting tougher. Thus, after every improvement the requirements shall be tightened by resetting higher targets leading to 'Re-specification of the requirements at slightly higher levels'. In the 'PDCA' cycle this resetting of objectives at higher levels results in a rising spiral instead of a closed loop and so shall bring about continual improvement.

Continual Improvement Methods:

a) **Break-through improvement** : This shall be carried out by cross-functional teams outside routine operations by:
(i) Defining the improvement targeted,
(ii) Analyzing the existing process to find out possible improvements,
(iii) Planning the improvement,
(iv) Verifying the improvement,
(v) Evaluating the improvement, and
(vi) Re-defining a higher improvement target.

b) **Small step on-going improvement** : This shall be carried out by the people within the process group themselves. Any idea 'or' suggestion for improvement shall be studied for feasibility and necessary resources shall be provided to the process for effecting the improvement.

All changes to product, process and system arising out of this procedure shall be approved, prioritized, planned, provisioned and controlled to enhance exceeding XYZ Corporation's current capabilities. In order to successfully effect such continual improvement, people shall be given control of their processes, and resources needed shall be provided including necessary training.

Issue No. 1	Issue Date: 29.09.2001	Page No. 2 of 3
Reviewed By:		Approved By:

<table>
<tr><td rowspan="3">XYZ Co.</td><td>XYZ CORPORATION</td><td>Doc. No. XYZQMS – 8.5.1/P-01</td></tr>
<tr><td>8. Measurement, Analysis and Improvement</td><td>Rev.No. Nil</td></tr>
<tr><td>Procedure for Continual Improvement</td><td>Rev.Date. Nil</td></tr>
</table>

Steps for Continual Improvement

(i) Determine areas where improvements are planned.
(ii) Ensure that the areas are strictly operating under control i.e. at standard conditions as per defined procedures, by trained personnel, using proper equipment.
(iii) Find out the best practices and means to adopt and practise them.
(iv) Identify the problems and parameters where improvements are possible.
(v) Set desired improvement goals.
(vi) Assess the symptoms and determine the root-cause of problem or poor performance.
(vii) Analyze the data from the problem area and determine options.
(viii) Develop possible solutions.
(ix) List resources needed and the cost implications.
(x) Verify which options give the best value for money.
(xi) Adopt the options and carry out trials.
(xii) Record test results as an evidence.
(xiii) Record obstacles and failures.
(xiv) Carry out trials on modification / correction.
(xv) Establish success of the improvement effected.
(xvi) Record improvement results.
(xvii) Stabilize the improved process.
(xviii) Repeat the above process.

Ref:

Issue No. 1	Issue Date: 29.09.2001	Page No. 3 of 3
Reviewed By:		Approved By:

ISO

twenty-two

Specimen Instructions, Specifications and Lists of XYZ Corporation (As Per ISO 9001:2000)

****

Plot No. 11, Street No. 08,

ABC Chambers, Hyderabad,

India

Ph. +91-40-110890

Fax. +91-40-290987

****

****

****

**

XYZ Co.	XYZ CORPORATION	Doc. No. XYZQMS – 4.2.3/P-01/I-XX/F-02
	Level 3 Documents	Rev. No. Nil
	Contents	Rev. Date. Nil

S.No	Document Number	Name of the Document	No. of Pages
1.	XYZQMS-7.5.1 /P-01/I-01	Work Instruction for operating a Gantry Crane	1
2.	XYZQMS-7.4.3 /P-01/I-01	Instruction for Inspection of Steel Sheets	1
3.	XYZQMS-7.6 /P-01/I-01	Instructions for Calibration of Pressure Gauges	1
4.	XYZQMS-7.4.2 /P-01/I-01	Specification for Hot Rolled Edge Trimmed Steel Sheets	1
5.	XYZQMS-7.6 /P-01/I-02	List of Measuring Equipment	1

Issue No. 1	Issue Date: 29.09.2001	Page No. 1 of 1
Reviewed By:	Approved By:	

<table>
<tr><td rowspan="3">XYZ
Co.</td><td>XYZ CORPORATION</td><td>Doc. No. XYZQMS – 4.2.3/P-01/I-XX/F-01</td></tr>
<tr><td>Level 3 Documents</td><td>Rev. No. Nil</td></tr>
<tr><td>Amendment Data Record</td><td>Rev. Date. Nil</td></tr>
</table>

S.No.	Doc. No.	Doc. Name	Page No. Of Doc. Changed	Issue No / Issue Date	Rev. No. / Rev. Date	Nature of change / Amendment

Issue No. 1	Issue Date: 29.09.2001	Page No. 1 of 1
Reviewed By:	Approved By:	

<table>
<tr><td rowspan="3">XYZ Co.</td><td>XYZ CORPORATION</td><td>Doc. No. XYZQMS –7.5.1 /P-01/I-01</td></tr>
<tr><td>7.5.1 Control of Production & Service Provisions</td><td>Rev. No. Nil</td></tr>
<tr><td>Work Instructions for operating a Gantry Crane</td><td>Rev. Date. Nil</td></tr>
</table>

Responsibility: Crane Operator

Machine used: Gantry Crane

Safety precautions:

- Ensure that rails are clear and free from any obstruction or material.
- Check the wire ropes for good condition and all clamping bolts for tightness.
- Do not operate the cross travel carriage beyond the limits.
- Operate the correct button for required movement.
- While operating the crane concentrate on the work and do not allow your attention to get diverted.
- Do not lift heavy objects to heights more than necessary.
- Never move the lifted objects by crossing over people.
- Ensure the lifted objects do not swing widely when moved.

Pre-Run Instructions:

(i) Switch on the power supply switch, on panel board and ensure the bulbs for all three phases are glowing.
(ii) Press the ON button on the remote to switch-on power supply.
(iii) Check all movements by pressing the respective push button on the remote to verify proper functioning of all movements.
(iv) Before transferring new objects into the yard, organize it.
(v) Switch off the crane after the work is completed.
(vi) Lift the weight just a little and stop the lifting to ensure that the weight stays in the same position under the brake clamping and it is not slipping. If the brake is slipping do not lift the weight and report immediately to the maintenance department.

Work Instructions :

(i) Use correct cross-section wire ropes and slings to lift weights.
(ii) Sling the wire rope 'through the weight or below the weight to be lifted' ensuring that it will not come off or slip and the weight will get lifted evenly and without tilting.
(iii) Lift the weight 'off the ground' to the height required to clear all obstacles and shift it to the required location carefully.
(iv) Lower the weight and place where required slowly.
(v) Switch off the crane when work gets over.

<table>
<tr><td>Issue No. 1</td><td>Issue Date: 29.09.2001</td><td>Page No. 1 of 1</td></tr>
<tr><td colspan="2">Reviewed By:</td><td>Approved By:</td></tr>
</table>

XYZ Co.	XYZ CORPORATION	Doc. No. XYZQMS – 7.4.3 /P-01/I-01
	7.4.3 Verification of Purchased Product	Rev. No. Nil
	Instructions for Inspection of Steel Sheets	Rev. Date. Nil

Responsibility: Receiving inspector

Inspection Details:	Parameter	Frequency	Sample Size	Test Equipment (min. least count required)
	Surface Defects	Each sheet	100%	Visual
	Dimensional	Random	10 Sheets	
	a. Length/Breadth			Steel Tape (1mm)
	b. Thickness			Micrometer (0.1mm)

Inspection

1. Verify the packing of the sheets is as per specification.
2. Verify for availability of mill test certificates.
3. Verify that the steel received conforms to the permitted specification.
4. Check each sheet for cast number and coil number marking.
5. Check 100 % of both sides of the sheets for visual defects like rust, pits, scratches, slivers, scour marks and other surface imperfections.
6. Check 10 sheets at random for dimensional conformity.
7. Maintain records using the lot inspection report proforma.

Decision Making Instructions :

Acceptance: If the lot is found conforming, send it for storage as an accepted lot or send it to the next stage of processing.

Rework: Sheets having shallow pits shall be segregated and such defective sheets shall be re inspected to ensure conformity or otherwise.

Rejections: Sheets having laminations, deep pits, heavily rusted surface shall be rejected.

Segregation: All defective sheets shall be kept in the area designated for NCP steel sheets.

Decision Criteria: If the defective sheets in a lot exceed the acceptable limits for NCP then immediately contact Head QC/D.G.M/E.D.

Remark: Acceptable limit for NCP is the total number of defective sheets:

1. Tolerated in this stage.
2. Not considered critical/alarming requiring "review and recording of the corrective action taken".

Note: In case of any doubts regarding actions to be taken, contact Head QC

Ref: Lot Inspection Report.

Issue No. 1	Issue Date: 29.09.2001	Page No. 1 of 1
Reviewed By:	Approved By:	

XYZ Co.	XYZ CORPORATION	Doc. No. XYZQMS – 7.6 /P-01/I-01
	7.6 Control of Monitoring & Measuring Devices	Rev. No. Nil
	Instructions for Calibration of Pressure Gauges	Rev. Date. Nil

Responsibility: Head Q C

Equipment Used:

1. Dead Weight Pressure Gauge (DWPG) calibrator.
2. Counter balance dead weights.

Safety Precautions:

1. Ensure that the pressure gauge needing calibration is fitted onto the DWPG calibrator stem correctly.
2. Ensure that the thread while engaging to the stem is correct and not cross, to prevent thread damage.

Pre-calibration instruction:

1. Check whether the DWPG calibrator is filled with oil to the top.
2. Manually operate the plunger of the DWPG Calibrator to bleed all air entrapped in the oil.
3. Check for leakages from joints.

Calibration Instructions:

1. Fit the gauge to be calibrated to the stem of the calibrator.
2. Place the "Counter Balance Dead Weight " of known value on the plate provided on the other stem of the calibrator.
3. Tighten the hand-operated screw which pushes oil inside until the dead weight on the plate rises and then stops.
4. Note the reading indicated by the pressure gauge.
5. Loosen the screw and allow the oil to get relieved so that the plate comes down.
6. Record the value of the dead weight and the corresponding readings of the pressure gauges
7. Repeat the above with another dead weight of known value.

Decision Making: The usability of the gauge depends upon the acceptability criteria.

Frequency of Calibration: Calibration of the pressure gauge for it's working range shall be done as frequently as necessary.

Ref : Pressure gauge calibration record

Issue No. 1	Issue Date: 29.09.2001	Page No. 1 of 1
Reviewed By:	Approved By:	

XYZ Co.	XYZ CORPORATION	Doc. No. XYZQMS – 7.4.2 /P-01/I-01
	7.4.2 Purchasing Information	Rev. No. Nil
	Specification for Hot Rolled Edge Trimmed Steel Sheets	Rev. Date. Nil

S.No.	Parameter	Requirement	Tolerance	Method of Test
1.	Dimensions a) Length b) Width c) Thickness	 2500 mm 1250 mm 2.9 mm	 +/- 2 mm +/- 2 mm +/- 0.1 mm	 Steel tape Steel tape Micrometer
2.	Edge condition	Clean cut and free from dents, cuts, nicks, etc	Edge burr of around 0.5 mm	Touch
3.	Surface Condition	Free from rolling defects	Defects not visually detected	Visual
4.	Soundness	Free from lamination	None	To be certified by the supplier
5.	Packing	Packed in bundles of 2000 kg and box strapped with corner and edge protection	–	Visual

Acceptance Criteria:

1) Conformance to IS 1079 Latest edition
2) Compliance to the above, and
3) Issuance of mill certificate.

Issue No. 1	Issue Date : 29.09.2001	Page No. 1 of 1
Reviewed By:	Approved By:	

XYZ Co.	XYZ CORPORATION	Doc. No. XYZQMS – 7.6 /P-01/I-02
	7.6 Control of Monitoring & Measuring Devices	Rev. No. Nil
	List of Measuring Equipment	Rev. Date. Nil

S.No.	Name of the Instrument	Identity Number	Least Count	Range	Calibration Frequency	Calibration Method
1.	Vernier calipers	VC 01	0.1 mm	0-150	1 Year	Outside
2.	Vernier calipers	VC 02	0.05 mm	0-150	1 Year	Outside
3.	Vernier calipers	VC 03	0.02 mm	0-300	6 Months	Outside
4.	Vernier calipers	VC 04	0.01 mm	0-300	1 Year	Outside
5.	Vernier calipers	VC 05	0.01 mm	0-500	2 Years	Outside
6.	Micrometer -flat	MM F01	0.001 mm	0-25	1Year	Outside
7.	Micrometer -flat	MM F02	0.001 mm	0-50	1Year	Outside
8.	Micrometer -flat	MM F03	0.001 mm	0-400	1Year	Outside
9.	Micrometer -ball	MM B01	0.002 mm	0-50	1Year	Outside
10.	Micrometer (digital)	MM D01	0.01 mm	0-50	1Year	Outside
11.	Steel rule	SR01	0.5 mm	0-150	1Year	Outside
12.	Steel rule	SR02	1 mm	0-300	1Year	Outside
13.	Steel rule	SR03	1 mm	0-500	1Year	Outside
14.	Steel rule	SR04	1 mm	0-500	1Year	Outside
15.	Steel tape	ST01	1 mm	3000	1Year	Outside
16.	Steel tape	ST02	1 mm	5000	1Year	Outside
17.	Pressure gauge	PG01	0.5 kg	0-7	1 Month	In-house
18.	Pressure gauge	PG02	1kg	0-10	1 Month	In-house
19.	Pressure gauge	PG03	1 kg	0-10	1 Month	In-house
20	Pressure gauge	PG04	1 kg	0-30	1 Month	In-house
21.	Pressure gauge	PG05	1 kg	0-30	1 Month	In-house
22.	Pressure gauge (digital)	PGD01	0.1 kg	0-10	1 Month	In-house
23.	Stop watch	SW01	0.01 sec	0-99	1 Year	Outside
24.	Dial gauge	DG01	0.01 mm	0-10	1 Year	Outside
25.	Slip gauges	SG01	0.5 mm	0.5-10	3 Years	Outside

Issue No. 1	Issue Date: 29.09.2001	Page No. 1 of 1
Reviewed By:	Approved By:	

twenty-three

ANALYSIS, DIAGRAMS, FLOWCHARTS AND TABLES FOR PROCESS APPROACH

1. ANALYSIS OF THE ORGANIZATIONAL PROCESS CHAIN

The inter-relationship of processes are shown through individual inter-relationship diagrams for each key Process of XYZ Corporation. This diagram for the key process "CUSTOMER CARE & SUPPORT" is prepared by treating it as the central key process for this diagram. These diagrams of the identified key central processes with other processes help the organization understand them for effective and efficient operations based on the process approach.

1.1 Selected Key Process "CUSTOMER CARE & SUPPORT"

'Quality is what the customer says it is, not what you write down as your product specifications and internal procedures, since quality is related to Customer Perceptions'.

Thus 'Customer Care & Support' process assumes significant importance and is the key process of the organization. If this process is simplified for the sake of understanding, it merely has to ensure the following two objectives from the customers:

1) They buy more and still more, and
2) They don't complain and if they do complain, it is less and still less.

1.2 Names of related PROCESSES in the PROCESS CHAIN

a) Key Processes

(i) Design & development

(ii) Marketing & sales

(iii) Purchasing

(iv) Product realization

(v) Delivery

b) Supporting Processes

1. Finance
2. Legal
3. Human resource
4. Infrastructure
5. Management
6. Information technology

1.3 Process Interrelationship Diagram

The Process relationship diagram for the key process *"CUSTOMER CARE & SUPPORT"* is prepared as shown in Fig. 12. by placing this process at the center of the diagram since it is the central key process for this diagram. All other key and supporting processes are placed around the central key process and link lines between them are drawn to depict the interrelationship through the flow of material and information. The interfaces are identified giving the authority details applicable at these link points

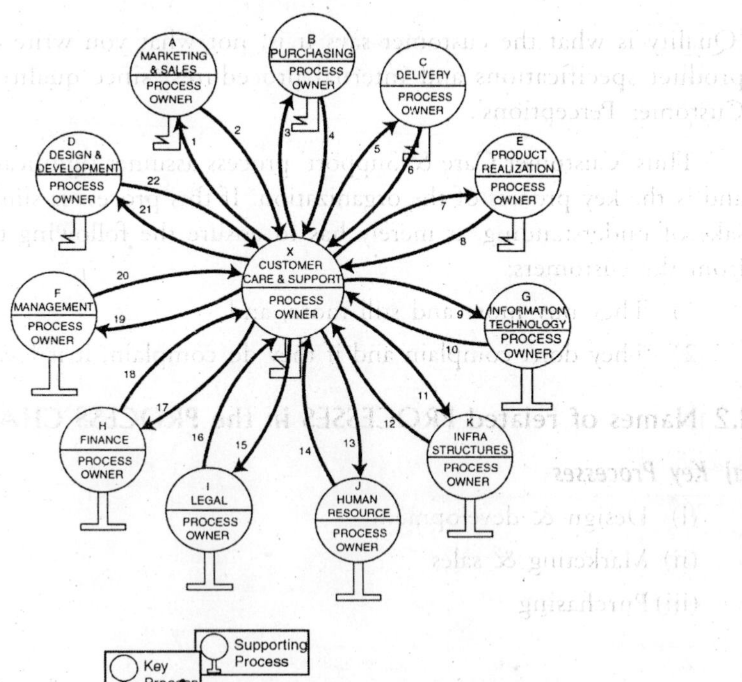

FIG. 12 *PROCESS INTERRELATIONSHIP FOR KEY CENTRAL PROCESS—CUSTOMER CARE AND SUPPORT*

TABLE 17

Process Interrelation details for Key Central Process

Arrow Number	Flow Direction		Type of Flow	Flow Details
	From	To		
1.	X.	A.	Information	Complaints, feedback
2.	A.	X.	Resource & Information	Free replacements, market conditions and demands, competitors & market leaders, market trends
3.	X.	B.	Information	Customer requirements for control and verification
4.	B.	X.	Information	Supplier information, supplier developments
5.	X.	C.	Information	Delivery requirements & expectations
6.	C.	X.	Information	Delivered product feedback
7.	E.	X.	Resource	Product
8.	X.	E.	Information	Product feedback and performance
9.	G.	X.	Information	Customer database information & data processing as per requirement
10.	X.	G.	Information	Customer information on satisfaction and performance
11.	K.	X.	Resources	Facilities and work environment
12.	X.	K.	Information	Infrastructure requirements
13.	J.	X.	Resource	Manpower of required competency
14.	X.	J.	Information	Human resource requirements
15.	X.	I.	Information	Details on claims and customer satisfaction with actions
16.	I.	X.	Resources & Information	Legal advise, settlement of claims, warranties, guarantees, etc.
17.	X.	H.	Information	Customer care costs, funds requirements
18.	H.	X.	Resources & Information	Funds, cost controls, etc.
19.	X.	F.	Information	Feedback on customer satisfaction, complaints and customer perceptions
20.	F.	X.	Resources & Information	Resources and support, to maintain and enhance customer satisfaction
21.	X.	D.	Information	Customer requirements details, expectations, delight features, performance feedback
22.	D.	X.	Information	Design and development data, advance information on features and attributes

2.14 ANALYSIS OF THE SELECTED KEY MACRO PROCESS

This analysis determines and diagrammatically depicts the sequence of the micro processes of this key macro process "CUSTOMER CARE & SUPPORT". It also shows in tabular form the process inputs, outputs, inter-linkages and controls at link-points for effective and efficient performance of the macro process.

2.1 Selected Macro Process: "CUSTOMER CARE & SUPPORT"

14.2.2 Purpose To ensure that external customer satisfaction and delight exists through maintenance of exactly the same level of standards of performance as in the internal supplier-customer relationship.

14.2.3 Functional Groups Involved

1. Research & Development
2. Production
3. Engineering
4. Quality Control
5. Purchase
6. Stores
7. Accounts
8. Personnel
9. Industrial engineering
10. Production planning & control
11. Marketing
12. Administration
13. Training

14.2.4 Process Boundaries The process of customer care & support, is all pervasive and takes priority over all other processes. It has impact on every function of XYZ Corporation.

14.2.5 Process Owner Performance and improvement of the cross-functional processes of XYZ Corporation, can occur only if all the senior persons with specific functional responsibilities form a cohesive team. Like any team this team would also need a team leader who should also be a member and contributor to the team effort. Ideally only a person with a 'stake' in a process can function as a true leader. Hence these leaders of the process shall be called process owners/champions / facilitators. Since XYZ Corporation has been functioning on the traditional structured functional lines and at present has no process owners, the process owners shall be selected from amongst the senior persons, since they are capable of managing the people and shall also be capable of influencing improvements. The responsibilities of these process owners in addition to their other responsibilities shall be as follows:

1) To guide the process and its people during operation and improvement of the process.
2) To monitor the process for its success in meeting customer requirements.
3) To report these findings to the top management.
4) To facilitate functional interaction and resolve link point issues.
5) To ensure that the process remains capable of meeting the primary goals of XYZ Corporation.

14.2.6 Human Resource Requirement Qualified, skilled, experienced, trained and competent people for careful, judicious and professional handling of the customers with a genuine concern for their interest at heart.

14.2.7 MICRO PROCESS within the selected MACRO PROCESS

1. Knowing the organizational policies for customer focus
2. Surveying customers for requirements
3. Analyzing the survey data
4. Determining customer's and other requirements
5. Assessing the requirements
6. Establishing requirements and expectations
7. Planning for meeting requirements and expectations
8. Designing the products as per plans
9. Developing processes capable of delivering Products
10. Producing the product as per design
11. Delivering the product as per design
12. Measuring and monitoring customer satisfaction
13. Assessing performance based on feedback
14. Acting on customer complaints
15. Evaluating performance based on complaints & feedback
16. Adjusting performance
17. Improving quality & performance
18. Re-establishing customer requirements & expectations
19. Building a passion for customer care & support

3. ANALYSIS OF THE SELECTED MICRO PROCESS

3.1 Selected Micro Process: "ACTING ON CUSTOMER COMPLAINTS"

3.1.1 Purpose To ensure that customer complaints are attended expeditiously, resolved satisfactorily and necessary 'corrective and preventive actions' are taken appropriately.

3.1.2 Inputs

- Customer Complaint
- Dissatisfaction with the product in meeting their requirement
- Non-fulfillment of expectation
- Feedback
- Observation
- Suggestion for change
- Expression of a viewpoint
- Merely an opinion
- Even only a feeling

3.1.3 Outputs

(i) Correction made - to rectify the defective product under complaint

(ii) Corrective actions - to rectify the defective process

(iii) Preventive actions - to anticipate and check other likely problems

(iv) Improvement actions - to improve upon the product, process and system

3.1.4 Names of the ACTIVITIES within the selected MICRO PROCESS

Activity 1: Receiving the customer complaint

Activity 2: Reassuring the complainant

Activity 3: Investigating the complaint

Activity 4: Analyzing the complaint

Activity 5: Taking necessary actions

Activity 6: Ensuring satisfaction

Activity 7: Preventing recurrence

3.1.5 Functional Groups Involved in the Activities

S.No.	Activity	Functional Group
1	Receiving customer complaint	Marketing, Personnel, Training
2	Reassuring the complainant	Marketing, Personnel, Training
3	Investigating the complaint	Quality Control, R & D,
4	Analyzing the complaint	Quality Control, R & D,
5	Taking necessary actions	Research & Development, purchase, engineering, production, quality control, stores, accounts, personnel, industrial engineering, marketing, production planning & control, administration, training, management
6.	Ensuring satisfaction	Research & Development, purchase, engineering, production, quality control, stores, accounts, personnel, industrial engineering, marketing, production planning & control, administration, training, management
7	Preventing recurrence	Research & Development, purchase, engineering, production, quality control, stores, accounts, personnel, industrial engineering, marketing, production planning & control, administration, training, management

3.1.6 Activity Flowchart

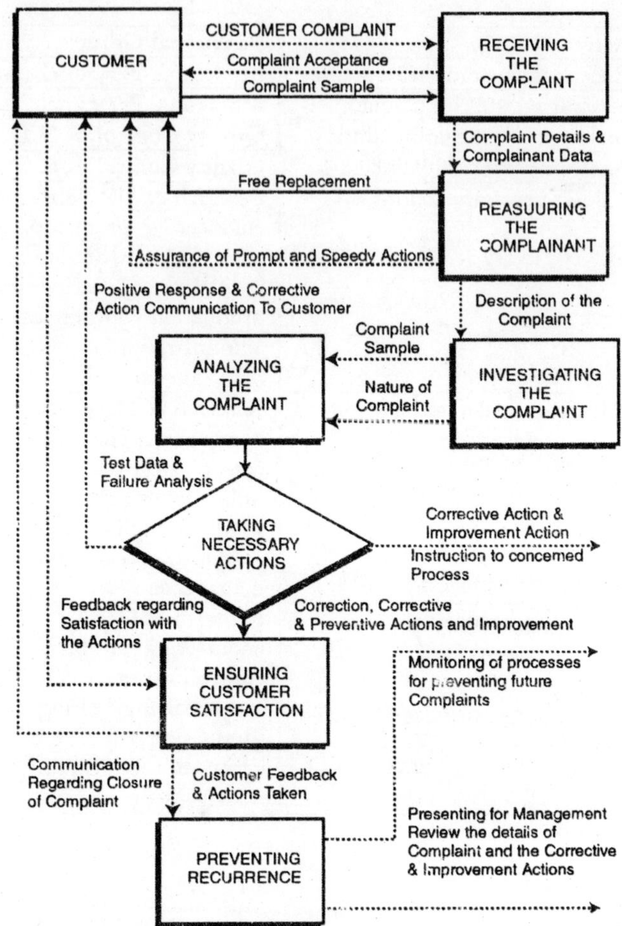

FIG. 13 *FLOWCHART FOR CUSTOMER COMPLAINT*

4. ANALYSIS OF THE ACTIVITIES

4.1 Names of the TASKS within the ACTIVITIES of the Selected Micro Process

Activity I: Receiving the Complaint

Task 1: Receive the complaint

Task 2: Elicit the details of the complaint with full sincerity

Task 3: Acknowledge the complaint/deficiency/ dissatisfaction/feedback

Task 4: Collect all relevant details of the problem including the sample (where applicable)

Activity 2: Reassuring the customer

Task 1: Give free replacement, where possible

Task 2: Thank the complainant for the information

Task 3: Give confidence to the customer regarding the organization's policy on assigning highest priority to complaints and their speedy redressal

Task 4: Register the complaint

Activity 3: Investigating the complaint

Task1: Investigate the complaint-sample for the 'unsatisfactory and any other related characteristic' against the specification requirement

Task 2: Test for the characteristic under complaint

(Note: In case of services, test the same characteristic in any other place of use and in case of goods test any other sample available including counter samples)

Activity 4: Analyzing the complaint

Task 1: Study the test results

Task 2: Analyze the cause of failure

Activity 5: Taking necessary actions

Task 1: Prepare report and propose alternatives for corrective actions

Task 2: Decide on the corrective actions and response to customer

Task 3: Take corrective actions to prevent recurrence

Task 4: Communicate to the customer in a positive way

Task 5: Follow-up on the corrections and improvements

Activity 6: Ensuring customer satisfaction

Task 1: Obtain feedback from customer regarding satisfaction

Task 2: Close the complaint

Task 3: Inform the customer regarding closure of the complaint

Activity 7: Preventing Recurrence

Task 1: Monitor future complaints for elimination of problem

Task 2: Present the complaint, improvements and preventive actions to the top management for review

4.2 TASKS within the selected ACTIVITY

TABLE 18

Task details for Activity "RECEIVING THE COMPLAINT"

Persons Responsible	Suppliers	Inputs	Time	Outputs	Actions
Task 1: Receive the complaint					
Every individual of XYZ Corpn.	External Or internal complainant	Product under complaint & written, verbal, telephonic, electronic media communication or even through a third person	Any time	Complainant & complaint data	Professional, prompt, and immediate attention
Task 2: Elicit the details of the complaint with full sincerity					
The receiver of the complaint	Receiver of the complaint	Complainant & complaint data	Without delay	Details and description of nature of complaint & complainant	Complete, correct & detailed information gathering
Task 3: Acknowledge the complaint / deficiency / dissatisfaction / feedback					
Verbally by the receiver of the complaint, preferably followed by a senior person in writing	Person eliciting the details	Details and description of nature of complaint & complainant	Without delay	Regret letter that acknowledges the complaint and assures of action and further information	Professional, prompt, and polite response.
Task 4: Collect all relevant details of the problem including the complaint sample (where applicable)					
Person responsible for this work who has knowledge of product	1.External or Internal complainant 2. Person eliciting the details	1. Complaint sample 2. Complaint details and data from the complainant	As soon as it can be done	Complaint details, sample and full information on the complaint	Ensure correctness & accuracy without adding or changing facts

Appendices

Appendix A
Process Performance

A.1 Definitions

A.1.1 Compliance Compliance is the adherence of the measurement to predetermined requirements. It is basically a 'GO NO-GO' type of approach to verification and considers meeting requirements as sufficient and adequate for demonstrating satisfactory performance.

A.1.2 Effectiveness Effectiveness as the dictionary defines is "having a definite or desired effect or result". As such although effectiveness relates to the output-side of the process it does not measure output but measures outcomes or consequences. Thus, effectiveness establishes through measurements, the degree of achievement of the desired results or objectives and could be applied for any attributes such as quality, quantity, time or cost.

Mathematically, effectiveness can be represented as follows:

$$\text{Effectiveness} = \frac{\text{Actual outcome}}{\text{Desired outcome}} \times 100$$

Thus, effectiveness is about doing the right thing. This describes what has been produced in relation to what the customers need or expect. Effectiveness of the organization can be enhanced, by improving the quality of the product being delivered to the customer. This requires improvement through redesigning of the process or product. It is a relative measure of what is delivered compared to what is expected. Effectiveness results in customer satisfaction and delight.

A.1.3 Efficiency Efficiency as the dictionary defines is "the ratio of the actual resource used to the total resource consumed for performing a work". Efficiency is therefore used to measure performance by assessing the 'input-side or the activity' of any process and measures 'degree of control on the utilization of inputs or activities' for achieving improved performance.

Mathematically, efficiency can be represented as follows:

$$\text{Efficiency} = \frac{\text{Actual utilization of input or actitivy}}{\text{Total resource used}} \times 100$$

Hence, efficiency is about doing things right. This describes how well the process performs. Efficiency can be increased only through process improvement. This requires elimination of waste, cost reduction, variability reduction, and cycle time reduction. It is process related and is measured within the process itself. It is a relative measure of the actual, compared to the theoretical. Efficiency results in cost control.

A.1.4 Effectiveness vs. Efficiency Effectiveness focuses on, "Quality of the result by comparing the achievement in relation to the target"

Efficiency focuses on, "Quality of the activity by comparing the input in relation to the output".

Effectiveness requires doing the right job
while
Efficiency requires doing the job right

It is therefore, quite possible to be doing a job very efficiently, but it may not be the right job and so would definitely lead to failure, despite the efficiency in the performance. Again one could be doing the right job, but if not done efficiently would again lead to failure. Hence, on its own, each is insufficient for organizational success, but in combination they work wonders.

A.1.5 Excellence Excellence as the dictionary defines is "superior quality of performance and output". It therefore refers to the achievement of a level of performance that is surpassing or outstanding. Excellence hence is a combination of effectiveness, efficiency supported by performance improvement. Any activity as such requires quality of performance, quality of result and continual improvement. To sumup, excellence is the state of surpassing requirements and expectations by:

(i) Performing at levels higher than expected,

(ii) Exceptionally good or proficient outputs, and

(iii) Continually improving upon the previous performance.

Excellence therefore requires:

(i) Meeting and exceeding all requirements and expectations,

(ii) Ensuring the right quality, right from design through production and delivery, to servicing,

(iii) Control on the inputs,

(iv) Proper utilization of time,

(v) Continuous monitoring of all activities for factual feedback, and

(vi) Constant effort for correction, prevention and improvement.

Excellence in any activity is therefore important for the simple reason that it helps set much better standards. Just as, 'human excellence' leads people to a belief in human capabilities and skills, so also, organizational excellence creates belief in its capabilities and skills. It provides sincere, honest, hard work needed to excel and gets its due recognition and rewards. In an organization, excellence is brought about from rewarding both individuals and teams for merit, performance, innovation, creativity, development, altruism, etc.

A.2 Understanding the Measures of Performance

The various Measures of performance are as follows:

1) Compliance
2) Effectiveness
3) Efficiency
4) Excellence

To understand these terms let us take the example of a target-shooter who is required to shoot ten shots within 120 seconds at a target-board 'X'. The quality of his shooting determines his performance. This is explained below.

A.2.1 Compliance If the shooter shoots all the ten shots at the target-board 'X' within 120 seconds and all 10 of his shots hit within any of the target-circles, his shooting is said to be in compliance with requirements irrespective of the following

(i) The width of scatter of shots on the board

(ii) The distances between each pair of consecutive shots on the board

(iii) The irregularity of the spacing of time between the shots

(iv) The total time used as long as it is less than 120 seconds (could even be just 12 seconds)

A.2.2 Effectiveness If he shoots all the ten shots at the target-board 'X' within 120 seconds, and even if 8 of his shots hit within only the outermost target-circles but 'all the 10 shots are clustered together', his shooting shall be said to be effective irrespective of the following:

1) The location of the cluster of the shots (could even be close to the outer boundary of the outermost circle)

2) The distances between each pair of consecutive shots on the board may be different,

3) The irregularity of spacing of time between the shots
4) The total time used as long as it is less than 120 seconds (could even be just 12 seconds).

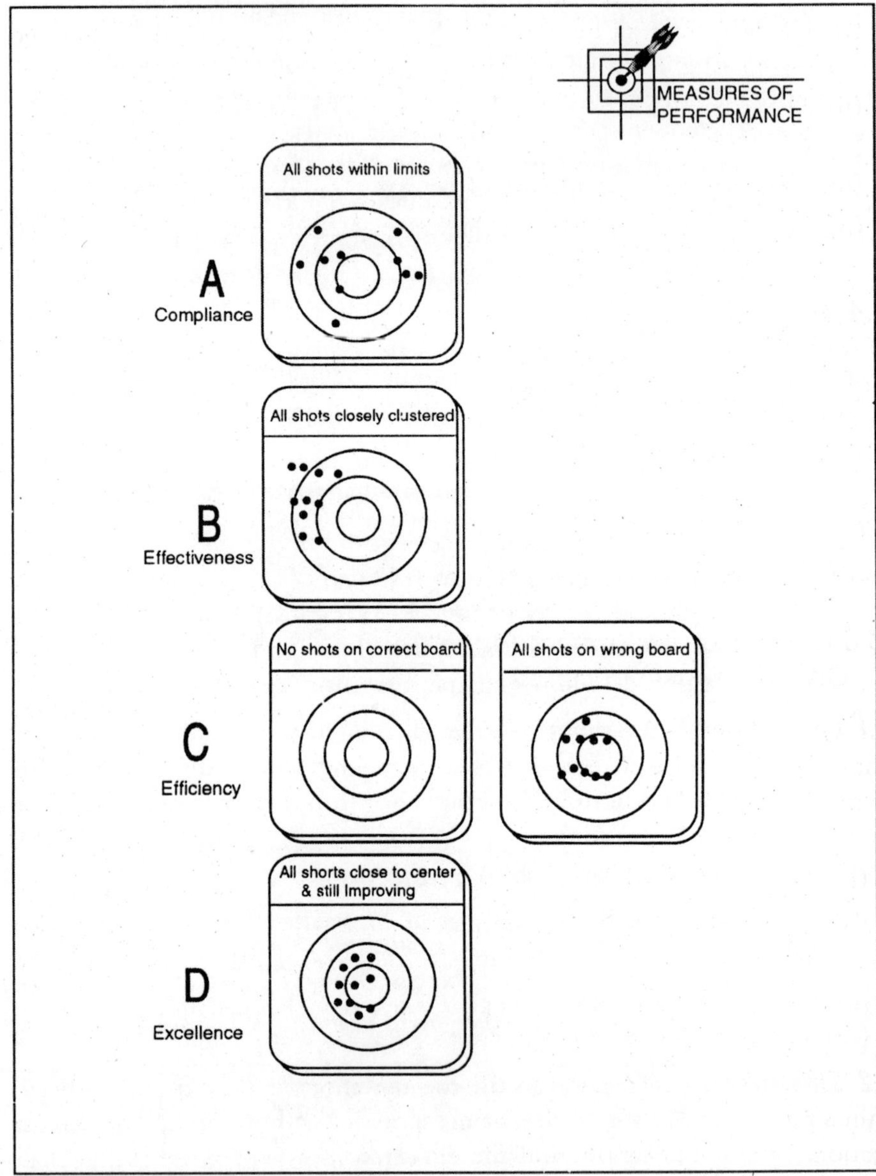

FIG. 14 *UNDERSTANDING THE MEASURES OF PERFORMANCE*

A.2.3 Efficiency If he shoots all the ten shots at any target-board within 120 seconds, and all 10 of his shots hit within the target-circles—'within the inner circle and the bull's eye circle', he shall be said to be efficient irrespective of the following; even if:

(i) He has placed all his shots at the adjoining target-board 'Y', instend of shooting at his board 'X'.

(ii) The distances between each pair of consecutive shots on the board varies,

(iii) The irregularity of spacing of time occurs between the shots, and

(iv) The total time used is less than 120 seconds (could even be just 12 seconds).

A.2.4 Excellence If he shoots all the ten shots at target-board 'A' within 120 seconds and all 10 of his shots hit within the target circles of the correct board, 'close together being near and within the bull's eye' and even within this cluster each subsequent shot is towards the center, and his shots are almost equally spaced in time as well on the board, then such shooting shall be said to be excellent irrespective of the following:

(i) Whether his final shot fails to reach the bulls-eye, and

(ii) The total time taken happens to be the full 120 seconds.

A.3 Measures of Performance in relation to Organizational Processes

A.3.1 Compliance In relation to the organizational processes, 'Compliance within a process' means that the measurements of the operating process exhibit deviations from specifications as shown in Fig. 15. and the deviations are such that,

(i) They are located on both sides of the specified mean value,

(ii) All of them are within the permissible control limits, right across from the Lower Control Limit (LCL) to the Upper Control Limit (UCL), and

(iii) All the measured values fluctuate at random from the mean value.

A.3.2 Effectiveness In relation to the organizational processes, 'Effectiveness within a process' means that the measurements of the operating process exhibit deviations from specifications and the deviations are such that,

(i) They are located only on one side of the mean value,

(ii) Most of then are within the permissible control limits, with a few lying outside, but even these are located in the same direction as those within the limits, and

(iii) All measured values are clustered even though far away from the mean value.

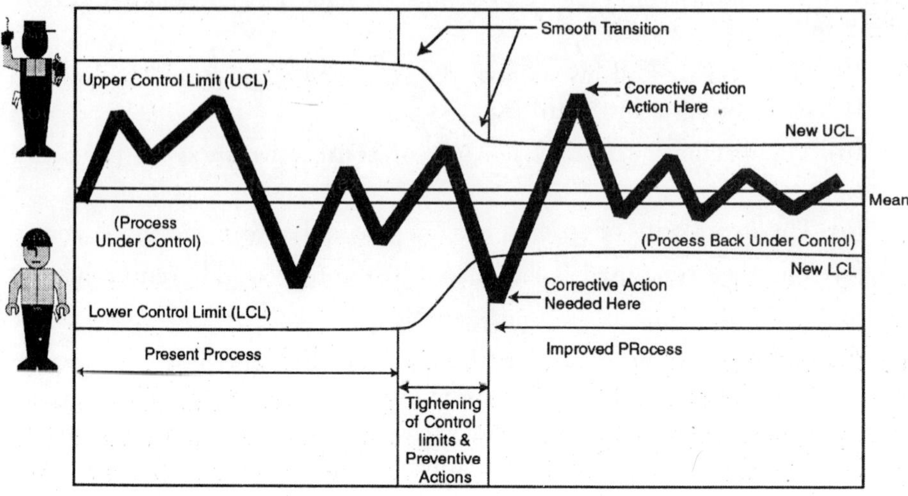

FIG. 15 *COMPLIANCE AND IMPROVEMENT IN PROCESS*

A.3.3 Efficiency In relation to the organizational processes, 'Efficiency within a process' means that the measurements of the operating process exhibit very little deviations from specifications but the deviations are such that,

(i) All the values are located close to the mean value,

(ii) Most of them are within an extremely narrow band, well within the limits, and

(iii) All measured values are however directed at an incorrect process.

A.3.4 Excellence In relation to the organizational processes, 'Excellence within a process' means that the measurements of the operating process do have some deviations from specifications but the deviations are such that,

(i) All of them are located on both sides but close to the mean value,

(ii) Most of them are minimal from the mean value, and

(iii) They gradually reduce with every operation displaying improvement.

Thus a process that is excellent in operation has the following characteristics:

(i) Efficiency through optimized cycle time, controlled costs, increased output per unit resource used and optimized people utilization.

(ii) Effectiveness through correctness and accuracy of performance, timeliness of delivery, compliance to all requirements and fulfillment of satisfaction requirements.

(iii) Improvability through flexibility and adaptability to change and process design.

Characteristics of Excellence in Organizations

(i) Obsession for proactive and reflective actions

(ii) Passion for customer care

(iii) Encouragement for innovative and creative ideas

(iv) Respect and value for people as human beings

(v) Leadership by example

(vi) Concentration on core competencies

(vii) Reduced bureaucracy

(viii) Visionary and strategic approach to planning

(ix) Ability to treat problems as opportunities

(x) Control on all forms of waste

(xi) Supplier relationship

(xii) Anticipatory problem solving

(xiii) Value for knowledge and skill

Appendix B
Questionnaire Preparation

B.1 Questionnaire

A questionnaire is a tool for collecting data for analysis, evaluation and assessment. Every 'field trial' makes use of this technique to collect data for study as a part of the field research process. A well-designed questionnaire can therefore, become an invaluable means for collecting valid, reliable, unbiased and representative data from respondents. A well-prepared questionnaire should be such that it is easy to understand and simple to answer. Only then is there a greater likelihood, of respondents filling it accurately, thereby serving its purpose and providing benefits. If however the same questionnaire is designed merely for the convenience of data user with a lot of technical jargon, the respondent may not be able to give the correct information. In fact it is quite likely that, he may not only not understand it, but actually misinterpret it, thereby providing inaccurate data. However being one of the cheapest and easiest means for collection of data through a structured approach, it is widely used. The only constraint on this method of collection is that the individuals should be willing to provide the data and should actually give the required information, accurately.

B.2 Purpose of Questionnaires

The objective of any questionnaire is not merely to determine the factual existing status of the study area but also to identify weaknesses, determine the comparative level in relation to others, look for possible scope for improvements and elicit new ideas. Depending upon the purpose for which the questionnaire is being designed it should be prepared by first identifying the key elements about which the information is required.

In obtaining information through this means, the best way to obtain a true and complete picture is to try and survey 100%. However, if the survey is to cover an unmanageably large base, a statistical sample being more appropriate is adopted and the target respondents selected so that they are representative of the lot, to get unbiased and reliable information.

In short the purpose can be listed as follows:

(i) To elicit accurate and true data and information

(ii) To create a structured framework for data collection

(iii) To have a standardized format for collection of data and information

(iv) To help in processing data collected

(v) To make the entire process respondent-friendly and also user-friendly

B.3 Features of Questionnaires

The questionnaire should have the following features:

(i) Identity of respondents and their responses should be kept confidential

(ii) It should be simple to understand and easy to answer

(iii) It should cover all areas

(iv) It should be logically arranged

(v) It should be possible to complete in about 30 to 35 minutes

(vi) It should be structured for the convenience of the respondent

(vii) It should be neutral in tone and not bias the respondent with the style of questioning

B.4 Structure of Questionnaires

1. Introduction

- It should specify the purpose and scope.
- It should specify the time for completing the questions and returning it.
- It should give a clear set of simple and precise instructions for answering the questionnaire.
- It should confirm that the identity of respondents and their responses shall be kept confidential.
- It should contain a request that all questions be answered.

2. Body

- Questions and instructions should be separately demarcated
- The questions should give scope for agreeing as well as disagreeing and preferably not be open-ended, since in such cases answers may not be forthcoming. However there are many instances where only use of open-ended questions will reveal the true facts and so they should be carefully worded and used.

- The closed -ended questions should preferably be answerable on a numerical sliding scale of 0 to 5

  where, 5 = strongly agree, 4 = agree, 3 = neither agree nor disagree, 2 = disagree, 1 = strongly disagree and 0 = not applicable.
- The instructions for rating the answers to questions on the scale should clearly specify number of responses to be given and whether the answer is to be circled, ticked, check marked, etc.
- Multiple choice questions may also be used but with care, to ensure that all valid responses are included.

3. Conclusion

- This should contain the method of presenting the results.
- If for the various answers a bar graph or a pie chart is used, its basic structure should be already drawn and only filling in of data should be required.
- In case responses to feedback given are required, the time period in which this will be done should be also stated.

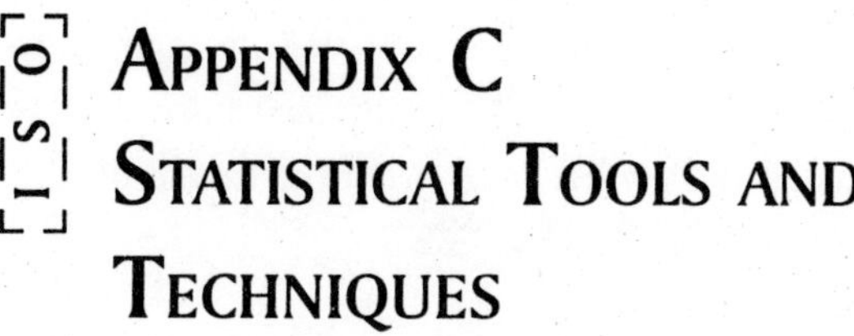

Appendix C Statistical Tools and Techniques

C.1 General

Statistical tools and techniques are scientific practical methods used for developing and establishing a fact-based approach to problem solving. They require the users to follow a structured approach, so as to guide them, right from determining the root-cause to developing a permanent solution. All data should be collected scientifically and analyzed statistically. Successfully solving problems based on facts, through the use of 'Statistical tools and techniques' should be the approach of every organization. Fear of the need for a high level of mathematical capability, as a prerequisite for understanding them should not deter the users. Actually logical understanding is sufficient to understand them.

C.2 Tools

Tools basically are, "data collection and analysis methods, that can be used without too much thought, mechanically". They have a narrow focus, clear-cut specific application utility and are used independently to facilitate a positive problem solution. Tools are simple to use and task specific.

C.3 Techniques

Techniques are, "skillful methods of practical application of the various tools used in combination based on purpose". They have a broader outlook, wider application and are used in varying contexts for different types of evaluations. Techniques usually require a certain amount of 'skill and training' in their use and assist in decision-making.

C.4 Application of Tools and Techniques

The key to successful application of the tool or technique is identifying and understanding the following:

- When to use them
- How to use them
- Which to use

C.5 When to Use Them

They should be used only when the situation demands and not just for the sake of fulfilling the ISO requirements.

C.6 How to Use Them

In practice for genuine problem-solving, tools are mostly used in isolation and techniques are used as a suitable combination of tools, for arriving at the best solutions. Their use should be preceded by training and practice sessions.

C.7 Which to Use

Application of the particular tool or technique to a problem situation should be based on the purpose. There are more than a 100 tools and techniques available and each can be applied to more than one phase of the problem-solving cycle. It is for the user to select the most appropriate tool or technique for a specific situation. Indian standards individually detail various tools and techniques available and are in fact also available in the form of the 'Indian Standard Handbook on Statistical Techniques'. These ought to be referred for guidance.

[ISO] BIBLIOGRAPHY

Books

- Aesop's Fables, *Great Illustrated Classics,* Baronet Books, New York.
- Al Ries , *Focus - The Future of Your Company Depends on It* , Harper Collins Publishers, London, 1997.
- Alasdair White, *Continuous Quality Improvement.*
- Armand V. Feigenbaum, *Leadership For TQM.*
- Armand V.Feigenbaum, *Total Quality Control,* McGraw-Hill Book Co, Singapore, Third Edition, Revised.
- Azzam Ali, *Concepts of Total Quality Management And ISO 9000.*
- Bharat Wakhlu, *Total Quality,* Wheeler Publishing, New Delhi, 1998.
- Bill Quirke, *Communicating Corporate Change.*
- Bryan D. Prescott, *Creating A World Class Quality Organisation.*
- BTEC Open Learning Foundation, *Organisation Structure & Process.*
- Bupendra K Modi, *Performance - A Manager's Challenge* , Tata Mcgraw-Hill Publishing Company Limited New Delhi, 1995.
- *Commitment and Leadership.*
- *Communication Skills For Information Systems.*
- *Communications and Training for Quality.*
- Dave Nelson, Patricia E. Moody & Jonathan Stegner, *The Purchasing Machine,* The Free Press, New York.
- David Hoyle, *ISO 9000 QS Development Handbook.*
- David Hoyle, *ISO 9000 Quality Systems Hand Book.*
- David Silk, *How To Communicate In Business.*
- David W. Hutton, *The Change Agents' Handbook,* Tata Mcgraw-Hill Publishing Company Limited, New Delhi, 1995.
- Dennis Green, *The Complete ISO 9000 Manual.*
- *Employee Involvement Makes TQM Work.*

- F.L. Lobo, *Gaining Advantage through Manufacturing,* Abhinav Publishing Industries Pvt. Ltd, New Delhi,1999.
- Frank W. Davis and Karl B Manrodt, *Customer Responsive Management*
- Gary E. Maclean, *Documenting Quality for ISO 9000 and Other Industrial Standards,* Tata Mcgraw-Hill Publishing Company Limited, New Delhi, 1996.
- Gayle Woodside, Patrick Aurrichio & Jeanne Yturri, ISO 14001 *Implementation Manual,* McGraw-Hill.
- Gopal K.Kanji & Mike Asher, *100 Methods For Total Quality Management,* Response Books , New Delhi, 1996.
- Gopal K.Kanji & Mike Asher, *Total Quality Management Process,* Productive Press (India) Pvt. Ltd., Chennai.
- Graham Wilson, *Problem Solving and Decision Making*
- H. James Harringtern, *From Compliance To Performance Improvement.*
- Harvard Business Review "On Breakthrough Thinking", Harvard Business School Press.
- Harvey Robbins & Micheal Finley, *Why Change Doesn't Work,* Orion Business, London, 1999.
- Helga Drummond, *The Quality Movement.*
- Hitoshi Kume, *Management by Quality*
- Hitoshi Kume, *Management By Quality,* Productivity Press (India) Pvt. Ltd., Chennai.
- International Trade Centre UNCTAD/GATT (Geneva), *Applying ISO 9000 Quality Management Systems,* D.L. Shah Trust., Mumbai M.K.Rustomji, Excellence in Management , India Book House Pvt.Ltd., Mumbai,1979.
- International Trade Centre UNCTAD/GATT (Geneva), *Total Quality Control at Enterprise Level,* D.L. Shah Trust., Mumbai.
- J.M. Juran, Juran on *Planning for Quality*
- J.M.Juran , Juran on *Leadership For Quality,* The Free Press, New York.
- J.M.Juran, Juran on *Planning For Quality,* The Free Press, New York.
- J.M.Juran, Juran on *Quality By Design,* The Free Press, New York.
- Jack Trout & Steve Rivkin, *The Power Of Simplicity,* Tata Mcgraw-Hill Publishing Company Limited, New Delhi,2000.
- Jacky Holloway, Jenny Lewis & Geoff Mallory, *Performance Measurement and Evaluation.*

- Jacqueline Dunckel and Brian Taylor, *Keeping Customers Happy*, Lancer Publishing Pvt. Ltd., New Delhi, 1994.
- Jeff Olson, *Cutting Costs*, Velocity Business Publishing Inc., Bristol - USA.
- Joel Ross, *Customer Focus And Satisfaction.*
- John Brandon, *Managing Change In Manufacturing Systems.*
- John C. Mawell, *The 21 Indispensable Qualities of A Leader*, Magna Publishing Co Ltd, Mumbai, 2000.
- John Gilbert,*How To Eat An Elephant*, Affiliated East-West Press Ltd, New Delhi, 1993.
- John Macdonald and John Piggot, *Global Quality*, Viva Books Private Limited, New Delhi ,1992.
- Joseph H. Boyette and Henry P. Conn, *Maximum Performance Management.*
- Lewis Caroll, *Alice in Wonderland.*
- Maeve Gallaher, *Continuous Improvement.*
- Mahendra S.Jakhar, *Spurious LPG Cylinders* , Times Of India.
- Malcom Mcdonald, *Marketing Plans How To Prepare Them : How To Use Them.*
- Martyn House, *Confessions of a Quality Expert*, Tudor Business Publishing Ltd, Great Britain, 1996.
- Masaaki Imai, Kaizen, *The Key To Japan's Competitive Success* , McGraw-Hill Book Co, Singapore, 1991.
- Mikel Harry, Ph.D & Richard Schroeder, *Six Sigma*, Doubleday, New York,2000.
- Navin S. Dedhia, *Quality from many perspectives* (Part - I), D.L. Shah Trust, Mumbai.
- NEBS *Management Development Super Series*, Auditing Quality
- Neil M. Glass, *Management Masterclass*, Nicholas Brealey Publishing, London, 1997.
- Paul F. Wilson and Richard D. Pearson, *Performance Based Assessments*, Tata Mcgraw-Hill Publishing Company Limited , New Delhi, 1996.
- Paul Spenley, *Step Change Total Quality.*
- Perry Johnson , *ISO 14000 The Business Manager's Complete Guide To Environment Management* , John Willey & Sons Inc., New York.
- Perry M.Smith, *Rules and Tools for Leaders*, Magna Publishing Co.Ltd, Mumbai, 1999.

- Peter D. Wickens, *The Ascendant Organisation.*
- Philip Crosby, *The Cost of Quality.*
- Philip E Atkinson, Creating Culture Change: *The Key To Successful Total Quality Management*, Productivity Press (India) Pvt Ltd., Chennai.
- Philip Sadler, *Leadership*, Crest Publishing House, New Delhi, 2001.
- Pradip N Khandwalla, *Organizational Designs for Excellence*, Tata Mcgraw-Hill Publishing Company Limited , New Delhi, 2001.
- Quality. Why Bother ?.
- Richard S Johnson, *Leadership For Quality Transformation*, Vision Books Pvt Ltd., New Delhi.
- Richard S Johnson, *Management Process For Quality Operations*, Vision Books Pvt Ltd., New Delhi.
- Richard S. Johnson, Lawrence E. Kazense, *The Mechanics Of Quality Process*, Vision Books, New Delhi.
- Robert Heibeler, Thomas B. Kelly and Charles Ketteman, *Best Practices - Building Your Business with Customer Focused Solutions*, Arthur Andersen, New York .
- Rohit Ramaswamy, *Design And Management Of Service Processes.*
- Rosemary Phipps and Craig Simmons, *Understanding Customers*
- Sandra Dawson, Analyzing Organizations.
- Sarah Austin & Sarah Caffyn, *Continuous Improvement in Action* by Maeve Gaallaher.
- Sohrab, *Mastering ISO 9000 Requirments*, Qprod Publishers, New Delhi.
- Stephan G. Haines with Katie McCoy , *Sustaining High Performance*
- Stephen Haires, *Sustaining High Performance.*
- Stuart Crainer, *The 75 Greatest Management Decisions Ever Made* , Amacom, New York .
- Sumantra Ghoshal, Gita Piramal & Christopher A. Bartlett, *Managing Radical Change*, Penguin Books India P Ltd., New Delhi,2000.
- Suresh Lulla, *Continuous Quality Improvement (Indian Experiences)* Part II, D.L. Shah Trust., Mumbai.
- Suresh Lulla, *ISO 9000 + CQI = Profit (Indian Experiences) D.L.* Shah Trust, Mumbai.
- Suresh M.Mody, *Advanced Tools for Quality Management*, D.L. Shah Trust, Mumbai.

- Suresh M.Mody, *Benchmarking And Process Improvement,* D.L.Shah Trust, Mumbai .
- Suresh M.Mody, *Creating Customer Satisfaction Excellences*, D.L. Shah Trust, Mumbai.
- Suresh M.Mody, *Self Assessment - A Tool For Continuous Improvement,* D.L. Shah Trust, Mumbai.
- Suresh M.Mody, *Statistical Process Control And Related Quality Tools,* D.L. Shah Trust, Mumbai.
- Suresh M.Mody, *World Class Competitiveness Through Total Quality Management,* D.L. Shah Trust., Mumbai.
- *The Basics of Coaching.*
- *The Practice Of Management.*
- *Total Quality Management.*
- TQM INTERNATIONAL Ltd, *Using Quality Tools and Techniques Successfully*
- *TQM Implementation.*
- Yoshikasu Tsuda, *Productivity, Quality, And Reengineering.*
- Walter J. Wadsworth, *Leadership*, Gemini Books, New Delhi.
- William Shaw and Graham Day, *Check It - Do It Checklists for Business*

Journals and Magazines

- All India Management Association, *People Management*, Maxcel Publishers Pvt. Ltd., New Delhi ,1999.
- "Business Opportunities", *The Times of India*, New Delhi, Aug 9-15, 2001.
- *Executive Excellence*, New Delhi, June 1999.
- *Industrial Safety Chronicle*, National Safety Council , Jul-Sep 2001.
- *Industrial Source*, Indian Express Newspapers (Bombay) Ltd, Dec-1999.
- *International Standard - ISO 9001 - Quality Management System Requirements,* ISO, Geneva.
- *Loss Prevention News*, Loss Prevention Association of India Ltd, Oct-Dec 1999.
- *MM The Industries Magazine*, July 99.
- *Quality Quest*, Essae Chandran Institute, Banglore, Apr - June 1991.
- *Quality Times*, Institute of Directors, New Delhi, March 2001.
- *Strategic Marketing*, Indian Institute of Management, Calcutta, Nov-Dec 98.

Index